THE TAO AND THE DAIMON

The Tao and the Daimon

Segments of a Religious Inquiry

Robert C. Neville
STATE UNIVERSITY OF NEW YORK AT STONY BROOK

State University of New York Press • Albany

Published by
State University of New York Press, Albany

© 1982 State University of New York

For information, address State University of New York Press, State University Plaza, Albany, N. Y., 12246

Library of Congress Cataloging in Publication Data

Neville, Robert C.
  The tao and the daimon.

  1. Religion – Philosophy. 2. Philosophical theology.
3. Creation. I. Title.
BL51.N444 1982   200'.1   82-5888
ISBN 0-87395-661-3   AACR2
ISBN 0-87395-662-1 (pbk.)

Dedicated to The Reverend William A. Tieck
Hero of the Tao and Servant of the Daimon

and to the Kingsbridge Community brought into History
by his love's long passion

Contents

Foreword

THE IDEA OF CREATION *ex nihilo* is one of those ancient intriguing notions that has survived a thousand refutations. Much of its fascination resides in the extreme way it combines abstractness and concreteness. If creation is *ex nihilo*, then there is nothing in the source of creation that determines creation's content, and *anything* can be created. Conversely, no matter what kind of world we find ours to be, it could be created *ex nihilo*, if that idea is plausible. The question whether the world is created *ex nihilo*, therefore, is most easily framed in terms of abstract consideration of problems such as the one and the many, problems that are indifferent to any possible world. On the other hand, if the world is created *ex nihilo*, then to find out anything interesting about the creative process, the creator, or the world as created, one must look concretely to the world itself. The religious or theological content of the idea of creation *ex nihilo* thus derives mainly from secular sources, in the literal sense of *secular*. The haecceities of history, of social and personal experience as well as the special positions of science and art, are the source material for philosophical theology.

There are two families of alternatives to the idea of creation *ex nihilo*, both of which lose the juxtaposition or contrast of the abstract and the concrete. The most obvious alternative is a total denial of any creation or ontological foundation; but, I believe, theories that do this fail to solve the abstract questions of metaphysics, such as the one and the many; they are unresponsive to awe and wonder at the fact that there is anything at all. A more serious alternative to creation *ex nihilo* is a theology that imputes an antecedent character or set of capabilities to a God such that the created world is to be taken to express divine nature in some sense. Such theories, I believe, also fail to solve the problem of the one and the many, because a definite God is one *of* the many, and there is no one *for* the many; or if there is, *that* would be God. Theologies with a God who is definite antecedent to creation also weaken the importance of secular concreteness because they tend to move from a revealed notion of what God's inner character is supposed to be to an interpretation of what the world has to be despite appearances. This has led again and again to mystification of affairs, to intellectual and social hypocrisy and to escapism. For reasons such as these, Nietzsche proclaimed the death of God. Even if unimpressed with Nietzsche's fussy indignation, most serious thinkers today are not moved by claims to revelation of a divine character antecedent to creation.

My own treatment of the idea of creation *ex nihilo* began with a highly abstract argument, in *God the Creator*, that the metaphysical problems of the one and the many, and of being-itself, find solution in my interpretation of creation. After a decade and a half, I still find no reason to take back the essence of that argument and recently found it reinforced in an extended study, *Creativity and God*, of process theology, a position that posits a definite character to God antecedent to (or independent of) creation. But even in that first book a great deficiency was apparent in the abstractness of the mode of argument – namely, that it offers few clues for moving out into concrete reflections in philosophy of religion, philosophical theology, theology of history, scripture studies, ethics, politics, comparative religions, and personal and social religious self-consciousness. Theologies whose God has a definite character antecedent to, and expressed in, creation have an enormous advantage here, for that character is the clue to what is religiously important in all those areas. Secular theories denying all creation have an opposite but equal advantage in saying that there is nothing religiously important there, a conclusion that is always tempting in the face of fustian or exhaustion. How can creation *ex nihilo* be conceived as a fruitful entry into religious thinking without denying its own integrity by sneaking in an illegitimate content?

To address this question I early turned from the abstract dialectic of *God the Creator* to a wide and deliberately dissociated set of fields of study. It seemed to me that part of the desired connection could come if questions within those diverse fields pushed back to creation *ex nihilo* for a plausible solution. Social ethics and problems of human freedom seemed at the opposite pole from the metaphysics of creation, and studies there resulted in *The Cosmology of Freedom*, *Soldier, Sage, Saint*, and a series of publications in the ethics of the life sciences. The Christian tradition, from which the idea of creation *ex nihilo* developed, is replete with interpretive content. Can creation *ex nihilo* provide an abstract theory that makes sense of some of that content? An even more crucial perspective is achieved when the same question is asked relative to the other great religions of the world, religions with metaphysical traditions that did not employ directly the concept of creation *ex nihilo*. Combining theological questions and comparative studies raises new questions about the nature of philosophical theology itself. Here again, I have found that creation *ex nihilo* is a valuable interpretive tool. Finally, I have come to see that religious reflection is always historically relative and definite. Our own historical position is one, I argue, in which the inner recesses of religious faith and practice have been penetrated by the Socratic daimon of critical reason. This process has progressed to the point where those religions still resisting the daimon must also resist engagement with the modern world, hence engagement with authentic spiritual relevance.

The present book begins with the encounter of the religious tao of faith and practice with the Socratic daimon. It argues that the encounter engenders a special sense of philosophical theology, the center of which is an abstract theory of creation *ex nihilo*. Finally, it calls upon considerations from all the fields of comparative studies, of interpretations of Christian orthodoxy, of ethics and of freedom. The selection of these supporting cases is, of course, idiosyncratic to my own limited interests. For that reason the book is subtiltled, "Segments of a Religious Inquiry." *The Tao and the Daimon* turns *God the Creator* inside out, as it were, not arguing for the theory of creation dialectically but stating it hypothetically as a resolution of problems arising elsewhere. Like the earlier book, however, it concludes that the abstract theory of creation is the best protection for the integrity of experience.

Acknowledgments

THE FIRST DEBT to be acknowledged here is to John E. Smith who, as my mentor in college and graduate school, convinced me of the absolute importance of experience, despite my own predilection for abstract dialectic. This book is a direct outgrowth of many early conversations with him; its strengths, whatever they might be, come from that friendship. Readers of his *Reason and God, Royce's Social Infinite, The Analogy of Experience, Religion and Empiricism,* or *Experience and God* will quickly recognize the extent of my debt to him. Paul Weiss taught me, on the other hand, that it is not only legitimate but imperative to follow out the free play of abstract dialectic in order to remain vulnerable in philosophical assertion. Since he published my first article over twenty years ago, he has been my most stringent, informed, and ruthless critic, and my most loyal, continuous, and effective supporter in dark times. Through him, I have known what it is like to be taken seriously; in trying to become mature by reciprocating, I have learned something of true philosophical companionship. Robert S. Brumbaugh, another early teacher, has not only been a friend but brilliantly exemplifies the two-handed juggling of concrete experience (often in the form of practical experimentation) and abstract theory. How I wish I could abandon my Germanic compulsion to say, yet again, for his Greek disposition simply to show!

Carl G. Vaught, a philosopher with a penchant for abstract dialectic as extreme as mine, was the first to lead me from that Empyrean through the dense matter of true religious quest. His recent *The Quest for Wholeness* sets a standard for combining the abstract and the concrete, and I wish I had written it. Hans Frei, Quentin Lauer (S.J.), Robert Johann, and Norris Clarke (S.J.) have been my main mentors in Christian theology. Elizabeth Salmon, William Richardson (S.J.), and Patrick Heelan (S.J.) each taught me important lessons in the philosophic approach to theology. Thomas J. J. Altizer and Peter Manchester were my

xiii

most serious critics from the standpoint of Christian orthodoxy (two kinds); I own my self-definition as a theologian largely to conversations with them. Robert Goldenberg and Jay Schulkin taught me to write something a Jew could respect.

Daniel Callahan, Willard Gaylin, and Robert Veatch, colleagues for several years at the Hastings Center, taught me the combination of concrete urgency and imaginative reflection appropriate to ethics. At a time when most philosophical ethicists were detached into meta-ethics, they invented the means and intellectual disciplines to bring ethics back to human life. Since those days in the early 1970s the rest of the intellectual community has come to adopt much of their approach.

From a personal standpoint, the crucial advance in my own education that led to this book was an introduction to non-Western religion and philosophy. For this, I am indebted, first and last, to Thomas Berry. At Fordham University one day in 1967, he asked me how I could teach history of philosophy (then my specialty) if I knew nothing about the Chinese and Indian traditions. Since I couldn't think of an answer, he committed me then and there to teach Indian and Chinese philosophies, which I have done ever since. Teaching those philosophies led to my learning them, initially under Berry's tutelage. He introduced me to sanskrit and arranged for me to learn some Chinese. I cannot conceive of religion now except as a set of worldwide phenomena, and I think Berry takes that to be a major step on the way to what he calls his own practice, that of being a geologian. Other colleagues were my mentors in non-Western religions, notably Sung-bae Park, Antonio deNicolas, and David Dilworth. David Hall and Kuang-ming Wu were my partners in developing ways of engaging non-Western philosophical and religious texts as sources for contemporary philosophy. Hall's recent *Eros and Irony* and Wu's *Chuang-tzu: World Philosopher at Play* are their very different alternatives to *The Tao and the Daimon*. Given my mode of entry into the non-Western field, challenging students have often been as important as challenging colleagues and teachers. I would like to acknowledge Warren Frisina, James Martorano, John Stahle, Joel Bennett, Boris Kiriako, James Warnock, and especially Steve Odin, now my colleague, whose *Process Metaphysics and Hwa-Yen Buddhism* does at length what Chapter 9 here sketches.

I would not have been able to write this book if I had not had some confidence that my peculiar approach had merit as theology. My great thanks to six people who gave me that confidence: Thomas J. J. Altizer, John B. Cobb, Jr., Langdon Gilkey, Ray L. Hart, Gordon Kaufman, and Paul van Buren.

Several chapters of this book went through many drafts, some of which were published in whole or part. Although all the chapters were rewritten for inclusion in this book, inevitably there are carry-overs in language and organization. For permission to print revisions of previously copyrighted material, I wish to thank the following:

James W. Felt (S.J.), editor of *Logos*, for permission to print, in Chapter 2, portions of "Authority and Experience in Religious Ethics," *Logos*, vol. 1, 1980, pp. 79–92.

James Wm. McClendon, Jr. and Axel D. Steuer, editors, and Abingdon Press, for permission to print, in Chapter 3, portions of "The Holy Spirit as God," from *Is God God?* (Nashville: Abingdon, 1981). Copyright © 1981 by Abingdon. Used by permission.

The editors of *Theological Studies* for permission to print, in Chapter 4, portions of "Creation and the Trinity," *Theological Studies*, vol. 30, no. 1 (March 1969), pp. 3–26.

The editors of *Harvard Theological Review* for permission to print, in Chapter 5, portions of "Can God Create Men and Address Them Too?", *Harvard Theological Review*, vol. 61, XXX (1968), pp. 603–23. Copyright 1968 by the President and Fellows of Harvard College. Reprinted by permission.

Robert J. Roth (S.J.), editor, and Fordham University Press, for permission to print, in Chapter 6, portions of "A Metaphysical Argument for Wholly Empirical Theology," from *God Knowable and Unknowable* (New York: Fordham Univ. Press, 1973). Copyright © 1973 by Fordham University Press, pp. 215–240.

The editors of *Philosophy East and West* and the University of Hawaii Press for permission to print, in Chapter 7, portions of "From Nothing to Being: The Notion of Creation in Chinese and Western Thought," vol. 30, no. 1 (January 1980), pp. 21–34.

The editors of *Process Studies* for permission to print, in Chapter 8, portions of "Wang Yang-ming's 'Inquiry on the *Great Learning*'," *Process Studies*, vol. 7, no. 4 (1977), pp. 217–37.

Introduction

THIS BOOK DEALS WITH three concepts and the realities to which they refer: the Socratic daimon of the Western intellect, the tao of religious faith and practice, and creation conceived as the ontological ground of all things.[1] The first two concepts refer to historical realities and therefore do not allow neat definition. The daimon symbolizes the protean forces of self-criticism that have infected and inspired nearly all forms of Western thinking since Socrates. The influence of the daimon involves an appreciation of the relativity of assertions, of irony in doctrine, and of the methodic necessity to be suspicious of all intellectual tools, even method.[2] Pure only in rare abstract dialectic, the daimon's needling whispers have affected nearly every mode of thought and writing in Western culture. Cumulatively, those whispers have resulted in the historical consciousness, the scientific methodologies, and the self-reflexive tools of interpretation that make up our contemporary intellectual habitus. The tao, almost by contrast, symbolizes participation in natural and spiritual forces, a participation disciplined by culturally institutionalized practices rather than by reflective comparison with alternatives. The tao is the way, or path, one follows to personal fulfillment. More broadly, each culture's representation of fulfillment or true life expresses the intelligibility and aspirations of its tao. Each historic religion is a binding (*re-ligere*) of personal and cultural elements into a path – a tao. One may speak indifferently of numerous "tao's" or, more collectively, of the tao of faith and practice manifested in many cultural patterns. The many paths of the world's cultures, the multifariousness of tao, can be grasped adequately only through historical understanding.

In history, the naive innocence of the tao of faith and practice has been destroyed by the sharp tongue of the daimon wherever they have met. The great religions of the West – Judaism, Christianity, and Islam – had their very origins in the daimonic Hellenic and post-Hellenic world. They can hardly be said ever to have been wholly traditional and innocent of the self-criticism of reflective abstractions. The problem of "faith versus reason" is addressed in the founding scriptures themselves. But with time, the daimon's reason has informed more and more elements of culture with its critical sensibilities. With the founding of Reform Judaism and the intellectual clean sweep of liberal hermeneutics in the early nineteenth century, the daimon's voice was acknowledged in the innermost sanctum of Judaism and Protestant Christianity. Roman Catholicism joined with the Modernist movement at the turn of the twentieth century, a joining that was ratified by Vatican II.[3] The Islamic world is currently rent by the division between fundamentalists who would preserve the integrity of the tao and liberals who seek to make Islam compatible with Western culture's daimonic rationalism. European intellectual currents swept India in the nineteenth century and China, Korea, and Japan in the twentieth. While manifestations of the "Eastern Tao" have appeared with increasing strength in the West, the voice of the Western daimon is even now transforming Eastern self-consciousness.

How may we, as students of religion, understand the tao of faith and practice? We would do violence to our own culture, to the aspirations of our own integrity, were we not to be guided by the daimon in its most developed manifestations. Thus a rigorous approach to religious studies includes not only traditional philosophical and theological reflection but also, today, paradigms of inquiry arising from Marxian, structuralist, poststructuralist, and functionalist theories, from physical and cultural anthropology, including archaeology, from both quantitative and narrative methods in history and art history, from philology and textual studies and from criticism in many forms. The arbitrariness of this list has no serious consequences. Other scholars would distinguish the disciplines differently. The point is that the critical intellect of the West is diverse, dynamic, contentious; although few scholars would assign equal weight to those methods, each of them, as well as others, opens new a perspective on religion. Although each is a perspective, a selection of factors to be noted, and therefore a complex abstraction, each can also demonstrate at least some importance, some value, in selection for consideration of what it does.

The result of understanding an innocent and naive tao of faith and practice through these daimonic approaches is to objectify it, to lay it out as a public thing, a patient etherized upon a table. True, we come to understand the object in many valuable ways. Hardly any field rewards inquiry better than religion. The social and cultural importance of religion is so enormous that it is irresponsible to neglect it in the academy. Critical inquiry does objectify, however. Now, as always, people originally immersed in a naively innocent tao, who come to see their faith and practice through one or several methods of critical inquiry, lose their innocence, sometimes their naiveté, and often their faith and practice.

In light of this phenomenon it is necessary to call attention to the modes of understanding and self-understanding *within* traditions of faith and practice that contrast with the products of Socrates' daimon. Obviously the tao is not without its own intelligence. Informed by myth and sacred narrative, selectively and discriminatively channeled by ritual and devotional practices, formed by institutions of discipleship and sometimes by explicit hierarchies of spiritual discernment, religious consciousness is as great a cultural achievement as any social organization, any art, literature, or science, including the main versions of the mature Western intellect itself. Those paths of faith and practice possessing highly developed commentarial traditions, such as Judaism and Buddhism, have an extraordinary degree of self-consciousness and understanding, even if the immediacy with which the self-consciousness identifies with commitments of faith and practice is vulnerable to the daimon's whispers.

When the tao of faith and practice is naively innocent, the understanding produced by the Socratic daimon not only differs from the tao's own self-understanding but sometimes opposes and undermines it. How can the Western mind, for instance, accept or fail to deflate the claims of yogis to special knowledge, to gnosis, based on years of disciplined meditation? The only way to check up in a self-critical manner is to undertake the yoga itself, which may require abandoning the detachment of the daimon. Of course the tradition of Socrates cannot simply accept that there are kinds of knowledge it cannot have; so it vacillates between imperiously forcing the intelligence of the tao into its own forms and declaring it to be nonknowledge. More than anything, this dilemma poses problems of historical justice.

Not many paths of faith and practice, however, are naively innocent any more. In varying degrees and ways the great world religions have met the daimon and internalized that encounter within their own self-understanding. In *Eros and Irony*, David Hall sharply contrasts the aesthetic and private immediacy of mystical religion to critical reason's appeal to consensus. What more clever daimonic strategy could religion employ to domesticate the daimon? The concrete problems of understanding most (though not all) living religions are *not* those of the opposition of self-critical objectivity to innocent sacred immediacy. Rather, they are problems arising out of detachment from commitments to the tao in contrast to the pious use of critical self-understanding in the service of the tao itself. These problems have enormous institutional dimensions – e.g., departments of religious studies versus seminaries – and existential ramifications – scholar versus seeker. They also have intellectual dimensions, and some are addressed in this book.

Philosophical theology, I shall argue, is the central discipline for this problem. When a tao of faith and practice begins to lose its innocence, it attempts to formulate its self-understanding in assertions with broader appeal than stories of individual commitment or divine encounter possess. This is the way to theology. In reflecting on the proper terms for such formulations, a tao encounters the even broader philosophical milieu of its culture. That makes theology philosophical. As early as Philo and Justin Martyr in the West, philosophical theology in this sense became integral to the paths of Judaism and Christianity, but admittedly more central to the latter. With proper cognizance given to different religious and historical experience and different philosophical cultures, some combination of philosophy and theology has been the vehicle for coping with the loss of innocence in the other major traditions as well, down to contemporary developments in Buddhism.

This traditional role of philosophical theology would not be enough to make it central today, however, were it not that it can be undertaken in solid critical continuity with the other modes of inquiry into religion that have developed under the daimon's promptings. Without suggesting that it is easy, I maintain that a philosophical theology which is an authentic contemporary philosophy must be able to engage appreciatively with the sociological, anthropological, historical, literary, and other ways of objectifying religious phenomena. Philosophical theology cannot be understood alone as the voice of a sophisticated tao of faith and practice expressing itself apologetically. It must also be understood as the mode of understanding by which the objectifying methods of the other forms of inquiry gain access to the mind of the tao.

The thesis of this book is that apparently we are entering a new historical situation in which the objectifying modes of Socratic detached, ironic, self-critical understanding have an opportunity to become internalized in a sophisticated, intelligent, pursuit of several taos of faith and practice. Furthermore, the immediacies of mythic, ceremonial, and commentarial thinking are not immature versions of the sciences of religion but partly independent access routes to experience and knowledge which philosophical theology can interpret in making other religious inquiries.

Philosophical theology can mediate between the daimon and the tao.

There is something prophetic, hopefully self-fulfilling but perhaps only fictitious in the announcement of a new historical situation, for surely there are few (or no) examples of philosophical theology functioning in the way advocated in the remarks just made. The true purpose of this book is to contribute the invention of the proper discipline of philosophical theology. In that regard, the thesis is that philosophical theology should be a dialectical movement back and forth between, on one hand, the self-advertised inner content of faith and practice and, on the other, the various suppositions, methods, and leading ideas of the modes of inquiry into religion. The method of this mediation is the relation of both sides to a highly abstract, speculative system of categories. The system needs to be precise, unified, and determinate. It also needs to be vague in the logical sense that, to be applied to the world, it requires further cultural expressions, specifically from the cultures of religion and disciplined inquiry. If the speculative system has merit, each religious claim can be elaborated as a version of that system, and so can the implications of the self-critical analytical intellect. The various specifications or versions of the abstract system may or may not be compatible. But at least, as related to the system, they are commensurable with one another and thus are mutually engagable. Furthermore, this dialectical method displays what is vaguely common to the many paths of faith and practice, as well as to the intellectual commitments of the West. If the great religions do indeed have elements in common, they do so only vaguely. Specifically, they *differ*. The advantage of this kind of philosophical theology is that it provides a context for inquiring whether the common points are important ones rather than disappointing lowest common denominators.[4]

What speculative system of categories would serve as the center of philosophical theology? In the past, the Platonic-Augustinian, Thomistic, Kantian, and Hegelian systems served something of this purpose in the Western world. Vendantic and Madhyamika systems were prominent in India, and China has developed taoist themes for systematic use in civilizing Buddhist and Neo-Confucian cults. Process philosophy is the most vigorous candidate today. An aim of this book, however, is to make a case for a systematic theory of divine creation, of God as creator. This label reveals the inevitable historical particularity of the system, for the concept of God as creator, or of creation *ex nihilo*, is the product of a specific tradition in the West. As developed here, the system is generalized as much as possible beyond that Western heritage and is stated abstractly to allow for specification by Indian and Chinese commitments as well as Western ones. My first attempt to develop that systematic conception was in *God the Creator*, a philosophic book whose abstractness has been a burden to its readers. But the book's very capacity for being abstractly stated and defended constitutes its usefulness in philosophical theology as advocated here.[5] Its abstractness may be recognized by contrasting the book with Langdon Gilkey's brilliant, roughly contemporary *Maker of Heaven and Earth: A Study of the Christian Doctrine of Creation*.[6] The biographical origins of our views are strikingly similar: reflection on the relation between creation *ex nihilo* and process philosophy. But, whereas Gilkey's theory is concretely Christian, mine is (I hope) now not much more Christian than Buddhist, though faithful to something important in both.[7] Buddhists have pointed out, however, that they would never call a generalization of their view, "God the creator"; hence the particularity in even a highly abstract system.

Not only is the abstract system particular, so are the expressions of both religion and inquiry to which it can be related. The case to be made for the systematic conception of creation, then, is that it can mediate fruitfully the particular paths of religion and modes of inquiry that constitute our problems. The most that could be said is that, if the mediation turns out to be fruitful, this particular, historically developed, abstract conception of creation mediates these particular expressions of religion and inquiry. It is foolish, though, to think that this kind of particularity is ever transcended or that it would be desirable to do so. Sad to say, as will be evident in the following chapters, the particularity of the discussion is already a highly general particularity. Nevertheless, the particularity accounts for the case-study approach taken.

If the argument that follows is only a small contribution to the development of an authentic philosophical theology, it is also a contribution to a new form of religion. At least that is its task, however far short of the goal it falls. For our contemporary living religions themselves need and are seeking to incorporate an authentic expression of Socrates' daimon. An authentic philosophical theology might become an element of religion's search for a contemporary voice of its own. Not only do non-Western religions seem dumb (or merely romantic) in the face of Western scientific culture, even Western religions, in those strains most closely incorporating the mature Western intellect, have lost the ability to speak a holy word or celebrate a sacred ritual. The most benign interpretation of the situation is that authentic religion lives on in individual personal lives, but this means private life in contrast to public life integrated with social and other cultural realities.[8] With the exception of

Latin America's liberation movements, the most public expressions of religion these days seem to be war and violence. In most cases—for instance, Ireland, India, Israel, and Iraq—the real sources of conflict are economic, political, and ethnic, not dominantly matters of religious faith and practice. Where the conflict is clearly religious, as in Iran, religious ideology stems from strains of the tao still naively innocent of the daimon, although acutely aware of its threat. If contemporary religions seek a voice with which to speak their now daimon-inspired tao, philosophical theology may be a crucial component. Thus the purpose of this book is not only to inquire into certain problems of religious understanding, not only to contribute to the development of an authentic philosophical theology, not only to justify (in part) the merits of a particular view of God and creation, but to help find a living tao.

The reason the argument consists of *segments* of a religious inquiry is that philosophical theology as sketched above extends without limit into all religions and all modes of religious studies. Only arbitrary cuts into the field are possible, resulting in segments. The segments, however, are arranged so as to constitute an argument that can be forecast.

The preparation for philosophical theology as conceived here requires disengaging it from its historical source in specifically Christian theology, theology at the service of the institutionalized Christian tao: confessional, dogmatic, kerygmatic, apologetic, systematic theology. The question of disengagement is not the denial of specifically Christian claims, though it involves viewing those claims in a wider context. Rather, disengagement is disengagement from the *authority* that sets arbitrary limits on the ironic reflections of the daimon. Chapter 1, therefore, is an essentially negative critique of confessional theology as having an authority not subject to Socratic dialectic and its relevant heirs. Chapter 2 makes a similar point with respect to religious authority in ethics.

Chapter 3 introduces the major components of the philosophical theology advocated. The chapter begins as an inquiry into a central Christian concept—the Holy Spirit—and presents the speculative theory of creation as a perspective from which to try to understand the Spirit. Then it examines the conditions under which the speculative theory might be considered true, picking up in a positive way the negative argument of Chapter 1. Finally, it discusses the dialectical significance of employing an abstract theory to interpret a traditional concept. Since the usefulness of the theory of creation depends partly on its persuasiveness, and since its persuasiveness depends on how well the theory brings difficult problems into focus, the next two chapters are "essays" on a creationist understanding of Christianity. Chapter 4 expands the discussion of the Holy Spirit to an examination of the doctrine of the Trinity, arguing that the creationist theory provides a way around many consequences of trinitarianism which Christian experience suggests are heretical. While orthodoxy has no virtue in historical perspective, plausibility is gained for the theory if it says what many others have tried to say. Chapter 5 raises the question of how a creator God, construed according to the speculative theory, can address persons in ways Western religions have articulated. A solution following from the creationist theory is offered to the old problem of free will and predestination.

If philosophical theology is to be genuinely sensitive to the claims even of Christianity, it must be able to see Christianity in a comparative light with other world religions. Consequently, it must at least attempt to be as sensitive to other religions as to Christianity. The attempt is likely to be vain because of the close historical connection of philosophical theology, particularly a creationist theory, with Western religion. Nevertheless, Chapter 6 restates the creationist theory as vaguely applicable to major world religions, emphasizing the abstract metaphysical character of the speculative theory in connection with the directly empirical character of the study of various religions as specifying the theory. Chapter 7 then questions in some detail how the creationist theory can be applied to classical Chinese taoism and Confucianism. They have no serious affinity for the Mesopotamian divine city lord whose personal will and individuality are the historical roots of the idea of the creator God in the West. The discussion, however, shows that the conceptions of nature and society in those Chinese sensibilities focus on and interpret aspects of reality that a creationist theory also raises. Chapter 7 also introduces the critical edge of Socratic questioning into the understanding of Confucianism and taoism, raising questions a Westerner would ask.

A dialectical interchange between the historical edge of the Western inquiry into religion and a tao of faith and practice is not merely a comparison. Without denigrating the important prior work of analysis and comparison, philosophical theology ought to be able to engage each side with the other so that both are strengthened and changed. Chapter 8 is an attempt at such a dialectic, criticizing certain major themes of Ming Neo-Confucianism (albeit intellectual themes rather than themes of devotion) from the standpoint of contemporary process philosophy, and then criticizing process philosophy from the standpoint of experiential insights of Neo-Confucianism. Neither side can be accepted as originally stated (surely many thinkers will object to my representations of both), and both can be made more cogent and sensitive by adopting features of the creationist theory. Chapter 9 attempts a similar dialectical encounter between process philosophy and Buddhism, engaging both Nagarjuna and Fa tsang as metaphysicians. Although chapters 8 and 9, more than the others, may be geared to the interests and language of specialists, in a sense they are dishes of the pudding in which the proof of the assertions of philosophical theology may lie.

Whereas Buddism and Neo-Confucianism can be approached as paths of faith and practice through their intellectual articulation, because they explicitly presented themselves that way, the question may be raised whether to do so does not skirt the *devotion* of faith and practice. For it may be that the dimension of faith which is amenable to the Socratic spirit is only preliminary and that religious development moves into a series of stages that self-critical irony cannot touch, stages from which there is no turning back. This, indeed, is claimed by certain strands of Mahayana Buddhism, and Chapter 10 undertakes a critical examination of this, as expressed in the *Awakening of Mahayana Faith*, paying special attention to problems of will as developed in the Augustinian tradition. Problems of will aside, perhaps it is simply necessary for scholars to have the disciplined experience of the "higher truths" in order to understand them; the commitment required for this experience might be incompatible with the daimon's self-critical promptings. Chapter 11 examines this experience as expressed in the Buddhist doctrine of the two truths and sketches a theory of religious conceptualization that identifies certain necessary roles for experience. The chapter concludes with the suggestion that piety before an alien tradition's experiential integrity is at the heart of an authentic religious sensibility in the contemporary, daimonically possessed world.

Just as the first chapter raises critical objections to major forms of theological authority, the Postscript asks what positive conditions must be present for religion itself to have the authority of compelling authenticity. There is no way in which sufficient conditions for authenticity can be defined because, as all the major religions say, in some sense that definition must be awaited, not constructed. Necessary conditions can be specified, however, which have to do with engaging religious thought and practice with the other vital elements of life. Religious paths can give off the sentiment of authenticity with compelling imagery. But if that imagery itself is incompatible with the imagery we perforce must employ in other areas, imagery developed under the promptings of the daimon, that tao of faith and practice may be limited to sentiment alone, which is incapable of the true feeling that binds personal and social experience into salvation. This judgment is not entirely pejorative. There is some merit in religious experience attained through drugs and hair shirts, just as there is some intellectual merit in facile cleverness in using a method. No one, and especially not philosophical theologians, can tell others what is the next appropriate step in their path. Surely all those individual steps are fragmentary and incapable of generalization in isolation from understanding both the tao and the culture of the daimon. Since, however, a tao of faith and practice transcends the private sphere and moves into the public, it should be possible to mention some conditions for authentic religious wholeness.

These chapters are obviously segments of what would be ideal contours of an essay on philosophical theology. No religious tradition is treated in great depth, and Judaism and Islam are barely mentioned. Furthermore, the disciplines of religious studies besides philosophical theology are rarely discussed directly, only presupposed as lying behind the sensibilities of the philosophy. No attempt is made to sort and weigh competing methodologies. In diverse ways, however, the chapters presented here bring together the daimon, the tao, and creation – symbols of three central concepts with which the study of religion must conjure.

Chapter One
Accountability in Theology

THEOLOGY IS NOT a timeless or transtemporal science but a discipline that has come to be what it is through a particular historical development. Understood historically, theology as it is generally identified today has been a Christian enterprise, cultured within the institutions of Christianity and responsive intellectually to historical affairs involving Christianity. It has few close parallels in the dominant forms of religious reflection in Chinese and Indian religions or in the rabbinic commentarial tradition of Judaism; although Islamic religious reflection has paralleled Christian theology as a discipline in the past, Christian theology has entered into modern critical scholarship in ways Islamic theology has not followed, at least not decisively.[1]

In dialogue with heirs of non-Christian traditions, Christian theologians are often justly accused of parochial bias when they assume that theology is the discipline within which truth about religious matters is to be sought. The modes of reflection Christians have in mind when they consider theology are not always, if ever, the important ways in which other religions have understood themselves and the religious matters that are the subject of theology.

When this is pointed out in ecumenical discussions, the typical response is one of historical relativism; each participant is supposed to acknowledge the integrity of the others' modes of religious reflection, practicing one's own while observing others practice theirs. Discussion, then, takes the form of comparing notes, usually leading to a greater understanding of other religions and perhaps to a broadening of one's own perspective. Religious studies, the field that contains theology among other disciplines, has its first responsibility in recognizing, articulating, and overcoming the alienation from other religions that characterizes beginning thinkers.[2]

The question of the truth of beliefs about the topics within the subject matter of theology cannot be raised in historicist framework, however.

Forced into a predetermined identity by historicistic respect for differences, a theologian cannot call the Christian position into question by asking whether it is true relative to other traditions. Unable to call specifically Christian theology into question, the theologian cannot become vulnerable to the other participants in the discussion. A similar invulnerability is forced on participants from other traditions. Without vulnerability, the dialogue is a sham, however much it may broaden individual perspectives. Historical relativists will say that's the way it is: Discussion profound enough to require human vulnerability simply cannot take place between widely different traditions. Nevertheless, although religion may be *mainly* a matter of cultic articulation of imagination, guided by beauty rather than truth, we need not be tempted to think it is that alone. On the contrary, religions make serious assertions which they purport to be true.

Another response to the Christian origins of theology is possible, however, for which I intend to argue here. Instead of the static positioning of differences typical of historical relativism, we may embrace theology as an ongoing historical enterprise. Theology has outgrown its Christian origins and become a discipline that ought intrinsically to be accountable to public norms for which one's inherited religious tradition makes no *final* difference. Because theology does insist on raising questions of truth, it allows for diverse religious traditions to take one another seriously in senses that depend on mutual vulnerability. Religious truth is, of course, not a simple matter; nor is accountability. To prize vulnerability and the dimensions of dialogue it makes possible is not universally held to be valuable. I shall remark on each of these dimensions in what follows. The conclusion toward which the argument tends is that philosophical theology can provide the means for a serious quest for truth in religious matters that is neither ultimately forestalled by the relativity of historical origins nor deficient in the vulnerability that defines the daimon's ironic objectivity.

Of course, theology does not do this to any extent at the present time. It will first have to develop specific forms, habits of reflection and sensibilities, that respect genuine historical differences. Before theology can go much further, non-Christian thinkers must enter the process of reconstructing it. But even Christians who practice theology should not be called Christian theologians, only theologians; for, as theologians they are ultimately accountable only to the public norms of inquiry, not to a Christian heritage or community except insofar as those are bench marks according to public norms of inquiry.

I. Theology

To make a case for this view, it is necessary to attempt a characterization of theology in the sense intended. Theology has developed as inquiry into divine or religious matters in light of the important topics of interest and modes of understanding of the day. This characterization has several components which must be discussed.

First, and perhaps most decisively, theology is inquiry. As inquiry, it differs from ritual, from spiritual practices such as prayer and meditation, from religious celebrations, from preaching and propaganda, from rehearsals of traditions and beliefs, and from teaching and inculcating religious heritages. Of course, all of these religious enterprises, as well as others, raise theological issues and in their practice often depend on theological results. But they are not essentially inquiry; for better or worse, they can be practiced in the absence of inquiry about the truth of their religious suppositions.

As inquiry, theology has two moments. On one hand, it is a questioning, a probing, of its topics, while on the other, it is the articulation and testing of answers to its questions. In some measure these two moments are conjoined. For instance, the questioning is often framed in terms of the interests and categories resulting from prior injury, and the theological positions adduced are the results of the questions asked, at least in part. One must beware, though, of overconflating the probing and the answering. Often the important, probing challenges to assumed positions come from outside the culture of theology. Early Christian theologians used Greek philosophy in their probing. St. Thomas did theology by using the newly discovered Aristotelian texts to do his questioning. The important questions in eighteenth-century theology were raised by the invention of historical hermeneutics. In the nineteenth century many of the crucial probings came from science, and in the twentieth, the Holocaust has brought most of Western religion into question. Similarly, innovative answers in the history of theology have often transformed the questions they address; consider St. Augustine's reconstruction of the topic of the person by his invention of the autobiography, or Friedrich Schleiermacher's reformulation of the question of the presence of God by his development of an ontology of religious experience.[3]

There is no one method to theological inquiry; rather, there are many methods. The appropriateness of a particular method or combination of methods rests on historical factors. For instance, how does one question the nature of God? By asking whether a theological statement about that nature is true? By asking how a passage of scripture interprets God? By a speculative hypothesis consistent with a larger theory of things? By comparing conceptions of God in different cultures? By analyzing the history of the concepts of God? By asking what God must or must not be if the Holocaust happened? Any of these and a host of other questions might serve the probing interests of theology. Then again, any such question might be used as sham inquiry, simulating but evading real questioning. Genuine probing is extremely difficult to accomplish, as Heidegger has made clear to our generation.

There is no single method for defending, demonstrating, or testing a theological answer. Rather, theology makes a case for a view by employing whatever methods are relevant. Deductive argument is helpful in the context of established premises. Evocation of decisive experiences may be relevant. Persuasive interpretations of history, texts, or common experiences might be appropriate. Perhaps most commonly today, theologians cite analogies and resonances with other areas of promising or successful inquiry.[4]

Because theology is inquiry its answers or results are always hypothetical. They rest upon the best case made out for them and are vulnerable to being overturned by a contradicting better case. To be sure, it is not easy to overturn a well-made case. In the context of given theological discussion, a wide variety of previous commitments are taken for granted in order to focus on the question at issue. As the context of discussion changes, those previous commitments themselves can come into question. After the initial articulation and acceptance of a good case for a theological hypothesis, it takes a genuine probing, a new and unsettling form of questioning, to unseat it. As history has shown, however, theological hypotheses are often unseated not by direct attacks or by reconsideration of the cases made for them, but by shifts in the overall context which the hypotheses have meaning. The hypothesis that the Bible is the infallible, literal word of God supported by the "harmony of the scriptures" and the fervent testimony of the heart was not overturned by dulling the heart or by finding contradictions unnoticed centuries earlier. Instead, it was overturned by the development of a historical critical method for dealing with documents that caused the scriptures to be viewed in new ways, ways that seemed more revealing and persuasive.

That theological claims have the logical status of hypotheses, and are therefore only stages in an ongoing process of inquiry, constitutes the vulnerability of theology. Analogously, a theologian's vulnerability consists in the requirement of framing claims so as to be open to further inquiry. Concerned with the truth of theological claims, genuine inquirers will "fund the opposition," as it were, encouraging new lines of probing that might overturn their own claims.

The characterization of theology as "inquiry into divine or religious matters in light of the important topics of interest and modes of understanding of the day" leaves vague the subject matter of theology. Theology is defined here not so much by its object as its discipline. Here, only two statements about theology's subject matter are pertinent.

First, by virtue of the historical character of theology, it is possible to begin to indicate its subject matter denotatively by saying that the subject matter is what Christian theology has taken its subject matter to be – for instance, the nature and reality of God, God's relation to the world, the ultimate meaning of the origins and destiny of human life, the significance of God's actions in history, and so on, as articulated in terms of scripture, tradition, and experience. In dialogue with other religions, the beliefs that constitute disagreement with the orientations of Christian theology are also theological. Although it is extraordinarily difficult to state just where disagreements lie, especially when similar symbols are used to express considerably different points, if Buddhism should reject the belief that there is a God, then theology includes atheistic alternatives to theism in its subject matter. Stated more positively, where other traditions reflect abstractly on themselves in ways to which Christian theology, in its historical expression, is a contradiction, alternative, or even opaque cipher, those reflections are theological. Religious intelligence becomes theological when it moves from mere assertion to assertion *as true*.

The second statement is that the nature and scope of the subject matter of theology are themselves points at issue within theological inquiry; therefore, they vary with changing historical developments and changing demands of inquiry. From a historical perspective there will be continuity of change in theological subject matter, with the continuity accounted for by the reasons for making changes.

To characterize theology as inquiry in the light of the important topics of interest and modes of understanding of the day is to emphasize both the historical positioning of theology and its relativity to interests that probe its subject matter and provide it with new concepts and new language. In the early centuries of Christianity the experience of personal alienation in the Roman Empire and the encounter with Greek philosophy shaped theology's orientation, one that had begun with the attempt to understand the implications of Jesus' life by people not already committed to Jewish law. The sudden enlargement of the Church's role as magisterium during the medieval period shaped its scholastic orientation, with the recovery of Aristotle and the encounter with Islamic theology contributing to its shaping. In the twentieth century theology has been decisively shaped by literature, so that now there is a subdiscipline called "theology and literature." The encounter of Christianity with the world's religions, which has intensified in the last half of the twentieth century, has brought a novel but inchoate agenda to theology's concerns; not only has theology new experience to assess and new positions to address but new people to respect. The result is a new scope for the theological community, one defined transtraditionally and accountable according to public norms, not parochially traditional ones.

II. Accountability and Inquiry

Accountability has some misleading connotations. I do not mean that a theologian is "accountable" to a particular community; it is always logically possible for a theologian's inquiry to lead to rejection of the legitimacy of the community. No, a theologian is accountable *within* a community; it is other members of the community who call the theologian to account. Nor do I mean that a theologian is accountable to a specifiable set of public norms of inquiry, because what those norms are, and the public forms they take, are themselves issues of theology and other modes of inquiry. Rather, a theologian is accountable in terms of the norms that can best be applied to the theological potentials of the day. Just what "can best be applied" is subject to future dispute within the community making the inquiry.

By *accountability*, I mean a theologian's obligation to inquire into the truth of the subject matter and justify the theological results as true. Perhaps there is no better expression than to say that theologians are accountable to the pursuit of truth. Of course, if all theological assertions are logically hypothetical, then there is no final truth, and the obligatory justifications are provisional. But a theologian can say: "As far as I can tell now, such and such is true because of these considerations, and these considerations are the relevant ones, given the public norms of theological inquiry as we best understand them now." The relevant considerations would include, of course, dealing with the counterarguments and alien perspectives that suggest such and such is false.

The central element in this reconstructed Enlightenment conception of accountability is that a theological assertion is presented as true only as long as it is connected to reasons for which an account can be given, and as vulnerable to being overthrown if the reasons are overthrown. Accountability to truth means readiness to make a case for assertions, and to alter or withdraw them if the results of inquiry so dictate. Some philosophers have identified the meaning of truth with the arguments that can be given for why such and such is true. By no means does this conception of accountability do that. Whatever truth is (and that is a problem of enormous complexity), it is not the same as the reasons to be adduced in inquiry for believing such and such to be true. The conception of accountability applies not to truth but to inquiry: Regardless of whether an assertion is true, to *assert* it *as* true is to be obliged to tie the assertion to the strength of the case that can be made for it.

The assertion of something as true is somewhat related to the meaning of truth itself. The sheer immediacy of experience – the subjective order of experiential representations, presentational immediacy, the material reality of a proposition – is not true or false except insofar as it represents that about which it might be true. A potential interpreter is necessary if anything – an idea, a feeling, or a metal straightedge – has the logical status of being true or false of something. Experience itself has no truth mode unless it has an assertoric element: "What is experienced now is what the world is." Thus there is no truth without assertibility and no true experience without assertive interpretation. There is a fundamental truth in Tarski's dictum that "snow is white" if and only if snow is white. But how does one separate an experience from the world so as to assert it? Not through Kant's method of distinguishing a publicly verifiable set of representations from among the larger set of subjective representation, for that supposes the entire world is representative. Kant's strategy, however, was basically correct: An experience is assertable if it is possible that a case can be made for it. The making of a case is the concrete insertion of a mediating link between assertion and its object, an assertion whose reality lies in the conceivable community to which the case is made. Nothing can be true without being assertable, and nothing can be assertable without supposing that making a case can both define a space and make a connection between the assertion and its object. To assert, then, is to be accountable for making a case.

This conception of accountability has a direct consequence for the conception of the community within which theology is accountable. Suppose a Christian says: "As a Christian I believe that an important element of salvation consists in perfecting the image of God in man and that this is done through the imitation of Christ." Suppose a Jew answers: "You are right about the importance of perfecting the image of God, but you are wrong about imitating Jesus; rather, you should live the life of the Torah to perfect the image of God." The Christian might then respond along one of two lines. The first might be: "I was speaking as a Christian. The role I ascribed to Jesus is an essential component of Christian theology." To this, the Jew would have to say: "Then you are not really making a theological assertion about God, salvation, or Jesus but rather a sociological or a historical assertion about what Christians believe, by noting that you are one of them." Yet this is likely not to have been the intent of one who speaks as the Christian first did; the intent, rather, was a theological one.

The Christian's other response might be one giving reasons for asserting that the imitation of Jesus is a crucial component in perfecting the image of God. What would constitute good reasons in this case? Good reasons are those that accord with norms of inquiry public enough to encompass the Jew. If, in the course of making the case, the Christian must resort to "this is what Christians believe," the inquiry has thereby excluded the Jew from the theological arena and, insofar as it publicly includes the Jew, transformed the discourse into sociology.

Public participation in inquiry makes all partners vulnerable. Suppose, after some frustrating arguments, the Christian says: "You wouldn't accept anything special about Jesus, no matter what I said, because you are a Jew and after centuries of persecution by Christians you define yourself as rejecting Christian claims about Jesus." How could the Jew respond? The most frequent response, for understandable historical reasons, would simply be to say: "Yes, as a Jew, nothing could convince me of a Christian view of Jesus." That is a sociological assertion, and many think that sociology and history define the realities of Jewish-Christian relations.

The Jew's response is not a theological assertion, however. A theological response would have to provide reasons concerning the image of God and salvation for rejecting the imitation of Jesus. Once the Christian recognizes that the theological assertion of Christian beliefs is conditional on a disputed case, and once the Jew recognizes that rejection of Christian beliefs may be conditional on a case in dispute, then both are profoundly vulnerable. Each recognizes that honest inquiry may require one or both to abandon the beliefs by which they were once identified. Theological inquiry may well be undertaken within a decisive historical tradition; but that tradition is always vulnerable, and the theologians' identities are conditional on the outcome of inquiry.

This hypothetical dispute between Christian and Jew illustrates a characteristic of the public community within which theology is accountable, that of coping with historically established and perceived contradictions. The encounter of Western theologies with Asian theologies presents numerous other problems, mainly those identifying where the real disputes about theological assertions lie. The underlying principle is the same, however: to make an assertion, one ties it to a case that ought to convince someone who otherwise would say it is mistaken. This entails working one's way to the inside of the other traditions' perspective, to locate such a case. That one's opponent is not convinced does not mean that the assertion is mistaken, only that it is vulnerable to overthrow.

This conception of inquiry, it should be remarked, is derived in large measure from that of Charles Peirce. Peirce's theory of inquiry as the foundation of community and his theory of community as the matrix of inquiry have been decisive developments in the transcendence of the American speculative tradition over the epistemological culs-de-sac of European philosophy.[5] My presentation of the concept of inquiry differs from Peirce's in a striking respect, however. Whereas Peirce expresses inquiry in the rhetoric of the scientific enterprise, I express it in the more general language of "making a case." Some cases are scientific ones, with formal theoretical predictions of observable outcomes. Other cases are hermeneutic ones of interpretation and understanding. Still others are moral arguments, aesthetic evocations, consciousness-raising, and so on. Peirce's own theory of signs is sufficiently general to include all instances of "making a case," but his rhetoric is not fair to the "humanistic" modes of thought most typical of theology.

Rooting the conception of theology as inquiry in pragmatism, however, even when it is expanded to encompass humanistic domains, appears to slight a traditional, defining element of theology. Theology has been written within religious communities, communities self-identified by faith and practice. Theology, therefore, has often been thought to stand under an obligation to be faithful to the community's founding revelation, to its convenant events in Western religions or to its paradigmatic yogic experiences in the East. It is thought that this requires theology to be fundamentally backward-looking even when it addresses hope and fear concerning the future. From this need to be faithful to the deposit of faith derives a need to be faithful to the religious community, making theology instrumental to religious ends, to preaching or practice or to gnostic salvation itself.

If theology is inquiry, then it is only accidentally apologetic, directive, or proclamatory (though theology has often served those purposes well). The concern of theology is for truth in religious matters, not for consistency with past belief even if that were possible. The pursuit of truth is valuable in its own right, and this value is distinctively registered in the fact that religious communities believe their beliefs to be true and sometimes pay theologians to prove it. Preachers want their doctrines not only to be old but sound. If a religious community is presented with clear alternatives between continuity with old beliefs, which had been its identifying ideology, and a contradictory theological result, which seems to have the best case on its side, its choice is not a theological but an existential one, pitting community continuity against perceived truth.

Religion, of course, is not a theological invention. One of the clearest norms of public inquiry is that theological assertions must be in touch with, interpret, and assess the historical and experiential roots of religion. A theologian often is asked to inquire into some grounding element of religious faith. But the norms for accountability in what to make of that element are the same for people within the tradition as for those without it. If, in making a case for his or her belief, the committed believer requires normative reference to being committed, then the topic has been shifted from considering the truth of the belief to a sociological comment on the believer's commitment. While it may seem at first glance that the requirement for public standards in theology is hard on thinkers committed within a community of faith, I believe its greatest hardship falls on those outside a given community of faith whose theology has genuinely to touch, interpret, and assess the foundations of that community. Public standards do not justify distance; they require full participation in whatever might count as part of a relevant case within inquiry.

If the conception of theology as inquiry does not slight faithfulness, it would surely seem to slight religious commitment. Even with the best of arguments, a theological position will have a vulnerable, hypothetical air about it; theology can never quite give up irony and skepticism. Yet the religious life is definite, a finite choice, and totally demanding in commitment. Therefore, theology seems incapable of being an honest mode of reflection within the religious life, however appropriate it may be for a neutral community of inquirers. About this point, I have three observations. First, it is true that theology must be more distant from organized, committed religious practice than it has often been in the past; it can be the servant of religious commitment only accidentally. Second, this is as it should be, since religious commitment would not want theology to tell it a lie when it asks for the truth. If religious commitment is possible without concern for the truth, it is better off without theology. But then it would be a tao without the daimon. Third, it is simply a characteristic tension of the modern age to have to act with commitment when understanding is tentative and uncertain. The example in religion is repeated in politics, ethics, law and with the engagement of society and culture itself. The tao is inescapable in modern and postmodern civilizations. If it is true, as William James thought, that intellectual commitment provides cognitive evidence for a belief that is inaccesible without the commitment, then the commitment is in some way required for a proper public assessment of the case. If contradictory commitments are required, the disbursing of responsibilities of inquiry within the community of inquiry is complicated beyond the capacity of the usual models. Here, though, the requirement of commitment comes from the public norms of inquiry, not from some intellectually irreducible demand of the community of religious faith.

David Hall has articulated a variant on these considerations by identifying religous experience with mystical experience, claiming that these two forms of experience are private rather than public ones, then saying that religious assertions about either experience should not be judged in terms of norms of inquiry that define ideal consensus.[6] The truth of religious assertions, Hall suggests, is closer to that of aesthetics than to science, because both religion and art constitute personal perspectives rather than communal contexts. Consensus is a myth, he says, when associated with important religious or aesthetic truths, however much it might be appropriate in morals or science. Contrary to Hall, it must be noted that religion is more than mystical experience, that it includes assertions about the way things are, and that among these assertions must be those justifying the analogy of religious and aesthetic experiences. Nevertheless, Hall is correct in his main point, that essential religious experience has a personal immediacy made dogmatic when translated into public assertions. But the reason for this is that religious experience in this sense is an affair of imagination, of primordially taking things as structured in the form of a world. Such experience is indeed normed by aesthetic criteria, not by truth. Questions of truth arise within a shared public world, not prior to it. Hence, religious imagination must become common, or public, before religious public assertions can be made. The ugliness but inevitable importance of religious dogma stems from its location at the boundary where imagination struggles to become public and public assertions struggle to be true to the demands of imaginatively having a world.

In one sense, the public norms of inquiry are those norms that have the potential for distinguishing between better and worse beliefs. The determination of these norms, and how they apply, is always relative to the community of inquirers at hand. In another sense, though, not all public norms for theological inquiry are as relative as the above remarks may indicate, for it is possible to distinguish some fairly steady dimensions of thinking that have come to be prized, and rightly so, as essential to inquiry.

For example, one dimension of thinking mentioned above is the work of imagination, which at its most basic level is the synthesis of causal impingements of the world so they become experiential elements. Through imagination, forces become feelings, indeterminate randomness becomes spontaneity, and inertia becomes intention. Imagination makes experiential engagement possible, and its public norms are those for perfecting engagement. Imagination – in theology, as elsewhere – is not the direct pursuit of truth but the pursuit of engagement. Its norms are aesthetic ones having to do with beauty, interest, and so on. Theology lacking the imaginative dimension is "scholastic" in the pejorative sense because it is not engaged with the realities of religion. This is recognized by the community.

Another dimension of thinking is the formal or systematic one. The function of systematic thinking is to provide a vision of the whole of things in terms of the abstract or logical elements of systematic theory. The logic of the theory allows one to get from one part of experience to the next without discontinuity. Theology that attends to system is philosophical theology. Systems are vague with respect to making direct claims about particular reality. They require lower-level, less vague claims to flesh them out. Without an integrating systematic vision, however, it is impossible to tell whether more specific claims that arise in religious reflection are compatible, complementary, or even relevant to each other. Public norms for the systematic dimension of theology are thus the familiar ones of formal cogency as a theory and proper relativity to what the community finds it worthwhile to systematize. Systematic theology also leads us to look for implications we might not otherwise think of. (We return to this theme in Chapter 3.)

Theology as inquiry has many other publicly recognized norms. In hermeneutic theology, for instance, norms like those for interpreting history and literature apply. It is difficult to say more about the norms for making a particular theological case without examination of the cases themselves. As has been argued, those norms are themselves much in dispute within the theological community as the community expands. But the defense to be made of norms for guiding and judging inquiry must have to do with showing that the norms do in fact guide and judge well; this defense is a logically indefinite process of normative self-evaluation requiring dialectical objectification of the community's state at each crucial point of the defense. It makes no sense to say that a norm is valid because it equates consistency with some tradition or past revelation, because consistency is not truth. That an assertion is consistent with another assertion may be a partial criterion of truth, but only if one has prior reason to believe that the assertion with which the one in question is consistent is itself true. To say something is true is to say that it asserts what is in fact the case and that an argument can be made to connect the assertion with its object.

III. Practical Implications

I have tried to indicate something of the multifariousness of theology and to build a case from many standpoints for the view that the theological community does indeed exercise critical judgment in terms of norms that are public, as well as determining what those norms are through processes of historical dialectic. There are practical implications of the directions my remarks have taken, which I would briefly like to indicate.

Whereas in the past the theological community may have been primarily Christian, now it includes thinkers from all religious traditions, or from none, who are concerned with and disciplined to pursue the truth in religious matters. The scope of the community is determined by interests anyone might have in the truth of theological issues. From this perspective it seems a little silly to say that inquiry into the truth of religious matters has been primarily a Christian concern; for surely there have been great inquirers in other traditions, perhaps greater than Christian theologians.

The paideia of theology will have to expand radically from what has been and still is traditional Christian theology. Instead of preoccupation with the history of Christian events and theology, the phenomenological sources in which theologians need to be steeped are the resources of all religious traditions. The history of religions or comparative religions or the phenomenology of religion needs to be developed to take the place of "church history" and "dogmatics" in Christian theology.

Even more striking than change in paideia is the change of venue required by the new historical stage of theology. Whereas theology formerly took place largely within organized religion (this is as true of other world religions as it is of Christianity), now it must find its home in a public context broad enough to encompass the entire community. This probably means that theology's home is the university. In the past there was uneasiness about the place of theology in universities, particularly public universities, because theology was thought to promote religion and to argue from a privileged bias. But because theology's norms have become public, it can no longer appeal to a privileged religious starting point unavailable to unbelievers or believers in other than locally established religions. Indeed, theology as a form of inquiry needs the pressure for objectivity that can and should come from other university departments. Insofar as organized religions have an interest in theology, they must develop a nontraditional relationship with university departments of religious studies. That, in fact, is already happening.

The historical development of theology-as-inquiry will have an impact on university curricula in religion. According to the old seminary model, the function of the university religion curriculum was to teach the university's religion. In reaction to this, the development of curricula of religious study stressed the historical and social-scientific study of religion. Theological questions were handled in the way I above dub "sociological," noting that for Jews one thing is true and that for Christians quite another thing is true. Now that theological questions themselves are on the agenda, they should be studied with the tools of critical scholarship and without the privileged position of a faith commitment to an answer in advance.

The upshot of these considerations is that theology has lost the authority it once had in Christianity and elsewhere as the intellectual voice of a self-certain community. Where self-certain communities exist today, theology is no more their voice than it is the voice of others. Where theology is faithful to the norms of truth and vulnerable inquiry, the self-certainty of a community can be an object of study and perhaps a conclusion of discussion; but it cannot be an authoritative source. The tao of faith and practice is not the "author" of theology; rather, its author is the tao of inquiry. That is, theology cannot be related to authority in any usual sense of the latter. If it could, it would lack the value of presenting the best case for truth, the very value the tao of faith and practice needs from theology.

The argument of this chapter is essentially a negative one intended to disengage theology from religious authority or confessionalism. The community of theological inquiry is described only briefly and then without serious exemplification. Chapter 3 attempts to make a positive case, arguing that theology finds a home in inquiry when it includes philosophical theology as described in the Introduction.

Before we take up the positive argument, however, we need to raise a systematic objection. The discussion of theology-as-inquiry is understandably academic, for the academy is where that kind of inquiry occurs most critically. But it might be argued, it is precisely the academic character of theology that obscures the real justification of the authority of the tao of faith and practice to determine theology. The authority of the tao of faith and practice extends directly to the practical life, not the theoretical. It is primarily an ethical authority and impinges on reflection only insofar as reflection is involved in ethics, in living well or poorly. Since theology obviously impinges on the ethical domain, it must, in some sense we have not discovered, be subject to the authority of the tao of faith and practice. So goes the counterargument to what I claim here.

Surely the norms of good thinking are a subspecies of the norms of good acting, since thinking is a form of acting. Furthermore, how we act depends largely on how we think. Therefore, we must inquire whether a tao of faith and practice contains an authority that binds ethics. Most religious traditions, in fact, are identifiable as *ethical* traditions. If there is such a thing as religious ethics in a normative sense, then the celebration here of public inquiry in theology must somehow be off the mark. My argument in this book is that ethics is subject to public norms of justification just as much as is theological inquiry, and to "secular" norms where that means the field of relevant good cases is more inclusive than any or all taos of faith and practice. The daimon, it will be remembered, goaded Socrates mostly in matters of moral substance.

Chapter Two
Authority and Experience
in Religious Ethics

THICS IS A SECULAR enterprise – thoroughly, finally, and ines-
capably secular. This is so despite the fact that, for most of the
civilizations of the Middle East and Europe, ethics is the child of
religion. Ethical duties usually have been seen as religious duties divinely
sanctioned. Even law and jurisprudence have been intimately associated
with religion, as they are today in some Islamic cultures. Where law has
separated itself from religion, usually it has separated itself from normative ethics as well. Throughout much of Western history the most
profound, thorough, and sensitive ethical thinking has been done under
the aegis of organized religion or under the direct, explicit inspiration of
religious ideas. The phrase "ethical tradition" calls to mind rabbinic
casuistry and the Christian moral magisterium. In the United States the
primary social function accorded religious institutions is the articulation
and promulgation of basic cultural values.

Yet ethics is a secular enterprise. I want to explore this thesis first,
then ask the obvious questions, What does religion contribute positively
to ethics? Is religion's contribution an authority that arbitrarily cuts off
the daimon of inquiry?

I. Decline of Authority

The migration of ethics from the religious to the secular arena is a
historical phenomenon of the modern era. It has to do with a shifting of
responsibility from a context of religious authority to one of personal experience. When ethics was contained within religion, recognition of the
authority embodied in religion colored every aspect of ethics. The enterprise of ethics has a great many aspects, to be sure, including at least the
following: identification of fundamental norms, extrapolations of the implications of the norms for typical cases, deliberation and judgment

27

about particular cases, acquisition of moral character by individuals and groups in accordance with their decisions and behavior, judgments of approval or guilt regarding moral character, and, of chief importance for contemporary social ethics, integration of all the above into complex personal and social responses to changing and novel moral situations. When ethics is considered in a religious context, all its aspects are colored by a respect for the authority ascribed to religion's holy elements. Identification of fundamental norms, for instance, can take its justification to be proof of divine sanction. Casuistry respects the authority of religious teachers, rabbis, and priests. Deliberation and judgment about particular cases can respect the limits of a permissible outcome set by religious figures. The quality of the moral life is construed as a matter of sin and salvation.

Religious authority was rarely absolute, however, even in the most religious periods of history. Political concerns generally have tempered religious ones. Disputes about interpreting fundamental claims temper the authority of basic norms. Recognition of the fallible human character of religious authorities insinuates some degree of suspicious worldliness into even the most authoritarian groups. The fact that respect for religious authority is rarely absolute, however, does not mean that it has not colored extensively ethical thought and action. In medieval Europe it was an insistent background against which apparently secular debates and struggles took place.

In the modern world that sense of authority has largely dropped away. No longer the background presupposition, in the few areas where appeal to it is still made, religious authority must be supported by arguments, claims of infallibility, or predictions of dire consequences should the authorities be forgotten – all of which indicate that religious authority is no longer genuinely authoritative. The daimon is chiefly responsible for this situation.

In the course of modern history a powerful principle has come to be valued as excluding religious authority, at least in ethics. It is that people *qua* persons are to be regarded as responsible for the values according to which they act. To ask only whether people act in accordance with their values is one thing. That is part of responsibility but not the most essential part. Even computers can be judged according to how well they make decisions on the basis of the values programmed into them. The more essential part of responsibility is that people are responsible for the values themselves according to which they guide their behavior.

Of course, no one begins with a value-neutral mind and arbitrarily fills it with norms. Rather, we discover ourselves already to be choosing and acting according to norms inherited from our culture or personal experience. When we discover ourselves to be acting according to norms that are challenged, however, it is part of responsibility to take responsibility for justifying them or to abandon them for alternatives. In intellectual matters this means justifying the criteria for making a good case.

It sometimes is very difficult to accept the notion that our basic norms can be questioned. Nevertheless, we prize that aspect of personhood which consists in the capacity to take responsibility for the basic norms directing action. When people lack that capacity, we limit the respect accorded them as persons by making excuses. If a family, for instance, is imbued with violent and mean-spirited values, we excuse the small children on the grounds that they lack the requisite capacity for self-consciousness. We may excuse the ancient reprobates on grounds of senility. We excuse feebleminded halfwits because they cannot understand the issues, and we excuse psychotics because they are lost in delusions. However humanely we treat those we excuse, the fact that we recognize excuses means that we qualify the sense in which we recognize them as responsible people. The violent and mean-spirited people for whom no excuses apply, we take with full human seriousness. They do not *have* to be guided by those poor values; if they never learned alternatives, that is ultimately their own fault. To condemn them for violent and mean-spirited lives is more humane and respectful than to conjure up some excuse that denies either their capacities or their autonomy.

The implication for ethics of the principle that people are themselves responsible for the values according to which they live is that there is no genuine authority other than responsible people themselves. People may look to a religious magisterium for advice, for skilled analysis, or for programs of cultivating the moral life; but responsibility for accepting the advice, the analysis, or the programs rests inalienably with the people who do the accepting. One may even will to accept a magisterium as an authority. Socrates, for instance, chose to be obedient to the laws of Athens. But, then,the authority of the magisterium derives from the individual's own authority. Whereas religions and cultural traditions can be massively and blindingly influential, they cannot be authoritative when that influence is challenged except by being posited as authoritative by the individual's personal authority. In other words, it is your responsibility what and whom you take to be authoritative, which means that the only true authority is your own authority, one that remains yours even when it is transferred to another. The classial meaning of *religious authority* is lost when the only authority is the individual's posited authority. Contrary to the supposition posited at the end of Chapter 1, a tao of faith and practice has no authority of its own except as it derives from individuals' autonomy. A tao that does not find driving authority within the autonomy of persons either has no driving authority or has only the psychological authority of subjective commitments.

Ethics is now a secular matter because responsibility rests on no otherworldly connection but only on individual self-constitution. Does this mean that religion has no bearing on ethics? If religion cannot function as an authority in ethical matters, has it no function whatsoever in ethics? It does – a function at the heart of autonomy itself.

II. Ontology and Cosmology in Religion

In keeping with the classical tradition in the philosophy of religion, let me begin the discussion with a metaphysical distinction. There are two perspectives from which the process of the world can be appreciated and understood, which I shall call the cosmological and the ontological. Every event or stretch of process can be exhaustively understood from both a cosmological and an ontological perspective. Anything with a cosmological aspect also has an ontological aspect, and vice versa. How can these aspects be characterized?

A thing's cosmological nature, its "what," is a function of its relations to other things. By *thing*, I mean not only an enduring object but anything with features, including situations, events, fields, possibilities, and ideas. To enter into a relation, a thing must be conditioned in some way by that to which it is related, and it must have essential features of its own. But the thing's character, its identity, consists in how it is related to other things so as to be different from them. A thing is, for instance, the set of roles it plays in various systems, its position in space relative to other things in space, its temporal and causal functions relative to other things, its relationship as a whole to its constituent parts, its relation as a part to the many wholes in which it functions. The cosmological analysis of a thing, therefore, is indefinitely complex. We can go indefinitely far back to its antecedents or project indefinitely far ahead to its consequences; we can penetrate indefinitely far into its components or extrapolate indefinitely far into its systematic or adventitious roles. Cosmological analysis is an analysis of the ways things are connected and the natures they have as they are related to each other. It explains, so far as we can understand, *what* things are. The stretch of a cosmological analysis is intrinsically indefinite and can be limited by functions of special interest. We can analyze a physical object in its setting or the setting itself with arbitrarily drawn limits; or we can analyze a cosmological process lasting a second, a year, or an eon.

An ontological analysis, by contrast, begins with any thing, any *what*, and asks about the fact *that* it is. No matter where the cosmological limits are arbitrarily set, *that* the complex exists is something to note. It is somewhat misleading to speak of an ontological analysis, because the dominant connotation of the word *analysis* is the division of the object into its parts and relations. Only cosmology admits of analysis in the ordinary sense. The ontological perspective, on the other hand, is a dimension of experience that cannot be reduced to the cosmological. There are times—crisis times—when the ordinary run of our minds through the relational, cosmological contour of things is arrested. With a shock we become aware of the fact of existence. We apprehend our intentions not by intending them but by suddenly becoming aware of them as detached phenomena. We feel the existential quality of something not through its causes, which are cosmologically related antecedents, but through its difference from absolute nothingness. If we attempt to flee from the ontological perspective (which we often do, because existential shocks are not always pleasant), we only proceed to more and more distant cosmological relations, earlier causes, finer components. The ontological shock travels along that entire flight; the thing *plus* its earliest causes or *reduced* to its finest components becomes the object of ontological wonder. "If I fly to the wings of the morning or dwell in the uttermost sea" (Psalm 139), the absolute fact of existence, shocking and holy, is there.

Now it is the ontological perspective on things with which religion has primarily to do. A tao of faith and practice is a way of addressing the fact of existence. Because the cosmological qualities of life differ, there are different taos for responding to the fact of life. The responses may be fundamentally different, but a tao is a tao because it addresses the positivity of existence itself. The shock of ontological existence is at the heart of holiness; it is the uncanny element in the sacred. The symbolisms of divinity orient the responses we make to the ontological fact. As a philosophical enterprise, ontology is a theoretical attempt to understand how and why there is what there is. In sophisticated religions, ontology is a central component of theology and contributes to the characterization of the religious object.

Before developing this point, however, it is necessary to relate ethics to the distinction between the cosmological and the ontological. In most respects, ethics is a cosmological matter. With regard to deliberation about cases, the identification of fundamental norms, and the casuistic elaboration of the implications of those norms, the cognitive aspects of ethics deal with actual situations, with ideal harmonies, and their inter-relations and alternatives. Cognitive ethics is concerned with what things are, what they should be, and what to do to make progress toward goals. With regard to choosing itself and acting according to choices, fulfilling obligations and taking responsibilities, ethics is again a matter of making and unmaking existential connections.

It is precisely because both the cognitive and the active elements of ethics are cosmological that ethics is truly a thoroughly secular enter-prise. Religious people as such have no special talent for analyzing a moral situation, for conceiving of alternate ways of harmonizing the situations, for articulating general normative harmonies, for cleaving to obligations or fulfilling responsibilities. Religion, however, contributes at least three elements to experience that have a profound bearing on ethics, especially social ethics.

It is my hypothesis that every major religion has a version of the three components: ritual, cosmology, and spiritual practices. What are they, and what is their relationship to ethics?

Ritual has often been construed as repetitive behavior on a continuum between magic and the reenactment of mythical, primal events. Doubtless there is something to this, but the more central element of ritual is that it epitomizes what the culture finds to be the actions that most engage life. Ritual actions are the epitome of the problematic in engagement. In paleolithic hunting societies, cave paintings indicate that rituals rehearsed stalking and killing prey and coping with violent death. In primitive agricultural societies rituals were concerned with fertility. In early urban societies they centered on the political stratifica-tion of power so as to order social classes. Gods in these societies were not earth mothers or baals but kings, and political kingship was ritualiz-ed to replicate divinity so conceived. In the early Christian era rituals in-volving the sacrifice of Jesus contained a deeply buried reference to the scapegoat rituals of a thousand years prior, and an overlay of reference to Isaiah's suffering-servant image of Israel; but the dominant sense for early Christian ritual was action that incorporated one in a life-giving God who transcends cultural differences. For the early Christians were primarily displaced people from parochial cultures who had to live in the cosmopolitan environment of the Roman empire. The Christian eucharist epitomized actions by which that world could be engaged authentically.

By cosmology, the second component of religion, I mean a vision or sense for the whole of things relative to one's own affairs. Cosmologies take many different forms. Some are mythological while others are framed in the language of science. Some are geographical pictures, others are histories or sagas. Some are inherited traditions and others are the creative works of genius or responses to decisive historical events. Most involve all these elements. How interesting it is in our own time to take part in the construction of a new cosmology by Jewish thinkers after the calamity of the Holocaust! The common element in religious cosmologies is that they function at the level of imagination prior to explicit judgment, sorting the items entering our experience into the groups it is important to respond to. The contours of the cosmology serve to throw the items of experience into the subliminal systems and causal relations that undergird the values by which experience is ordered. It might be tempting to say that cosmologies indicate the place of human reality in the cosmos, but that would be too optimistic a generalization. Cosmologies may tell us that mankind has no place, that the cosmos is fragmented, that life is meaningless, even that, though life has meaning, we have lost our chance and armageddon is upon us. Cosmologies give shape and symbolic articulation to rituals, and rituals, by their very repetition, reinforce the significance of cosmologies in our imaginative engagement of the world.

The third component, spiritual practices, involves ritual elements and is symbolically articulated by cosmologies. Spiritual practices, however, are aimed at cultivating spiritual perfection in individuals. They include the familiar practices of prayer and meditation, reflective confession, fasting, and penance. Spiritual practices also include ideal conceptions of the goals of spiritual perfection, often implying a series of stages through which one should progress. Sometimes there is an organized hierarchy of spiritual masters. Spiritual practices – unlike rituals, which seem to require a continuity of culture over long periods, with each period leaving a sediment of engaging action, and unlike cosmologies, which rise, shift, and fall under the impact of new information – can be transferred with some ease from one culture to another and can slough one cosmological rationale for another without fundamentally changing shape. Witness the current adaptation of Zen meditation techniques to Jewish and Christian piety. This happened probably because spiritual practices have such quick and local responses within the experience of practicing individuals.

So far I have indicated something of the nature of ritual, cosmology, and spiritual practices, focusing on what could be called their cosmological elements. Let me now indicate what makes them religious, what makes them responsive to the ontological perspective.

The religious quality of ritual can be understood in terms of the old distinction between spiritual life and spiritual death, a distinction common to both European and Asian religions. A spiritually dead person is not biologically or culturally dead. He or she can be involved in all the cosmological affairs of nurturance, production, leisure, even the pursuit of moral quality. Because the spiritually dead person has not responded to the ontological fact of existence, though, there is a quality of disengagement from participation in life. However energetic and well intentioned they may be, spiritually dead people tend to be reactive, not existentially engaged. Ritual, if it is authentic, focuses a person's imagination on the modes of action that are genuinely engaging. True participation in a ritual is an act of spiritual life. Of course, because rituals contain "sedimentary" actions that are no longer the epitome of engagement, participation in ritual can be spiritually dead. The standard criticism of ritual as formal, as "killing the spirit," reflects that widespread belief that rituals sometimes fail to epitomize those actions that indeed would be engaging for the culture and the people at hand. Although rituals sometimes are not related to the ontological perspective and thus lose their genuinely religious function, they can, on the other hand, succeed, directing people's imaginations to incorporate the ontological perspective in the ways these people engage the world.

The religious quality of cosmology can be distinguished from the philosophical or scientific quality of cosmology. Philosophically, a cosmology allows a person to create a certain kind of cognitive experience, one that constitutes the knower as someone with a whole vision. Scientifically, a cosmology lets one understand what things are and how they work on a cosmic scale. The religious function of a cosmology is to articulate and sharpen the contrast between *what* the world is and *that* the world is. Without a sense of the coherence of all the "what's," more particularly of all the "valuable what's," it is difficult to grasp the stark holiness of the world's sheer existence. Although a cosmology might be constructed through explicit inquiry and art, it functions in imagination prior to judgment. Therefore, the religious function of cosmology is to make possible the feeling of the contrast between the character of the world and its existence. Religious cosmology is the work of the imagination making both emotional and cognitive sense of the shocking ontological perspective on things.

The religious quality of spiritual practices is somewhat clearer, although spiritual practices can be construed reductively as mere psychological therapies. At root, spiritual practices are aimed at disciplining people individually to be fully responsive to the ontological perspective. They cultivate psychic integrity, which removes the cosmological interests of the ego from blocking an open response. They cultivate sagacity or directness of feeling, exhibiting particularly the contrast between the relativities of the world and the ontological absoluteness of its existence. They also cultivate purity of heart and love, so that one's desires are not functions of one's own needs but of the desirability of their objects.

III. Cosmological Ethics, Ontological Religion

Ritual, cosmology, and spiritual practices together constitute religion as a complex of responses to the fact that our ordinary cosmological perspective can always be contrasted with a corresponding ontological contrast. I have characterized these ideals in terms of ideal functions, and it is not difficult to assess our actual religious conditions with respect to them. Here, though, I want to focus on the relation between religion and ethics.

The first point to emphasize is that the contribution of religion to life is principally at the level of imagination and therefore religion operates prior to the level of critical judgment and responsible action which is the domain of ethics. In light of the ontological perspective, religion formulates the structures of imagination by which we engage life or by which we fail to do so. More exactly, most of us engage life in partial and fragmentary ways because authentic religion, for us, is only partial and fragmentary.

The second point to be emphasized is the converse of the first: any aspect of religion can be objectified, lifted out of its immediate imaginative functioning, and subjected to ethical criticism. The priority of religion's home in imagination does not mean priority in order of judgment and criticism. Fertility rites involving human sacrifice, for instance, however authentic they once were for epitomizing the sacrifices necessary for fertility, are immoral and ought not be practiced. It would be a confusion, for example, for an anthropologist to defend cannibalism on the grounds that it is an authentic religious ritual for the tribe in question; that argument confuses authentic religion with morality. The same is true of cosmologies. A biblical fundamentalist cosmology may serve someone's religious imagination, allowing them to make a profound apprehension of the contingent ontological status of the world; but it cannot accept the mass of information and critical judgment that proves it to be cognitively in error. Thus it ought not to be believed. Spiritual practices, too, may be effective in personal cultivation but ethically selfish or destructive to others or the community. Where elements of religion can be brought from the immediacy of imagination to the mediated status of objects of judgment, the ethics of judgment and of action proceeding from judgment demands that persons take responsibility for the best possible assessment and self-control.

This point provides another perspective on the shift in ethics from religious authority to secular experience. Religion was, is, and will be the mother, the matrix, of ethics in the sense that critical judgment arises from and presupposes the experiential bed of imagination; but when the forms of religion were immediate and their status was unconscious within the imagination, they seemed authoritative. Insofar as ethics was separated from its imaginative base and the religious forms were still immediate, religious forms seemed authoritative over ethics. When the daimon devised means through critical thinking in psychology, history, economics, and philosophy to objectify the contents of imagination and bring them to critical judgment, the authority of religion faded. Now, we may—must—ask whether our rituals *ought* to be celebrated or whether some others should be invented, whether our cosmologies are true and our spiritual practices moral. This is not to reduce them to ethical concerns, for their function is still in the imagination prior to ethical judgment; what it does say is that they are at least ethical concerns because they can be recognized and in part controlled and therefore should be influenced for better rather than worse.

The third point about the relation of religion to ethics is that ethics needs religion in its imaginative ground. Not only is religion in imagination prior to ethics in critical judgment, it is necessary. Put more directly, to the extent that religious imagination fails to engage one in the world with the intensity that comes from feeling the contrast between the cosmological perspective and the ontological perspective, ethical life also fails to be engaged, however valid its judgments and well intentioned its efforts. This can be illustrated with regard to ritual, cosmology, and spiritual practices.

For technologically advanced countries, many of the actions that would authentically engage the world are those having to do with justice, particularly distributive justice. Ritual actions for productivity, social order, even finding identity in a universalistic culture have already been laid down and are no longer the focal point of engagement. Social justice and fairness in the distribution of resources are now what move us as people, what marks the actions by which we spiritually live or die. Consider the ritual mourning that took place after the death of Martin Luther King, Jr. A ritual engagement of the religious imagination does not alter any of our ethical judgments about how to achieve justice; it introduces no new premises or rules of inference. It does not even add anything to that ethical motive that consists in the attractiveness or rightness of obligation. What it does mean is that social justice as a domain of ethics becomes a medium of spiritual life or death. If one wakes up to the ontological perspective and seeks a life that reflects it, for our time and place, that means engagement in the struggle for social justice. The struggle for justice is worthwhile and commanding on its own merits; but it can be undertaken with spiritual life or with spiritual deadlines. The quality of religion is what makes the difference.

Regarding cosmology, the relation between ethics and religion is confused. The reason is that most of the intellectual factors which in times past contributed to a unified, coherent view of the world now suggest that the world is not unified and coherent. The cosmological truth seems to be fragmentation, and the means of systematizing these findings seem far from a vision that can symbolically structure the imagination. Most theologians seem to have abandoned the cosmological parts of their enterprise and focused their attention on interpretation, the very discipline that sparked the belief in fragmentation. Yet the older religious visions have far more profound symbols for fragmentation than the optimistic cosmologies inherited by the scientific heritage from Aristotle. In Genesis 1, for instance, Yahweh creates a fragile world out of roiling water and wind and repeatedly threatens to let things slip back into chaos.

The problem for contemporary thinkers at this point is not a religious problem but an intellectual one in the critical sense. We simply have failed to acquire a systematic cosmological understanding that articulates incomplete and partial relations, the threat of chaos, and the dissociation of our modes of analyzing things. If the intellectuals could do their work, complicated as it is by the vast increase in information and cultural perspectives that must be integrated, we might expect that an intellectually satisfying cosmology could find symbolic expression in the imagination so as to make possible the feeling of cosmic existence. Lacking both intellectual and religious cosmology, however, ethics not only is fragmentary but is unconscious of the fragments. How often do we find in ethical discussions today that problems have been driven back to basic issues about the place of human life in the cosmos, the significance of its very existence? Obviously, the abortion problem does this; but the question of medical use of behavior-control technology does it just as surely. Religious cosmology will not provide an answer to these questions that is not already available to plain reflection. It will, however, provide a context for orienting our imaginative sense to what is important. Without that, ethics has no sense of perspective, no balance; every issue seems as important as every other, especially to those directly involved in pleading a case. Without the contrasting ontological perspective that cosmology makes possible, the relativity of ethics itself can be lost sight of.

Ethics' need for spiritual practices is hard to formulate, for spiritual development is not the same as developing good moral character. Both involve changing conventional habits and developing capacities that do not exist without special cultivation. But there *is* a difference. When moral character is built without the development of spiritual underpinnings, monstrosities can result. Psychic integrity in ethical matters, for instance, consists in rigor, loyalty to ideals, and a sense of responsibility. Without the abandonment of ego in which spiritual psychic integrity consists, moral integrity flirts with fanaticism and megalomania. Wisdom in ethical matters consists in appreciation of profound values and in prudential skill at analyzing affairs in order to see what is important. Without the spiritual sagacity of identification with the world, in its ontological perspective from which all outcomes seem indifferent, moral wisdom can develop a frantic mode that seeks satisfaction in total control. The moral development of good character and habits, noteworthy goals and admirable life-styles are to be desired. But without the spiritual perfection of desires so that goods are pursued for their own sake rather than because they bring virtue to the pursuer, the heroic moral character is a pain in the fundament.

In summary, religion can make ethics an enterprise in which life is fundamentally engaged, or it can leave ethics as a mere discernment and pursuit of good. Whereas authentic ritual, religious cosmology, and spiritual practices have no authority over ethics, contributing neither new ethical propositions nor ethical motivations and rewards, they make life in its ethical pursuits more responsive to reality than it would be otherwise. They save it from the monstrosities of the religious unresponsiveness to which it is prone: fanaticism, unbalanced valuing of the importance of ethics, and pomposity. By abandoning false authoritarianism, religion makes contributions to the secular world of ethics that are all the clearer.

Let us return now to the question with which Chapter 1 left the argument. Does the tao of faith and practice have authority in ethics that indirectly gives it authority in theological inquiry? The answer is clearly no, because the terms of the question are ill formed. Religion is not one sphere of life alongside, and perhaps dominant over, ethics and inquiry. Rather, the argument of Chapter 2 is that there is a hierarchical but non-prejudicial relation of religion to other areas. Religion deals with the ontological fact of existence; it does so at the level of imagination where people's very world-orientation is constructed. Its function is authentic engagement with reality as a fact, not judgment as to the cosmological nature of reality. Although the terms of this engagment can be subjected to judgment, both intellectual and moral, judgment always presupposes some such set of imaginative terms. If religion is interpreted as making moral or truth claims, inquiry into justification of those claims is accountable to the norms of inquiry, not to higher-level, religious, authoritative assertion. The norms for imaginative engagement are not the same as those for true inquiry; pursuit of each presupposes the other. Whereas the tao of faith and practice can assert no authority over the assertions of inquiry, every inquiry rests more or less authentically on one tao or another as its orientation to the ontological fact of existence. Inquiry resting on alienating rather than engaging religion is not, per se, mistaken in its assertions but disengaged from and disoriented toward its own reality.

The hypothesis that characterizes religion in part through the contrast between the cosmological and the ontological aspects of things suggests a further integration of the tao and the daimon. This hypothesis suggests that the cosmological activity of the daimon willy-nilly is nested in a tao with ontological significance. That, of course, is what Plato thought. How, then, can we conceive of the religious character of people so their ontological center manifests itself in their cosmological activities? The ontological center can no more "determine" people's cosmological activities than the tao of faith and practice can determine authoritatively the activities guided by the daimon. But then, there can be no simple separation of separate spheres of life.

In the Christian tradition the presence of God in human life has been interpreted according to the symbol of the Holy Spirit. By examining that symbol the ontological question can be raised in a serious way. This examination also needs, at least generally, to illustrate the method of philosophical theology, for that is the point at which the positive connection of the tao with the daimon becomes evident.

Chapter Three
Philosophical Theology:
The Case of the Holy Spirit

T HE CONCEPT OF the Holy Spirit can be articulated as an understanding of the presence of God as creator in the world. Because of the multiple layers of presuppositions involved in this, however, articulation has several levels of generality. Section I presents a relatively naive hypothesis about the creator's presence, discussing briefly how that presence relates to certain operations traditionally associated with the Holy Spirit. Section I constitutes what Peirce might have called a "humble argument," one to be followed by a more sophisticated consideration of the suppositions of the argument. Each succeeding section except the last is a "humble argument" for the one that follows.[1] Section II presents a speculative hypothesis about God as creator whose presence in the world might be as depicted in Section I; that is the system to which the Introduction refers us for philosophical theology. Section III discusses the nature of systematic speculation relative to the theological problem of the Holy Spirit as God. Section IV treats the issue of using the Christian notion of the Holy Spirit in public meta-Christian inquiry about God, returning to problems raised in chapters 1 and 2.

I. The Holy Spirit as the Creator's Presence

Within the Christian tradition the Holy Spirit has come to be the concept with which to articulate any activity of God in a present moment. The activities range from the stirrings of individual hearts through guidance of history to the sanctity of nature. To generalize the notion of the Holy Spirit in such a way took many centuries. Perhaps the concept did not reach its greatest intellectual power until Hegel's *Phenomenology of Spirit*. The concrete experiences the notion was intended to interpret, however, were recognized in ancient times – for instance, the experiences at Pentecost, Jesus' baptism, Elijah's still small voice, the founding activities Job learned about from the whirlwind, the voice from the burning bush, Jesus' promise to send his spirit as a guide, the divine spirit in prophecy.

The intellectual development of the concept of the Holy Spirit was inextricably involved with development of the concept of the triune God: Father–Son–Spirit. If the concept of the Holy Spirit is to be helpful in understanding God in the contemporary situation, its articulation requires a systematic concept of God.[2]

To appreciate what is special about the Holy Spirit, we must have a concept of the world in and to which God as Spirit might be present, a concept that can articulate divine presence. If there were no such concept, there would be no cognitive way of envisioning how the various alleged manifestations of the Spirit would be *one*. A concept of the world, or philosophical cosmology, is thus a prerequisite for articulating divine presence.

A philosophical cosmology cannot be constructed just for the purpose of articulating divine presence; that would be ad hoc and lacking in force. Rather, it must arise from, and prove itself in, all areas of inquiry relevant to basic philosophic conceptions of the world. In the twentieth century the revolution in the scientific view of the physical universe is perhaps the most decisive contributor to philosophical cosmology. The historical recognition of evil and human responsibility and the development of abstraction in the arts are also decisive. The cosmological tradition of process philosophy is the most highly developed and sensitive contemporary approach to cosmological questions. A variant of that tradition is sketched here in connection with the Holy Spirit as the presence of the creator.[3] No attempt is made here to justify the hypothesis except as it helps make sense of issues concerning the Spirit. I should point out that the cosmology presented here completely rejects the concept of God in Whitehead's process cosmology and bears little relation to process theology.[4] The deviations in this hypothesis from central process conceptions stem mainly from the need to amend the views of Whitehead and his followers with a significantly different conception of God.[5]

Divine presence in existence

The most distinctive process conception is that the world consists of occasions, or events. An event is a happening in which previous events, given as completed facts, are transformed and arranged in a new way with the definiteness of an individual event. When an event has happened, it too becomes an accomplished fact. While it is happening, however, it is not an existing fact but a fact coming into existence.

The concept of *causation* in the process view roughly divides into two components. On one hand are past facts which function as conditions for an event. They are the material with which things happen in an event. Limits are imposed on the event by the past events from which it arises. But past events do not *act* once they are over and have become facts. Action, on the other hand, is an expression of the present creativity within an event whereby it brings itself into existence as a definite new fact. A present happening must incorporate past events and give them places in its own resolution. This conception of causation is Whitehead's most important contribution to thought.

The *character* of an event derives from two sources. Some of the character derives from past events taken up as conditions. Other elements of the character derive from the process internal to the event of integrating those diverse past conditions in a unified, definite new fact. The elements of character deriving from the past illustrate the regularities and systematic patterns of the environment of events within which the emerging event takes place. Further, the elements of character deriving from the internal process must fall within the limits imposed by environmental regularities; otherwise the event could not come to factual existence in harmony with its environment. Within those limits, though, and from the perspective of antecedent predictable regularities and patterns, internal integration is spontaneous. Here, *spontaneity* means "not determined according to antecedent regularities"; this may be called "character spontaneity" because it refers to spontaneous elements of character.[6]

There is a larger sense of spontaneity, however, one that can be called "existential spontaneity," referring to the creative process of bringing the event into existence, the process of integration itself. Whereas the character of the integration might be determined by the extremely strict limits set by the encompassing facts from which the event arises, those facts do not produce their integration in the new event. Production of the new event, however determined, is the spontaneous essential quality of the event itself. Existential spontaneity is the *making present* of the event; reference to existential spontaneity is made in accounting for the fact *that* the event occurs. The character of the event is *what* it is, and character spontaneity might exist within an event along with elements of character determined by other events, together comprising the event.[7]

Existential spontaneity is *decisive* for the formation of an event.

Without it, there would be no new event, only the finished events that are potential conditions. If the antecedent conditions allow alternate integrations, some elements in the character produced by the existential spontaneity will exhibit character spontanteity. All elements in the character of an event derive either from the decisions of its own character spontaneity or from decisions that decided the past events conditioning it. Each past event has characters decided either by their own character spontaneity or by that of their antecedents, and so on *ad indefinitum.*

The character of an event is a relative matter, relative to antecedent conditions, future consequences, the products of its own character spontaneity. In the course of ordinary human affairs we attend to the actual, emerging, potential character of things, and we do so from a relative perspective. One may reflect, however, on the fact *that* some event or set of events exist is coming to exist or that it will exist. The events, of course, have characters; understanding their characters consists in tracing their relative connections. Appreciating or inquiring into the *thatness* of the events, however, points to their absolute or ontological dimension.[8]

Inquiring into the ontology of events we may say that the Holy Spirit is their existential spontaneity, God creating each thing. The Holy Spirit as existential spontaneity within an event operates within the limits set by the antecedent conditions given for integration. But then, each antecedent condition had its own existential spontaneity that operated within the limits of still other prior events, and so forth. Therefore, as existential spontaneity, the Holy Spirit is God creating each event in both kinds of character – that resulting from integration of given conditions (present existential spontaneity) and that from the given conditions themselves (past existential spontaneity). From the standpoint of each event, the Holy Spirit is actively present in each, in its own time. The Spirit thus operates at different times and places. Yet, because the character of any event is a function largely of its connections with conditions (and with the future things for which it will later be a condition, a theme not developed here), the diverse times and places of the Spirit's action exhibit a mutual relevance in the creative activity of the Spirit.[9]

The concept of existential spontaneity within events articulates that most general sense of the Holy Spirit as creator or ground of all things. That the existential spontaneity deserves to be described in the language of divinity derives in part from the sense of wonder and awe we sometimes exhibit at the fact that things exist at all. Although *what* the world is might not be sacred, there is something sacred about the fact *that* the world exists.

Another characteristic of the Holy Spirit follows immediately. That part of an event's existential spontaneity which is also character-spontaneous introduces novelty into affairs. Deriving not from antecedent determinations of character but solely from the event's existential spontaneity, the characters of integration produced in what was called character spontaneity are the Spirit's guidance of affairs in some measure of freedom from antecendent commitments. The Holy Spirit thus not only grounds and sustains but also leads. If the order of nature has evolved from the least possible order, then the Holy Spirit has directed the entire evolution by introducing each novel component of order.

Divine presence in life

According to the hypothesis of process cosmology, an enduring object is a series of events, each of which exhibits much the same character as the others and each of which derives the character as a condition from antecedents within the series (this does not apply to the first member, if there is one). Sameness of character is a matter of degree; often, whether a series of events is called one enduring object or two is arbitrary. Each event in the series may have many characters unique to itself that derive from individual relationships to a changing environment. A *living* thing combines events in well-patterned, enduring elements with events having a significant degree of novelty, where the novelty is relevant to the enduring pattern. Most novelty, it may be presumed, is *ir*relevant to the surrounding events and leaves no marks, conditioning little if anything. The novelty involved in a living thing, however, affects the pattern of many elements in the series, so that novelty is related organically to patterns fixed by antecedent. A novel event in a living thing requires a well-patterned environment to which it can be relevant.

The Holy Spirit can be conceived of as the source of life in the sense that the existential spontaneity in the novel event is mutually relevant with the existential spontaneity in past, contemporary, and future environing events in the enduring live thing. The Spirit is the source of that peculiar and poignant mutual relevance of novelty and continuity in which life consists. Death is either the cessation of novelty associated with an enduring organism or a radical diminishment of the relevance of the novelty to the overall organic pattern. Decay involves novelty relevant not to the overall pattern but to separable parts. The Holy Spirit as existential spontaneity is in those events that constitute death, including the less-than-organically relevant novelty; the Lord gives and the Lord takes away. But the Spirit makes a particularly valuable contribution to the mutual relevance of novelty and patterned continuity that make up the breath of life itself.

Divine presence in human experience

The question of the operation of the Holy Spirit (God-creating) in the more complicated structures of human life cannot be separated from questions about *what* is created. If God is creatively present in the existential spontaneity of everything, it is almost trivial to point out the Holy Spirit here, there, or some other place unless that Spirit has an interesting character. Yet the character of the Spirit consists in what is created, a point reflected in the traditional Christian trinitarian view that the Holy Spirit is the spirit of the Son.

The character of what is created is an empirical matter to be determined.[10] It is clear that the world has *some* order to it; what is not so clear is that the order is as tightly integrated as is necessary to make it legitimate for us to say that "the world" is what we would expect of a personal agent. The Spirit is God creating at least the most interesting structured things we know. There are, of course, many schemes regarding the most basic and interesting structures of human life. Since the validity of any such structure depends on the evidence that can be marshalled for it, and not from anything antecedent in the concept of the Holy Spirit, any structure can be chosen to *illustrate* the symbolic faithfulness of this concept of the spirit.

An outstanding trait of human experience is the fundamental distinction between actual process and norms. The integration of events in the past, the processes of integration in the present, and the potential for integration in the future are all matters of past, present, or future harmonies.[11] *Harmony* is a notion connoting relative degrees, however; in principle, it is always possible to ask whether integration in any event or set of events is the best harmony, the most harmonious harmony. In some spheres of experience, in fact, we imagine alternate harmonies which we recognize as more harmonious than what actually happens. Experience is evaluative when there is recognition of the logical character of degrees of harmony.

One dimension of normative human activity is experiential *engagement* with the world, the transformation of mere causal relations with the environment into experience of the environment. As Kant argued, this engagement is largely the work of imagination. The images with which experience is formed, filtering that which we respond to from what is screened out, are more primordial than any categories that may be true or false. Our fundamental, experiential images are not without norms, however; they either engage us well with the world or they alienate experience, and in multifarious ways. Religions have long known that authentic life requires engaging images. Much of ritual, prayer, music, meditation, and other spiritual disciplines is practiced for the sake of cultivation and disciplining primordial imagination. From the meditative absorption in a mandala to the habitual imitation of Christ, imagination is formed so as to engage the world according to what religion takes to be the world's most important structures. The Holy Spirit is God creating within the imagination that engages the world according to some image, and the successful attainment of a spiritual image can be felt as a special grace of the Holy Spirit.

Another normative dimension is *hermeneutic truth*, faithful interpretation of the world. Among the most complicated intellectual concerns, truth, in knowledge and practice, involves a special mutual relevance of intentionality with the ways and worth of things. Although it may be said that propositions and actions informed by propositions may be true, truth requires diverse, special orientations of experience to the world. From a religious standpoint it can be said that to know the truth one must be "in the truth," which is a function of the public and private aspects of inquiry. As the guide of the interpreting community, the Holy Spirit is the existential spontaneity creating things with the mutual relevance required for openness to truth.

Yet another normative dimension is *envisagement* of the world, grasp of the world in mystical vision. Any kind of envisagement involves seeing something as a whole by virtue of selecting some logically coherent features as important elements and suppressing the other features as details not needing articulation in vision. When the entire order created is the object of envisagement, the formerly important elements are those of the structure of creation itself, as well as of the creator – the mystical vision of God. The existential spontaneity involved in this ruthless experiential focus on what is most important is the Holy Spirit in envisagement.

Perhaps the most inclusive normative dimension is the pursuit of *goodness*—not just imagining, interpreting, and envisaging well but doing and being well. Although the objectivity of the norms involved is controversial, it can be argued that the most basic normative element in human experience is to be *responsible*. Religiously, this has been articulated as a commitment to life—"Choose life that you may live!" Attainment of responsibility is closely related to the problem of salvation; the problem of salvation is that of being responsible to the fact of existing as such, to the absolute dimension of the relative process within which we have particular responsibilities. The Holy Spirit is existential spontaneity creating experience in that mutual relevance with the ontological fact of creation that constitutes one's life relative to salvation.

The concepts of these four normative dimensions of activity are expansions on the four dimensions of thinking discussed in Chapter 1. There are also important normative dimensions of expression, religiously important, which relate to *history* and *community*. History and community, however, are vastly more complex than the more individual dimensions of experience already mentioned and need to be developed as topics on their own. Also, whereas the various religious traditions share some vaguely common views about the dimension discussed, they are widely separated regarding history and community. Let us here be content, then, with the remark that, whatever the role of history and community in experience, the Spirit as existential spontaneity lies behind them as their divine origin.

Divine presence and human freedom

The inference is frequently made that, if God creates everything, there is no freedom or responsibility attributable to created persons. This inference is especially tempting when the creating Spirit is interpreted as existential spontaneity in both present and past components of existence. Within the Christian tradition the inference led Reformation theologians to adopt deterministic theories of human action and to characterize God's sovereignty in terms of complete responsibility for all that happens. It also led contemporary process theologians to assert that God is not the creator in a strict sense but an actual entity separate from the world who grasps the world after its subjective present and guides it only with tempting lures.

But the inference need not follow. The integrity of a thing in the world, including a human being, consists in its being the character it is.[12] That character is a function of the conditions of the events constituting the character plus the various processes of integrating the conditions. A thing is not a secret core which possesses its character; a thing is its character. Human freedom has numerous dimensions; one of the most important is often alleged to be a certain indeterminacy. If a person is to be responsible for some action, and the responsibility is not to be traced back reductively to antecedent conditions, the future must in some features be indeterminate with respect to what the antecedent conditions require. Furthermore, the actual decisive process within the person, starting from the antecedent conditions, must determine what possible outcomes will happen; otherwise, chance, not the person, is responsible.[13]

In principle, there is nothing that requires events of the world to be completely determinate with regard to their consequences. There is a certain observed order and regularity to things, but we have not observed that there is complete regularity as would be required for determinism. In the face of moral experience it seems wise to assume that there is enough of the right indeterminacy for individuals to make a moral difference.

Moreover, there is nothing, in principle, excluding from the events making up human experience the kinds of features that, on one hand, determine future consequences and, on the other, are not determined by antecedent conditions. In other words, it is possible for there to be character spontaneity in events. Character spontaneity is the coming into existence of elements of an event's character not determined by antecedent events that enter as conditions. Whether, in fact, there is any character spontaneity, or any of the right sort for moral experience, is an empirical matter, not one required by cosmology or by scientific assumptions necessary for finding regularities where regularities are. The existence of moral experience does, however, make a prima facie case for such character spontaneity.

A person *is* the character of the events making up the past, present, and future of life. A person exercising freedom consists in certain decisive events that contain morally relevant character-spontaneous features. Responsibility for the consequences goes to that person and not to the person's antecedents, because those character-spontaneous elements were what made the difference. Sometimes people think they are free in this sense when they are not; that is because the truly decisive factors are factors other than those affected by any character-spontaneous features people might have. We have vast experiential evidence for thinking that people, in many situations, *are* free in this sense. Chapter 5 explores a special version of the issue whether people can be free to respond to God.

Throughout the process of integration within an event, character-spontaneous features come into existence through existential spontaneity. In this sense, God the creator is responsible for them and for the free responsibility to which they contribute. But since the freedom and responsibility of a person consists of those character-spontaneous features (in harmony with all other elements of character), the person is responsible, too. One's free choice consists partly in constituting oneself as the determinant of this alternative rather than another determinant. It is not free to be completely determined in one's choice on the basis of antecedent reasons. Instead, free choice involves determining oneself with an action that transforms into decisive motives certain reasons antecedently entertained, rather than other reasons that were also potential motives. The sense in which a person is freely responsible for choices is the sense in which the person *is the choosing*, where the choosing is what determines an otherwise undetermined consequence. This makes sense of the profound observation that God (as Holy Spirit) is closer to me than I am to myself.

The discussion in this section attempts to illustrate various senses in which the Holy Spirit can be construed as God creating in the world. The principal vehicle for this is a brief elucidation of a cosmology. The cosmology itself is not strictly dependent on the need to illustrate a concept of the Holy Spirit, but it could be accepted on its own merits by people who completely reject the Christian religious symbolism involved in the notion of the Spirit. Further, it should be noted that the experiential phenomena discussed – such as engagement, interpretation, envisagement, and responsible pursuit of goodness – are widely recognized. The problem of freedom has been treated hypothetically. It has been shown to be possible, though not necessarily actual and compatible with the cosmological involvement of the creator in the world.

What has not been discussed, however, but merely asserted, is the claim that God is indeed creator of the cosmos. Whether this or some other hypothesized cosmology is true, can sense be made of the claim that the world is created? Since, in at least this cosmology, the Holy Spirit can be used with many of its traditional associations to interpret the existential quality of affairs, how does that relate to the overall conception of God as creator? By what speculative hypothesis may we conceive God as creator?

II. God the Creator and Trinity

Let us suppose, *ex hypothesi*, that everything determinate is created and that we call the creator "God."[14]

Because everything determinate is created, the creator must be indeterminate except insofar as the creator acquires a character from the act of creation. The character acquired by creating is itself a created, determinate affair. By analogy, a parent is not a parent except as a child is produced; but this analogy has a limitation: Parenting is understood partly in terms of prior potential for parenting; the creator cannot be said to have any potential "prior" to creation, since that potential would be determinate. Because potential alone prior to parenting is not enough to make a person a parent, the analogy holds with respect to the belief that the act of producing offspring (transforming former potential) is what makes a person a parent, similar to the way the act of creating determinate things makes the creator a creator.

Because God's character, whatever it might be, derives from the creation, this hypothesis is an "economic" speculative one, an economic trinitarianism, as we shall see.[15] God's character is a function solely of God's creation. Apart from creating, God cannot be said to have a character, to be determinate, to be existent, one, good, true, beautiful distinguishable from nothingness, or "God" in any sense. This claim itself is a logical implication of the hypothesized creation relation—namely, that God creates everything determinate. Appreciation of this logical implication perhaps lies behind the experience of God as the Abyss, the aboriginal fire, the ultimate Nothing from which creation springs. But since there *is* creation (and even to deny this is to acknowledge the determinateness of intelligibility), God is *not* Nothing but the creator of this world, with at least the creatorly characteristics of being a this-worldly creator. Because the pure divine aseity would be unintelligible, we would have to say that God *could* not be Nothing. In fact, there is no reason to say God *is* Nothing, since God is determinate as creator of this determinate world.[16]

A distinction should be clearly drawn between cosmological causation and ontological creation. Cosmological causation is any of various ways determinate things in the cosmos influence each other, as one event conditions another. It is *cosmological* in that it pertains to relations between created things in the cosmos. Ontological or divine, creation is the bringing into being of determinate things.[17] Cosmological causal relations are themselves ontologically created; for instance, an event has as part of its determinate character that it is conditioned in various specific ways by other things and that it is a potential condition for other things. Created things need not be determinate in all respects; temporal events may be indeterminate with respect to how they will later be conditions for other things. Yet insofar as they are determinate at all they are created, and insofar as they will later condition other things, this conditioning is part of the created, determinate nature of those later things. Temporal relations, with all the change and novelty involved in the process, are themselves created. The cosmological hypothesis about process mentioned above indicates how, in at least one hypothesis, the creator is present, creating, in temporal things.

To be a thing is to be determinate or at least partially determinate. A thing is determinate by virtue of at least two features: *conditional* features, by virtue of which that thing is related to other things as being different from them; and *essential* features, by virtue of which the thing's conditional features are not mere reflections of other things but modifications of other things from the standpoint of the thing itself.[18] The essential features would be the thing's own nature if it were not that a determinate nature must be determinate with *respect to something else*. Conditional features are derived from those other things so that it can be determinate with respect to them. The conditional features would be the ways a thing is related to other things; but that supposes the thing has a character of its own to be related or conditioned. A thing's true nature is a harmony which necessarily includes both essential and conditional features. In terms of the cosmology discussed in Section I, the antecedent conditional events would be conditional features and the characters arising from their integration would be essential.

How can the connection between essential features and conditional features be accounted for? Not by antecedent causes or goals, or abstract forms or material components, because each of those causes, at most, could account for conditional features alone. Even then, the difference the essential features make to the conditional ones is not accounted for. Thus cosmological relations, causal and otherwise, are insufficient to account for the harmony of essential and conditional features that is the being of a thing. The being of a thing must be ontologically created; part of what that means is that the de facto harmony of its essential and conditional features is simply "made to be."

For a thing to have conditional features with regard to something else, both things must be in a context of mutual relevance. That is, the being of one thing must be mutually relevant to the being of the other for one to condition the other. The cosmological character of the conditioning itself – for instance, causal conditioning – would not be possible if there were not an ontological context of mutual relevance. The ontological context of mutual relevance cannot be reduced to the cosmological relations of conditional features because the being of any conditional feature requires harmony with the essential features of the thing whose feature it is. Therefore, the ontological context of mutual relevance includes the essential features of diverse things, whereas, cosmologically, they are connected only conditionally. Consequently, to be determinate means to be with other things with respect to which a thing is determinate, and that means to be created in an ontological context of mutual relevance.

The creative act by which the diverse things of the world are ontologically created is unified in the sense that its product has the character of the context of mutual relevance. It is diversely located, in that each thing is created as a harmony of its own essential and conditional features. That the creative act is unified does not mean its product is *totum simul*, only that past-present-future things are in an ontological context of mutual relevance.

Does the created world have an integrity over against the creator? Cosmologically, such integrity is necessary for freedom. In ascertaining what a thing (or set of things) is, one looks to the characters it has de facto. Upon analysis, some features of those characters are conditional on other relevant things. Scientific inquiry, among other kinds, can trace out these conditional connections. Other features of the characters are ownmost to the things themselves, to be apprehended by attaining the perspective of the things through intuition or empathy. Generally, the humanities focus on understanding these essential features. Of course, there is the unique harmony that makes up a thing's own real character. Such harmonies can be presented imaginatively to experience by the arts and by many other avenues of inquiry. In no sense, though, need one go outside the realm of created determinate things to understand or account for their character. *What* things are is a function of their determining conditions and of idiosyncratic self-realization. The question of the ontological creation of things arises only when one wonders *that* things are. The question of the ontological existence of a thing is not the same as whether there are cosmological causes that bring it into existence. Rather, it is whether there is an ontological context of mutual relevance in which the thing is (was, or will be) real, a context requiring appropriate conditional causes, to be sure, but also the appropriate essential features and the harmony of both. Divine creation thus can never be cited as a reason for a thing being one way rather than another or why the course of events goes one direction rather than another, except in the general and usually trivial sense that God is the creator of everything. The particular course of history is to be understood according to historical causes of the sort historians cite. God is indeed the creator of that history; if the historical causes had been different, however, and the course of history different, God would have been the creator of that instead.

What are the implications for the character of God of this analysis of the speculative hypothesis of divine creation? As is remarked above, we may not speak of God as a being apart from the creation relation with the world, for that would be indeterminate. Rather, we must speak of God as characterized within the creation relationship. Within that relationship, God has a tripartite character; no part can be understood without the other two parts, yet no part can be completely defined by the other parts.[19]

First, as creator, God is the source of all determinate being. As creator, God is not contingent *in the way* determinate things are. That is, God is not a composite of essential and conditional features; there is no ontological context of mutual relevance in which God is together with other things. God is like a parent in being the source; unlike a parent, God has no nature apart from creating which would explain how God could create. God is not anything except creator. In trinitarian terms, God can be called "father" (although the exclusive gender connotations of the word may not be a healthy contribution to contemporary public inquiry, however natural it was in comfortably patriarchal societies).

Second, as creator, God cannot be separated from the product of creation, and must be identified with the product. There is no determinate medium in which the realm of determinations can be separated from the creator that creates them. God, therefore, is the created world insofar as the divine character is the end product or products of the creative act. To say that God is the created world is extremely vague. To be at all helpful religiously, this part of the hypothesis should be specified by a more concrete interpretation of what this world actually is. The importance of specifying this *part* of the divine character is far greater than specifying the sense in which God is source. Indeed, the way to make that part of the hypothesis more specific is to specify that of which God is the source. From the perspective of this vague hypothesis, it seems equally plausible to specify God's identity in the world with the metaphors of Maya, the dance of Shiva, the Absolute aspect of the Mahayana One Mind, or the Incarnate logos.

Third, God is the activity of creating itself. That activity has no form or nature of its own other than that of the determinations created. If the traditional Christian story is essentially correct, and the Christ is the redeeming perfection of fact and norm, then the central, or paradigmatic, character of the creative activity can be called "the mind of Christ." But this historical characterization cannot be made out until after a proper Christology has specified the speculative hypothesis and has independently justified itself. From the standpoint of the hypothesis, the creative activity has the character of its product, as an action by a human person has the character of what the action does. Whereas human action always proceeds in part from antecedent potential, giving it a nature which in part must include the past in present action, the activity of ontological creation has no such character stemming from the past.

On the other hand, one of the more universal or transcendental products of creation is the determinate metaphysical character of creation itself. Within this character, the activity serves as a mediator linking the source and the product. The source could not create the product without the creative activity; the product could have no being without the creative activity. The creative activity could not end in its determinate product without the otherwise indeterminate source, because its own determinate nature as creative activity would have to be created. The creative activity could not be the activity or expression of the source without issuing in the determinate world; otherwise, there would be no creating.

The creating activity is related to the world and to the source in ways strikingly parallel to the Holy Spirit as understood in trinitarian theology. Of course, trinitarian theology is equally expressive of the experience of Jesus and is based on a Christology which will not be investigated here. What *has* been investigated (in Section I) is how much the creative act resembles the Holy Spirit when the act is specified by a cosmology otherwise attractive in public discussion.

It may now be suggested that what the Christian tradition has called the Holy Spirit is both a plausible category for interpreting the ontological dimensions of experience, as revealed in the discussion of cosmology, and a coherent symbol within a speculative notion of God as creator. We have not, however, inquired into the nature of the intellectual strategy of treating the Holy Spirit according to the hypotheses of the speculative conception of God and the philosophical cosmology. Is it not an arrogant impiety to "reduce" the concrete witness of Christians about the Spirit to hypotheses?

III. The Holy Spirit as a Systematic Speculative Problem

The Holy Spirit traditionally can be identified in a variety of matrices. According to the New Testament, the Holy Spirit had a historical identity, expressing divine commentary on Jesus' baptism, for instance, and appearing at the day of Pentecost. The Holy Spirit was identified by Jesus as part of his promise; the Spirit sent by God after Jesus' death has a quasi-historical identity. Then there is the Spirit that manifests itself with potential universality in the life of communities of Christians, a Spirit with a capacity for pervasive or multiple location. The Holy Spirit also has been looked to as a testor of personal spirits and as an interpreter of scripture and doctrine.

At the same time that there are all these relatively concrete matrices for identifying the Holy Spirit, there is also the matrix of conceiving the Holy Spirit as divine, as part of God or as divinity itself. This matrix has its own special complications, connecting and unifying a wide variety of relatively concrete identities of the Holy Spirit and connecting them with other things that should be said about God. The proper matrix for conceiving of the Holy Spirit as God is philosophical theology. Because speculative philosophical theology (or speculative philosophy dealing with God) has not popularly been practiced, it is important to say something about it, because to do so provides a vantage point for reflecting on the discussion above.

Speculation is an attempt to envision the whole of one's subject matter. Envisagement requires selection of the important elements to keep in view, as distinct from the relatively more trivial elements that can be disregarded. The important elements are articulated in categories that indicate their bearing on one another in logical, causal, and all other ways that contribute to the importance in question.

Speculation thus can take two directions.[20] One direction is that of moving from the relatively disorganized welter of experience to the systematic categories that articulate what is important in experience. The other is to move from systematic categories back to experience, as now interpreted by the categories. Both directions are necessary for each other and are implicit in any genuine, speculative endeavor. Speculation frequently has been identified as merely movement away from experience toward systematic categories. Sometimes it has even been identified as logical thinking *within* the system of categories itself. But the categories themselves are vague and do not articulate what is important *in experience* unless movement from the categories to the experience of the subject matter is made as part of systematic thinking. A speculative "system" might be identified as the systematic categories construed according to its formal structure. But *system* as adjectival to speculative *thinking* refers to the responsibility for moving from experience to categories and from the categories to experience, with each move reinterpreting and correcting the other.

What is the relation of the system of speculative categories to the experience constituting its subject matter? There are five points about this relation, which also indicate the role of speculation in public inquiry:

1. The system of categories collectively, and the categories individually, are *hypotheses* about the subject matter. The subject matter could be simplified and articulated in various ways, perhaps. It is hypothetical whether any given simplification of categories is better than another. That the categories are hypothetical means that certain formal requirements obtain about them – namely, that they be consistent and coherent.

The move from experience to categories does not proceed according to logical rules, but rather from what Peirce called "a guess at the riddle."[21] The categories, therefore, must be relevant to the subject matter, though judgments about relevance can be made only after articulation of the categories. With a history of speculation, the guesses are "educated." The historical dialectic of systematic answers to basic philosophical and theological questions provides a rich background for the contemporary speculator, and there are enough standard moves to indicate the general advantages and disadvantages attending the types of category.

A hypothesis, although imaginatively produced as a guess, must be articulated internally to become applicable to experience. Again, there are no rules for preliminary parsing of speculative categories, but the end product of the analysis of categories ought to be articulation in logical form, so categories will be expressed in what logicians call "well-formed formulas." Once the categories are articulated with formal precision, it is possible to make logical deductions from them; this cannot be done before articulation.

At best, a hypothesis can be highly plausible. To see how plausible, one deduces experiential consequences that ought to follow if the hypothesis is true and then tests to see whether the hypothesis as specified is applicable to experience. Then one can see whether the hypothesis is adequate to experience, or whether there are some things it should entail that it does not. Hypotheses can never be certain. They can never be deductions from experience, because experience provides no well-formed formulas from which they can be deduced. Such "geometrical" thinkers as Spinoza did not deduce their theories from experience but from some allegedly indubitable, logically well-formed first principles. Nor can speculative hypotheses ever become certain by having complete plausibility, though concrete particular doubts can be removed, at least for the time being.

2. A hypothetical system of speculative categories is logically *vague*. As a logical notion, *vagueness* does not mean "fuzzy." It means that the vague proposition is insufficiently determinate to specify the objects to which it refers, and that it requires supplementary propositions to identify the objects. For instance, the proposition "someone is about to die" is vague because it does not *specify the person*. The proposition "things are going well" is vague because it does not specify what things and because it is compatible in everyday language with "some other things aren't going well."

Vagueness contrasts with *generality*. A proposition is general if it refers not directly to individuals but to a class, yet is determinate about the class of individuals it refers to. "All men are mortal" is general because it refers to anything that is a man.

Hypotheses as described above may be general, vague, or particular. Scientific hypotheses aim to be general because it is hoped that they can thereby be tested by particular critical experiments. For instance, a hypothesis about electrons that is vague as to what counts as an electron would be difficult to test. Speculative hypotheses, however, should be vague. A speculative hypothesis about God cannot refer to particular experiential manifestations of divinity without intermediate, interpreting hypotheses. These intermediate hypotheses might be historical accounts of God in human affairs or interpretation of religious experience, of a divine grounding for moral judgment, or of a host of other interpretations. Because the interpreting hypotheses themselves may be vague in their own way, the set of hypotheses relating speculative systems to concrete experience might be ordered hierarchically, partially overlapping, historically contingent in their relations, following the sage of hermeneutic development.

3. One advantage of vagueness in speculative hypotheses is that vagueness directs attention to various positive tasks of specifying the hypotheses so as to determine objects. The hypotheses *must* be supplemented by interpretive propositions arising from considerations *other than those directly forming the speculative hypotheses*. In particular, if God is hypothesized to be the creator of the world, further interpretive theories about just what is created, how creation takes place, the difference between divine creation and intraworldly causation, and many

similar issues must be developed before the creator hypothesis determines God. Further, these midrange interpretive theories might not be consistent with each other. For example, the creator hypothesis might be made specific by claiming that the cosmos created is an Aristotelian substance world. Or it might be claimed (as it is in Section I) that it is a Whiteheadian process world. Let us suppose that these two midrange theories are incompatible. They cannot both be true. Which one is preferable cannot be deduced from the supervening, vague creator hypothesis, for the creator hypothesis is true if either (or some other) midrange hypothesis is true. The probation of the claims of the midrange hypotheses must be made on their own terms according to criteria appropriate to the middle range. In fact, there are many midrange hypotheses, with many connections, involved in specifying a vague hypothesis.

Because it is logically required that vague, speculative hypotheses be specified positively, diverse religious traditions and incompletely congruent strains within single traditions necessarily have potential contributions to make to the inquiry about God *from the speculative standpoint*. If the hypothesis is properly vague, then *any plausible positive interpretive experience of God must be capable of specifying it*. The truth of that specifying religious statement must be made out on its own account; it cannot be derived from the vaguer hypothesis. Neither can it be falsified by the vaguer hypothesis. Proponents of the midrange position have no immediate reason to fear that the speculative hypothesis would prejudice the plausibility of their position. If their position is a possible specification of the vague hypothesis, it has at least been demonstrated to the public community as a possibility. The Christian claim, that God created the world *ex nihilo* is not obvious to everyone even as a possibility; the speculative creator hypothesis would show that it is a possibility. In the short run, if the speculative hypothesis does not show the midrange claim to be a possibility, there is a fault in the vagueness of the speculative hypothesis. In the long run, it might be found to be impossible to arrive at speculative hypothesis that shows a midrange view or a particular religious claim to be a possibility. It might also be found that the speculative hypothesis that receives overwhelming support from other areas of experience is incompatible with a hypothesis that does allow for the possibility of the less vague position. But this only amounts to saying that the particular religious position is found to be implausible in the long run, a fate to which any interpretation of anything is liable: it is unable to sustain itself in public inquiry.

4. Another advantage of vague speculative hypotheses is that they lay

the foundation for testing the universality of proposals required for public inquiry. Suppose that a vague hypothesis about God is specified in each direction proposed by the major theological traditions (by no means an easy matter, but let us *suppose* it can be done). Whereas the presentations of each tradition in the terms internal to itself are somewhat incommensurable with each other, as specifications of a vaguer speculative hypothesis it would be possible to see how they relate. They might be complementary, irrelevant to each other but compatible, or contradictory and irreconcilable. Perhaps the traditions are related in some of each way. For instance, it might be discovered that the Buddhas of Mahayana, the avatars of Hinduism, and Jesus the Incarnate logos are overlapping, compatible models of divinity in human affairs but that the Christian claim that Jesus is the exclusive or supreme figure is incompatible with the other traditions. This discovery, by itself, does not say that the Christian claim is right or wrong, only that it is incompatible with the rest. It might be discovered that the Jewish and Christian views of criteria for the Messiah are different though compatible but that the conclusions the traditions draw about the relation of their communities to their respective messiahs are irreconcilable. With a properly vague but variously specified speculative hypothesis, it is possible to locate some issues in public inquiry that are otherwise hard to find.

Furthermore, awareness of the problem of developing an adequate speculative hypothesis in conjunction with the possible specializations of the hypothesis by the less vague positions represented in dialogue serves as a regulative principle of public inquiry. Speculative hypotheses are potentially universal, capable of illustrating any religious claim that can sustain its plausibility. Finally, it may generally be supposed that any tradition with massively interpreted experience of the divine, which has sustained itself through a long period of its own internal responses to affairs, is plausible in its main contentions.

5. The truth conditions for a speculative hypothesis can now be summarized. A hypothesis is true if, in the judgment of an infinitely critical community of inquirers, the following conditions hold:

a.   The hypothesis is formally consistent and coherent.

b.   The hypothesis is dialectically superior to alternate hypotheses on formal grounds.

c.   The hypothesis can be compatibly specified by all true claims of lesser vagueness (however the truth of those claims is established).

d. Some plausible claims of lesser vagueness specify the hypothesis.
e. If the plausible claims are incompatible specifications of the hypothesis, no other speculative hypothesis satisfying conditions a to d would make them compatible and the hypothesis could be consistently specified by a world-range of claims compatible with the falseness of one side of the contradicting, plausible claims.

If a speculative hypothesis is supported by specification of a plausible view that eventually becomes implausible, the hypothesis is not necessarily falsified; it does, however, require plausibility from elsewhere and must be specifiable by whatever view becomes plausible instead of the first. Otherwise, the speculative hypothesis must be altered. The history of thought has shown that plausible, speculative hypotheses that function in partial ways to constitute the background for public discussion have themselves developed through the dialectic of inquiry. There is no reasonable expectation that any speculative hypothesis, however attractive it is today, will have much staying power. But that does not denigrate its usefulness to present public inquiry, whose positive existential needs must be met for the purposes of our own discussion.

The Holy Spirit is a speculative-specified problem in the following way. In the tradition of Christian theology, the Holy Spirit has been an integral part of the concept of God. The Spirit, in turn, has been specified by various identities of the sort mentioned at the beginning of this section. Sections I and II present a vague, speculative hypothesis about God as the creator of everything determinate, as well as a somewhat less vague, speculative cosmology specifying the creation theory, which, on independent grounds, interprets the main domains of experience in the twentieth century. It was argued that a certain economic trinitarian view from the Christian tradition specifies the hypothesis of God in ways that reinforce and elaborate the cosmology, with special relevance for the notion of the Holy Spirit. The Holy Spirit is the way the speculative hypothesis suggests God is present in the world as creator, specifying the hypothesis with the Christian tradition. It is now possible to see, at least in part, how this conception of the Holy Spirit is an enlightening interpretation of central experiences, how it is a contribution to public inquiry about God. It remains an open, but opened, question whether the historic and symbolic associations of the notion of the Holy Spirit are publicly valuable or whether their worth remains limited to the Christian tradition.

IV. God and the Holy Spirit in Public Inquiry

The "problem of God" is a public question for our times. It is formulated in various, related ways. What is God's nature? Is there a divine element in experience? Is there a divine word for us? Can spiritual practices have spiritual (rather than merely technological) results? Is there an unconditional standpoint of moral judgment on human affairs? Is there generally an unconditional dimension of things? Is there a meaningful unconditioned ground for the world? A meaningful unconditioned goal? In what way is the problem of God a *public* issue.

These questions are asked not only by traditionally commissioned theologians but also by philosophers, scientists, public figures, intellectuals, and artists. All of the questions are, of course, conditioned by religious traditions within individual cultures. It seems to be characteristic of our period, however, that raising the question of God in any of these forms makes problematic the inquirer's relation to the traditions of the surrounding culture. Furthermore, the context of inquiry today is affected by dramatic encounters of Chinese, Indian, Islamic, and Western cultures, each with its own religious strands. Inquirers from any of these traditions find themselves sharing the inquiry with those whose cultures are formed by other traditions.

If it is to be serious, inquiry into the problem of God should reflect the public context of the discussion. This normative thesis stems from a logical observation: Inquiry into the problem of God has God and related matters as the subject matter about which it seeks to discover some truth. To put forth an assertion, however hypothetical it may be, requires presenting it so that the evidence for its plausibility is potentially accessible to the other interested inquirers.

Here, one must stress the *potential* accessibility in order to do justice to the profound particularity of cultivation involved in deep experience and skilled, wise thinking. Not everyone has the capacity or preparation for critical inquiry into the validity of quantum mechanics, the veracity of Wallace Stevens's poetry, the integrity of Begin–Sadat negotiations, or the spiritual depth of Martin Buber or Thomas Merton. Moreover, it is always necessary to acknowledge the indefinite ambiguities of the rhetorical context of dialogue; most inquiry is taken up with clarifying questions and making explicit the associations and suppositions brought to the discussion.

If one puts forward a proposal about God in the public context of inquiry, however, one must make it and its evidence potentially accessible. Here, *evidence* means not only critical experiential variables and rational proofs but also the cultural and linguistic context of interpretation, the motives behind the proposal, and the potentials of all these for further critical examination. Part of the meaning of a public proposal is that, when grasped from the perspective of all the evidence, it is "evident" to all inquirers that the subject matter is as proposed. Not to make it potentially accessible is to say that the proposal is "true for those in privileged position X." This, however, is to change the subject matter of the proposed hypothesis, for "true for those in privileged position X" means "those in privileged position X consider the proposal true." The latter clause is not about the subject matter, God, but about those in the privileged position. It is one thing to note that some inquirers do not have access to the evidence. In this case, the proposal cannot be completely asserted as true, only that it is potentially true. It is another thing to assert the proposal to be true for those in a privileged position; that would be to covertly change the subject.

The logical argument sketched above is not without controversy. It might be objected, for instance, that with all the talk about evidence and dialogue for the clarification of meaning, *truth* means "provable within an actual community with a common language (for practical purposes) and a common, steady sense of what counts as proof, good evidence, and argument." Indeed, some philosophers of science have put the point that way.[22] " 'Electrons exist' is true" means " 'electrons exist' is provable in L," where L is a language spoken by a properly qualified community. In "L_1," a different language with a different community, "electrons exist" is not provable and therefore is not true. Since all inquiry takes place in one language or another, there is no language-neutral inquiry about electrons. Therefore, we cannot inquire whether electrons "really exist" but only whether they are provable in L, L_1, L_2, etc. There is no truth about electrons, only truth in L_X. There are, in fact, no electrons to be referred to except through the references whose publicity is language-specific.

Hardly any scientists accept this analysis, since they are interested in electrons. They treat the above observation as true for theories but not for the discourse of scientific inquiry. Theories may be altered or traded off according to evaluative considerations that are broader than any theory or finite set of theories. The language-specific theory of truth, however, is taken far more seriously in religious discussions. In this century it has been the epistemological position of many neoorthodox theologians and more recently of some who defend "particularism" in Judaism. The former maintain, for instance, that the kerygmatic proclamation is the norm that defines the truth of what the content proclaims ("Jesus is the Christ" is true within the proclamation of the Gospel). The normative status of the proclamation itself is not a function of the truth of its content but of something else, namely, that the proclamation was a divine revelatory act. To accept the proposition that the proclamation is normative is already to be within the community defined by its content. Jewish particularism is sometimes articulated as the view that some things are true within Jewish tradition (for instance, that Jesus is not the Christ) which are not true within the Christian tradition, and that the two traditions should coexist, each with its own truth. Since there is no truth apart from some tradition, the claims about Jesus are not contradictory. This position is maintained after dialogue has shown that the traditions use different criteria for messiahship and after each of the differing interpretations of the historical sources are admitted to have prima facie validity. Because the language-specific (or religious tradition-specific) theory of truth is taken seriously in theology, it is important to argue against it if one wants to assert the notion of a public community of inquirers suggested above.

The first argument against the language-specific theory of theological truth is that it is a betrayal of the very traditions it intends to protect by guarded isolation. It was because the early Christians thought Jesus was the Christ that they thought the circumstances, events, and proximate impact of his life had the status of divinely revelatory proclamation. Only in later centuries, when ecclesiastical authority of teaching had become an issue, did people seriously entertain the veiw that the normative status of the proclamation defined the truth of its content. Even then, the "infidels" who denied that Jesus was the Christ did so because they were thought to be *mistaken* about the normative status of the proclamation, not because they had some other proclamation. In the Thomistic solution, truth somehow has to be one, and argument always helps. In neoorthodox particularism, often the arbitrariness of "picking up the stone" of the proclamation is just as arbitrary as the accident of being born into a particular linguistic or traditional community. Similarly, for this historical point, at least until the emancipation and the Enlightenment, Jewish thinkers believed Jesus wasn't really the Christ. The reason for that belief was not that they were Jews but, rather, they were faithful Jews partly because they thought it was true that Jesus was not the Messiah.

The second argument is that inquiry within a tradition, if the tradition is a living one, is always partly normative for that tradition. Inquiry often implies recommendations about what to value, what to believe, what to do to achieve the excellence of the tradition. Over time, this constitutes change. It supposes that there are criteria for appeal to judge what is worthwhile within the tradition that are not completely bound to any finite section of the tradition; for if they were, there could be no claim that "*M* is worthwhile," only that "*M* is regarded as worthwhile according to the criteria of the tradition at privileged moment *X*." To say that moment *X* is privileged is to define the tradition as nonliving beyond that moment.

The third argument is the Hegelian point that to state the theory that claims of truth are specific to languages or traditions presupposes a theory of reference and truth contradicted by the theory asserted. One may attempt to get around this argument with a theory of levels or "orders of discourse," allowing that propositions may be true on a higher level which are false on a lower level. At what level are the propositions religiously significant, however? Suppose the first-order proposition is "Jesus is the Christ," and the second-order proposition is "Jesus is the Christ for Christians but not for Jews." Can one say that only the first-order proposition has religious significance, and that this significance is rich enough to enhance religious life? There are several ways to respond to this question.

1. The dogmatic way is to read the second-order proposition as really of the first order, translating roughly: "Jesus is the Christ, as Christians know. Jews are mistaken in not believing what he is." If this is the beginning of the inquiry rather than a possible conclusion, a dogmatic reading fails to respect the integrity of the alien inquirers and thus reduces to the second-order point the belief that Jesus is the Christ for Christians.

2. A social-science way is to read the first-order proposition as exhaustively contained within the second order, translating as follows: " 'Jesus is the Christ' is something one believes because one is a Christian; if one is a Jew, one believes the contrary." The "because" here says that there are no first-order evidential justifications for the belief, only sociological explanations. But this position is false if a participant in the inquiry holds a belief for reason of evidence or, more strikingly, if the participant changes belief and sociological affiliations because of the evidence.

3. A theologically inquiring way of responding to the first- and second-order observations is to transfer the religious significance of the first to the second, and potentially beyond. This way can be translated thus: "Although Christians believe that Jesus is the Christ, the fact that (other) Jews who also had access to the same material believe the contrary makes the whole situation problematical." The situation of religious belief is therefore regarded as being in the middle of inquiry.

Inquiry may settle on the view that Jesus is the Christ or it may settle on the opposite view. Most likely, the inquiry will redefine the religiously significant terms so as to transcend the controversy. Perhaps it will not, and a general conversion to one position will take place.[23]

The topic of this chapter can now be set in the context of this long postlude. How does the conception of the Holy Spirit contribute to public theological inquiry concerning God? The notion of the "Holy Spirit" is at once a historical artifact developed over centuries of Christian thought, a philosophical concept defined through various theological controversies, and a symbol pointing beyond what its meanings explicitly describe. Can it contribute to our understanding of God?

The topic is not the historical question, What is the notion of the Holy Spirit? or how the notion developed. That important topic is one for a separate discussion. Nor is the topic the dogmatic question, What should Christians believe about God as Holy Spirit? What Christians should believe about God as Holy Spirit is what *anyone* should believe, and that depends on the validity of the notion of the Holy Spirit, however it is understood in its proper historical context.

The key to the contemporary worth of the notion of the Holy Spirit lies in the speculative development of its conceptual form. This is the central, general thesis. The historical and symbolic aspects of the notion are, of course, much broader than the speculative conceptual component. Perhaps the conceptual element alone has little, if any, religious significance. But a proper respeculation of the conceptual form is what can render the other elements viable and valuable for contemporary inquiry into the question of God.

A final reflective question can be posed about the Holy Spirit as God. Within the Christian tradition the Holy Spirit has often been viewed in a historical dimension. The Spirit was to have been sent by Jesus to guide us to the end. The thesis has sometimes been urged that we are now, or soon will be or must wait for, the historical dominion of the Spirit. Since we now live in an age when many normative characteristics of the community of public inquiry have come to consciousness, it can be said that God is most clearly present in the immediacies of that inquiry and in the norms of justice it entails. No longer is the authority of the transcendent source of creation recognized beyond what is revealed immediately in public inquiry. No longer do historic events of revelation carry authority in themselves apart from the Spirit's testimony, which consists in the way things stand in public inquiry.

Is the presence of the Spirit in public inquiry, however, sufficiently numinous to be spiritually transforming? Is an understanding of the

Spirit as an indissoluble part of the trinity sufficiently numinous? Josiah Royce and others have tried to interpret the reality of the presence of God as the community guided by the norms of inquiry; few have responded to this symbolism as religiously powerful. Perhaps the age of the Spirit does away with religiously powerful symbolism. Perhaps public inquiry is not numinous except for those engaged in the more individual spiritual practices of prayer and meditation. Whatever the answers to these questions, testimonies to the Spirit's numinous divinity lie in the Spirit's own operation.

This last point illustrates the interplay of tao and daimon mentioned at the end of Chapter 2. Theological inquiry depends for its engagement with genuine religious phenomena in part on having authenticity in its own tao of faith and practice. It cannot appeal to that tao for certification of its claims; nor can it impose faith and practice in the tao on inquirers in other branches of religious study. Its own engagement as inquiry, however, is better or worse, depending on the vitality with which its religious imagination is home for religious phenomena.

Philosophical theology includes a speculative dimension by which theological inquiry moves back and forth from phenomena to system, passing through numerous levels of vagueness and specificity. Other disciplines for the study of religion neither simply repeat phenomena of faith and practice or deal explicitly with the most abstract systematic categories. Instead, they constitute various specifications of those categories, selecting from the phenomena according to principles revealed in specification of the categories. The discussion of the Holy Spirit, a concept of midrange specificity derived from the ancient discipline of ecclesiastical thought management (the magisterium), is interpreted here both as a generalizing experience in the Christian tao and as uniquely specifying more abstract categories concerned with creation. In illustrating the concept of the Holy Spirit, the discussion introduced systematically the categories of creation. Chapters 4 and 5 make these systematic categories more specific, Chapter 4 by sorting out problems within orthodox trinitarianism and Chapter 5 by expanding on the problem of divine creation and human freedom. Although the theory of creation doubtless will remain controversial, these two chapters attempt to make a case for the theory being able to articulate important elements of the Christian tao. Subsequent chapters inquire whether the theory is sufficiently abstract to be specified in alternate ways by the taos of other traditions.

Chapter Four
Creation and the Trinity

T HE DOCTRINE OF of the Trinity is elaborated in this chapter in a way that demands philosophical theology. It is maintained that the doctrine stems from *both* revelational *and* speculative roots and that its defense must appeal to and acknowledge both. Here is the classic meeting point of the tao and the daimon in the West. The argument begins with a set of speculative notions that articulate a new slant on the abstract metaphysical theory of creation. Then the traditional conception of the Trinity is related to the speculative categories, first in general and later with reference to certain dilemmas crucial to the orthodoxy of Trinitarian formulations – for instance, economic versus immanent Trinitarianism, modalism and monarchianism, the distinction between creating and begetting. By the end of the chapter it should be apparent, at least in outline, that the particularities and unique claims of the Trinitarian doctrine that stem from the history of Christian theology can be given vague and critical (though not particular and demonstrative) articulation in the notions of the creation theory. That is, the speculative theory makes only vague statements about the Trinitarian persons and unity; it makes vague statements that are liable to particular specification by precisely the elements exhibited in the historical tao.[1]

Speculation can make no claim that proves a revelational thesis, one that arises from the tao of faith and practice; yet it can demonstrate that the revelational claim is neither contradictory nor unintelligent by articulating the general features of the claim in an abstract and consistent set of categories. Most arguments *against* revelational doctrines (such as that of the Trinity) do, in fact, try to show the doctrines as self-contradictory or unintelligent.[2] Further, the speculative interpretation of a doctrine rooted in revelation relates the doctrines to the other elements of experience with which the speculation is connected. This does not, of course, prove the revelation or even make it more plausible than otherwise, as some have thought. The revelation has to be *received* to be related to anything else, and the authenticity of its reception in a living tao is the critical element. Speculative articulation, however, does elaborate its meaning and show what abstract connections stand or fall with the truth of the doctrine.

The chief contribution of speculation to the self-expression of a tao is precisely the abstract precision with which it can state the doctrine. The articulated doctrine of the Trinity is already several steps away from the revelatory events themselves. The reason theology is driven to systematic interpretation in the first place is that the relatively immediate responsive utterances, even at several removes from the event, are too concrete to be precise.[3] Precision is called for when the problem of error arises or received formulations are questioned. The history of development of the doctrine of the Trinity is an example. Definition of the doctrine came directly from the controversies over heretical interpretations of tradition and scripture.[4]. Heretics usually had good traditional and scriptural sources on their side, but the orthodox won because they were able to articulate the heart of Christian doctrine more consistently and comprehensively in terms of their partially speculative Trinitarian concepts. In fact, the difficulty that has always been felt with the Trinitarian terminology of the great councils is that it is not precise enough. Even those who reject the speculative terms of Trinitarian distinctions often do so not because they are speculative in the first instance but because they lack the speculative virtues of precision and consistency.[5]

I. The Metaphysics of Creation

The argument is that speculation about creation furnishes a general model for interpreting the Trinity; thus we must begin with the theory of creation. The remarks in this section should be taken as a restatement of the philosophical hypothesis introduced in Chapter 3, with a new emphasis. Chapters 5 though 8 also restate the theory of creation, each from a different perspective.

Suppose that *God is the creator of everything that has determinate identity.* What does this entail about the character of God in relation to the created order?[6] Three features allow for specialization in Trinitarian thinking. The first is that God is the creator or source of everything determinate. The determinations not only are *what* they are but *are* what they are because of their dependence on God as creator; they are totally conditioned by their relation to their creator. On the other hand, because determinations derive their whole being from God, God's *aseity* cannot be conditioned by them. Precisely because the determinations depend wholly on God, God must be independent of them. By creating them, God becomes creator, a relative feature of divinity; but the presupposition of creation is the independent reality of the creator. Strictly speaking, our knowledge of God's abysmal aseity is knowledge of the implications of divine created relations with the world as creator, not of divine aseity taken as an object.[7]

The second feature is more complex. There is a sense in which the created determinations are themselves a feature of God, the same sense in which a person's deeds are part of the person's identity. People, of course, have effects they can walk away from. Dependence of the determinations on God, however, is so nearly complete that the determinations cannot be without the divine creative presence; therefore, so long as there is a determinate world, God is constituted as the creator of a certain kind of world.

But what kind of identity is this? Determinations are always determinate relative to each other and therefore are all complex, each comprised both of features that relate to some other determinations and of features unique to itself.[8] As a unified complex, each determination is a harmony of a plurality of components; thus it is a transcendental property of everything determinate to be some sort of harmony. An analysis of harmony gives a clue as to what constitutes God's identity in the created product.

Specifically, two principles with metaphysical status are involved in harmony. The first principle is that every harmony supposes plurality. Therefore we can say about the creator that God creates a world with plurality in it. But that is not much to know about God. Plurality in itself is thoroughly indefinite; what pluralities are depends on how they are harmonized, not on the fact that they are pluralities. Since many have claimed that the absurdity in the world stems from plurality, it may be comforting to know that God is its creator. Still, that says little about God except to hint that God's creation may be absurd or fragmentary.

The second principle is that there are certain norms for harmonizing things. Not all kinds of features can be harmonized. The formal norms that determine what can be harmonized, and in what ways, are presupposed by all structural harmonies and given instantiation in them. The norms are not reducible to the harmonies, however, since they are normative for any possible determinate structure. Thus we may speak of norms in several ordered senses. The primary sense refers to the norms that make all structures formally harmonious. In themselves, the norms are indeterminate because they are prior to and presupposed by determination. In a secondary sense, we can speak of a particular determination's harmonic structure as a normative way of measuring or combining its components. In this sense, every determination is a "good," because it is a normative way of unifying its plurality. The reason it is normative is that its structure, simply because it is harmonious, embodies norms in the primary sense. A normative ideal is a third sense of norm, usually mistaken as the primary sense. We can speak of determinate ideals as imagined ways of getting more harmony in the arrangement of given things than there is in the things merely given.[9]

What can we conclude about God from the norms of harmony? In the primary sense, norms, *taken by themselves*, say nothing, since, by transcending structure, they are indeterminate. But norms in the secondary sense, as normative measures of the components of created harmonies, are the expressions of God (John 1:1–3). The reason those secondary norms are expressions of God, however, is that they are instantiations or specifications of norms in the primary sense. Norms in the primary sense are uncreated, since they are indeterminate; they are what gives harmonious structure to all that is created. Therefore, interpreting tradition and anticipating the argument below, we can call norms in the primary sense the Word of God; norms in the second sense constitute the Word "spoken," as it were, in creation. As a person's identity is constituted by the determinate character of what the person does and says, so God's identity is constituted by the determinate character of the divine spoken Word, the created order that expresses God in its harmonies.

The third feature of God is the very act whereby God creates. This act relates the abysmal creator to the determinations created. Furthermore, the act accomplishes the creation of both the plurality in determinations and the determinate, normative elements in harmony. The former gives no *special* character to the creative act, but the latter makes the act that which constitutes the determinations to be normative expressions of the creator. The act, therefore, has a mediative function promising to relate not only the created order with God but also, to use Christian terms, the Son or normative expression with the Father.[10]

We encounter a problem, however, when we ask what the nature of the act is. A finite person's act consists in its accomplishment of an end through a series of steps or stages, the order for which can be formulated as a blueprint for action. There are no stages or steps in divine creation, however, since there can be no determinate medium through which the creation of all determinations occurs. Creation *ex nihilo* is immediate. A person's act has the character of producing its product. If the product were all that is determinately involved, the nature of the act would be nothing but the nature of the product considered as being produced (*natura naturans*). Thus, with God's act, its only nature is the nature of its product considered as divinely produced, that is, the product as the normatively measured expression of the creator.

These three features of God—being the source of the creative act, the normative terminus of it, and the act itself—are implications of the speculative hypothesis that God creates everything determintate. They are features God possesses because of God's relation to the created order. Many other things can be stated about the created order that stem from the order's relation to God, but they are not pertinent here.

II. Trinitarian Persons

The suggestions provided by the creation theory for interpreting the persons of the trinity are: God the Father is the creator, God the Son is the determinate product of the creative act *in its character as the normative expression of the creator*, and God the Holy Spirit is the creative act itself mediating normatively between creator and product.

The Father

In early Christian writings the Father was nearly always identified with the creator.[11] The identification of Father and creator as interpreted in the present theory differs in one crucial respect from the view of certain early writers who supposed that the creator-Father is the real whole God of whom the Son and Spirit are elements or extensions.[12] Rather, as will become apparent, the creator in the present theory is on a par with the normative product and the created act. In later Christian thought Father, Son, and Spirit are identified as each a person of the Godhead, and it is this more orthodox position that creation theory supports.

The motive behind the church fathers' interpretation was an acute sense of monotheism, of the need to recognize the unity of God behind all distinctions.[13] This problem may be posed in terms of the speculative creation theory by asking whether the creator is closer than the other persons to the sense of divinity that is independent of a connection with the creation. The nature of the creator by definition means that the creator must be independent in reality of what is created, since what

God creates is dependent solely on God, and since the character of being creator depends on the actual creation of something (without creating something, God is not creator), there would seem to be a transcendent ground beyond the feature of being creator toward which that feature is the closest step.

To be sure, the reality of God must transcend God's character as creator. But this transcendent reality is utterly and necessarily indeterminate, known only by the implications of the determinate nature of creatorship. The transcendent ground is a mystery in terms of its transcendence of God's determinate character – but only in these terms. Beyond, or apart from, transcending the determinate character of God as Father, Son, and Spirit there is nothing, not even mystery, for us. Speculatively, God is *not* apart from the divine determinate character but in it, because God has created. Because God is not creator except in that God creates something through the divine creative act, the act and the created things are as close to the transcendent ground as the ground's character of being creator. It is God's immediate connection with the creative act and product that makes God also creator. If the act and the product can be identified successfully with Spirit and the Son, it will be plain that God is as much Spirit and Son as creator-Father. Either one entails the other. (It should be recognized that to call the transcendence of God beyond determinate creatorship a "ground" is to cheat; *ground* means the same thing as creator, and we are only pointing out the transself-referential character of the notion of *creator*.)

The Son

The doctrine of Jesus as the Son of God is a central claim, especially when New Testament sources are read in the light of later Trinitarian controversies. In its general form, the Christological thesis is that Jesus is the Son of God because he is the incarnation of the creative Word (Col. 1:13–20).

The creative Word must be spoken of in two senses, corresponding to the first two senses in which we may speak of norms. In the primary sense the Word *unspoken* is the form of pure normativeness, indeterminate in itself, that is embodied in anything with a harmonious structure. In the secondary sense the Word *"spoken"* is the determinate expression of the creator, the harmonies created. What expresses the creator in determinate things is their formally normative way of combining their components. The Word is not determinate except as it is spoken, as embodied in things and as expressing the Father. It makes no sense to think of the Word of God as anything characteristic of the Father or determinate itself if the Father is not actually expressed in the creations that are the Father's products.

That there is a Word of God is not a uniquely Christian claim; Jewish Wisdom literature is filled with it.[14] The Christian claim is that the Word is incarnate in Jesus, and its logical force is unheralded in either Greek or Jewish thought, the Hebrew scripture's prophecies notwithstanding.[15] The force of the claim is underscored by contrasting it with an interpretation of Jesus characteristic of popular piety.

In the minds of many Christians, Jesus is the incarnation of the Word *because* he is perfect. What perfection in this context means can easily be interpreted by the creation theory: Determinate harmonies have varying degrees of richness. The richer ones can be called more harmonious than the poorer ones. Consequently, whereas every harmony expresses the Father just because it is harmonious, some harmonies are more expressive than others, Jesus being somehow the best. What perfection means concretely can be interpreted in terms of the moral and aesthetic traditions of Greece and Israel and is part of the common sense of our own culture. But to be perfect in a moral or aesthetic sense is not ipso facto to be an incarnation. A crucial distinction must be drawn between being a maximal instance of an ideal form or norm (perfection) and being God in the flesh (incarnation). That *embodiment* is a synonym for both *instantiation* and *incarnation* only compounds the confusion. To say that Jesus is the incarnate Word is to say that he personally is the normative condition for the created order in the same sense the formal norms or harmony are the incarnate word on a more general level. In other words, Jesus personally must be that "through which all things that are created, are created" as the formal normative condition for their possibility. Jesus must be the Word according to which the creator structures his creation (John 1:3); he must be the transcendental condition according to which the created order expresses the creator.[16]

Therefore, we must look at the specifics of the historical life of Jesus to see what it means to be the incarnation of the Word. The Christian claim is that by participation in Jesus' life the whole world attains or is restored to the acme of its created status, so that it expresses the Father according to its proper glory (Eph. 1-2; 1 Pet. 4:11, 5:10; cf. 2 Pet. 1:3; Rom. 8:19-22; Heb. 2:10). The biography of Jesus is a cosmological account. Jesus is the divine, incarnate Word precisely because according to the Christian tao, his biography and the world's history relative to that biography accomplish the creation and redemption. The Christological question now becomes: Is Jesus of Nazareth one through whom the entire creation glorifies God properly? To answer the question, we examine Jesus' historical identity as a candidate Jewish messiah, since that apparently is the historical figure who would redeem the world. The *specific* form of the central Christological thesis is that Jesus is the incarnate Word because he is the Christ, the Messiah.[17]

This development is opposite the history of Christian understanding. Jesus was first called "Messiah." Only later was the term recognized as involving the incarnate Word.[18] But if the historical *Jesus* is the Messiah, then the Messiah is not what the Jewish tradition historically expected. Jews balk at Christian doctrine today, not so much because of Jesus' humiliation but because of the cosmological implications concerning incarnation drawn for historical messiahship.[19] The cosmological claim is not merely that Jesus is the best instance of the formal norms of harmony but that he is the norms themselves, doing for the created order what they do. The Christian response to Jewish charges of idolatry regarding Jesus has been to increase the claim, not to retreat.

To speak of the normativeness in the harmonies of things is to speak abstractly and vaguely. We understand normativeness on the vague level perhaps by analogy with mathematics and art. To see what normativeness really is, to see what the determinate expression of the creator is in detail, we must look at the entire domain of determinate things bit by bit.[20] In human affairs we must look to history, especially the history of Jews and Christians. Specifically, Christians say God is humanly and divinely present perfectly in Jesus. Jesus not only *shows* but *is* himself the Word. If, on reflection, Christianity is implausible, it is because of the great difficulty in thinking of a person as carrying this metaphysical burden.

The Spirit

God the Holy Spirit is the creative act mediating between the creator and created product, i.e., between the Father and the Son.[21] The Spirit mediates through actual creation. What is mediated, however, is normativeness.[22] By creating something, the creator gives determinate structure to the normativeness or harmony of which God apart from creation is the indeterminate form. Conversely, it is through the creative act that the created determinations are normative expressions of the creator. Only by virtue of its creation can the created world contain the divine Word. Thus it is from the Holy Spirit that the world's sanctity is derived.

The speculative thesis that the creative act mediates between the creator and the creator's normative expression can be made concrete in the Christian doctrine of the Spirit only by reference to the historical Christ, since the Holy Spirit is Christ's historical Spirit (1 Pet. 1:11). This reference can be made economically through a discussion of certain standard Christological problems.[23]

First is the heretical Ebionite claim that Jesus could at most be a perfect human being.[24] That he is a perfect human being need not be denied, but his perfection constitutes the true divinity of the second person of the trinity. Jesus is the human incarnation of normativeness in God's. creative act. Because of this, the whole world glorifies God and expresses the creator by participating in Jesus through the Holy Spirit. It is not the structural fact that Jesus is the incarnation that is in itself important but, rather, the implication that the entire created domain can fulfill itself as the terminus of the divine creative act through participation in Jesus (2 Cor. 5:17-19). The surprise of the Incarnation is that it shows that all the rest of the world cannot be fulfilled in its created status without participating in Christ (Rom. 8:20-39). Although this is not deductive from the theory of creation, it is consistent with the theory and is what is apparent from Christian examination of what creation in historical detail reveals itself to be. If Jesus' actual identity as a perfect being has this eschatological significance, then being that kind of perfect man is no small thing and is not to be taken as excluding divinity.

The second problem is the opposite heretical claim of Docetism – that Jesus Christ could not have been an actual human being, but only the appearance of one.[25] This claim is easily rebutted within the creation theory because of its identification of the second person of the Trinity with normativeness in actual created things. It would be no indignity to the second person of the Trinity to be a real live human being. Obviously, the tender spot of the present interpretation is to show sufficient distinction between the second person and the world.

The third problem is the adoptionists' claim that Jesus was a mere man who was sanctified by the Spirit to become Lord and Savior.[26] True, it is because of the Spirit's mediation through creation that Jesus is divine; but that is not something overlaid on an ordinary human nature. It is by the Spirit's creative activity that every created thing embodies to some degree the normativeness of the second person of the Trinity. Likewise, it is through the Spirit's creative activity that Jesus is the perfect incarnation in whom the world is fulfilled. The adoptionists are right in saying that if Jesus had done someting wrong, if he had been disobedient, unfaithful, or arrogant, he would not have been the Christ. They are also right in saying that the reason he did *not* do something wrong was that the Spirit was present to him. But they are wrong in not seeing that the perfect presence of the Spirit constituted the very being of Jesus because he was by nature the Christ. It was because of the Spirit that Jesus was the divine Christ, and it was because he was the divine Christ that the Spirit was present to him.

The fourth problem is the Patripassianist claim that Jesus' suffering (and life) was a combination merely of human pain and the suffering of the Father present in Christ by the Spirit.[27] This claim attributes divinity to Jesus only in the sense that the Father is present to him; hence, the only *divine* suffering is that of the Father in Christ. But it is Jesus Christ himself who is the second person of the trinity; his human suffering itself is the suffering of the second person. The Father in the Spirit makes Jesus the suffering Christ. The eschatological significance of this is that we participate through the Spirit in the suffering of the Son (1 Pet. 4:13–14).

III. Economy and Immanence

Let us now take up several traditional problems of the Trinity as a whole. Classically, the contrast has been made between the economic view of the Trinity and the immanent view. According to the immanent view, the distinctions between the persons are in God in aseity;[28] according to the economic view, they are, rather, in God's revelation to the world or at least God's connection with the world.[29] The orthodox position has been to hold to both views. If one holds to the immanent view, the economic view usually follows; but many people have held the economic without the immanent.

My own suggestion attributes the distinction of the persons to God immanently in the following way. God's determinate character comprises the threefold totality of being (1) creator, (2) normative terminus of the creative act, and (3) creative act. This determinate character is Trinitarian. Indeed, to show that this is an immanent, or "essential," doctrine of the trinity, two steps must be taken. First, it must be indicated that all three elements in the Trinitarian distinction are properly and equally divine. Second, it must be made clear that the locus of the Trinitarian distinctions is the real and true God and not just an economic appearance of some god who lies behind all three characters of creator, act, and product.

The task of showing all persons of the Trinity to be equally divine seems different in the case of each person, for it would seem that everyone would accept the claim that the creator is divine and probably the act as well. Most thinkers, however, would initially reject the claim that the product, as the expression of the creator, is divine, precisely on the ground that being the created product is the essence of the contrast to being divine. It would seem that what is meant by saying something is not divine is that it is created instead. It is argued here that the case for all three persons is the same: if the creator is properly divine, so are the other persons. This is a denial of the Christian heresy of subordinationism. Below we consider the thesis that no person is divine, but for now we assume that the creator is divine.

In traditional Trinitarian theology the divine unity of the persons has long been attributed to the mediating function of the Holy Spirit, interpreted in our categories as the creative act. So it is with our model. The creator is creator by virtue – and only by virtue – of exercising the creative act. The character as creator is constituted by creative acting. Therefore, the Spirit act is divine in precisely the same sense that the creator is divine, since they are mutually constituting features.

Now, is there any sense in which the product can be detached from the creator and creative act? If there is no such sense, we are allowed to say that the product is divine, since that is what makes the act a doing of something and the creator an actual creator. An act that produced nothing would not be an act, nor a creator who created nothing a creator.

I submit that there is no sense in which the product can be detached from or disunited with the other persons, since it would need an independent being to be detached. Yet, by definition the whole being of the created product depends on its connection with the creator and act. In the human analogy, we distinguish a person's deeds from the person's person by a kind of detachment or disunity. That is because the person's actions take place in a medium of space, time, and other things which give the deeds and the results of actions a locus other than the person. A person can walk away from deeds. Furthermore, human actions always partly share the character of the medium or environment in which they occur; thus we can attribute responsibility for a deed to a person, although we cannot attribute to the person the power to create it *ex nihilo*. In the case of God, however, there is no medium for actions; the product is produced immediately. To make a difference, a medium would have to be determinate, hence created, and therefore could not be a condition of creation as such. Further, there can be no features of the creator's deeds that the creator did not create, since every feature is determinate and every determination created. Consequently, the created product is of a piece with the creative act and the creator. Its nature is immanent in the natures of creator and act in the sense that they could not be what they are *at all* (not even a little bit of a creator or a feeble effort of act) without the created product. The product constitutes the natures of the other persons. To deny this requires acknowledgment of an independent status for it that would deny the creatorship of creator and act. In other words, the creation theory of God is essentially Trinitarian. God cannot be conceived simply as a creator over against a world created.

In light of the attempt above to show that the created product qua created is within the divine Trinity, it is likely that the strongest charge to be brought against the general suggestion is that it is no immanent doctrine of the Trinity at all but, rather, a solely economic view in disguise. If the created product is divine, the kind of divinity involved must be inferior. Since we have acknowledged that the creator must have some reality independent of the character of being creator, the implicit assumption of this view is that the creator's transcendent independence is the true divinity and that the whole of the determinate Trinity is derivative because it is dependent on the creative act that makes all determinte things. Finally, so the charge goes, the chief trait of the merely economic view is that the distinction between the persons of the Trinity depends solely on the connection with the world; this is all that underlies *our* Trinitarian distinction.

First, let it be answered that God's divinity lies in the Trinitarian nature, not in an independent reality beyond Trinitarian distinctions. Given the reality of the creation, with the Trinitarian distinctions there is no *further* reality to God. God does not have some primordial nature *beyond* the Trinitarian one. God's reality as an independent source of the being of the created realm is transformed into and contained within the divine nature as creator, act, and product. The transself-referential character of creatorship means only that there can be no determinate necessity that God be creator. There is no necessity for God having any nature whatsoever, since any determinate necessity depends on God having the peculiar character of creator; this is the truth of the claim for transcendence. After the fact, so to speak, we can say, nonetheless, that God has a Trinitarian nature. Given God's self-determination as creator, act, and product, there is no need to search for anything else divine. If *anything* is divine, it is the Trinity.

If God did not create anything, including even the determinate structure of intelligibility, there would be no basis for saying God has a nature. Specifically, there would be no basis for saying God has a divine nature. Divinity is a meaningful character only in relation to determinate things. If there are no determinate things and hence no relation to them, God could not be divine or anything else. God makes divinity in creating, in the only meaningful sense of the word *divinity*. Of course, this claim would not be correct if we did not also claim that everything determinate, including the structure of intelligibility and possibility, is created. If, prior to creating, there were a possibility of God creating the world, God would have to possess some nature in order to have the possibility, and that nature would have to be divine. The belief that God did or could have such a possibility stems from a misleading analogy with human creativity. The creative acts of human persons are conditioned not only by the media and by the nature of the things acted on but by the prior character of the persons. People are discursive individuals such that every act is conditioned by feedback concerning the nature of earlier acts. That, however, is an element of the finitude of human acts which God's perfectly free and infinitely self-constituting creative act does not share. In rejecting the analogy with human acts at this point, it is not at the same time strange to say that God has no nature prior to self-naturing, that once God's reality has a Trinitarian nature, that is the whole of its nature. This denial of a transcendent, determinate character constitutes the potential affinity of Christian belief with conceptions in Hinduism, Buddhism, and taoism.

It might be thought that the distinction between the unspoken and the spoken Word holds a clue for distinguishing an immanent Trinity from an economic one. It would seem that the Word unspoken is internal to the Godhead and is unconnected with the world, whereas the spoken Word is God present in the world. But the Word unspoken is indeterminate and, consequently, is indistinguishable from any other person in the Godhead. We can talk about the unspoken Word only by inference from the determinate and normative spoken Word expressing the Father. This is exactly parallel to the distinction between the transcendent, indeterminate divinity that makes itself creator and the determinate creator it makes itself. Just as God is not transcendently indeterminate, having become determined, so the Word is not unspoken but spoken. The Word is not some "what" before it is spoken; it is precisely "what" *is* spoken.

The second part of the criticism of our view is that God, in the transcendence of divine nature as creator, is more divine than the divinity of derivative Trinitarian nature. My reply to this is implicit in what is stated above: Divinity cannot apply to anything beyond the Trinitarian nature. The question whether the Trinitarian nature itself is derivative is an important one, however. True, it is made or constituted by God in transcendent reality. But it is not derivative from or made out of any transcendent primordial God-stuff, for there is no such thing. God is nothing except as Trinitarian creator. Were God not creator, divinity would be indeterminate and indistinguishable from nothing. Divine transcendence of creatorship and Trinity means only that what God is, God did not have to be, that God self-natures freely.

The last part of the criticism is that the distinction of the persons of the Trinity depends on the connection of God with the world and that this is a merely economic view of Trinity. True, I claim that the distinction between the persons depends on the creation of the world. But the claim is also that the world, *in the respect that is crucial to distinctions between the persons*, is not merely mundane but also divine, a part of the divinity of the other persons of the Trinity. What is rejected is the view that God is on one side and the world is on the other, that creative activity is a bridge between the two. If the distinction between the persons depended solely on the bridge as conceived, the persons would not be immanent to God's own nature. Since I reject the Aristotelian substantialist model of God and world as separate and conjoined, the notion that the connection between God and world constitutes the distinction of Trinitarian persons does not mean that my view is merely an economic one. The connection between God and world is internal to God.

Ironically, the most difficult problem for our Trinitarian suggestion is the defense of the economic side, not the immanent side. The real test comes in making a distinction between the begotten Son and the world. If this test is failed, no meaning can be attached to the revelation of God to what is other than God. That is the problem to which economic Trinitarianism is addressed. The truth in the economic view is that God is indeed present in three persons to the world. If the world cannot be distinguished from God, however, then being present is very strange.

The focus of the problem of Christian theology is the claim that Jesus is the Christ. The problem is that Jesus, a creature like humans, is also the divine Lord, "begotten, not made." Therefore, just as the life of faith is focused on the problem of grasping Christ as both human and divine, so more abstract theology ought to have its focus centered on the problem of distinguishing and grasping together the created world and begotten divinity. Speculative theories that begin with an antecedent begotten Son and try to meld him onto a separately created world do not reflect the proper locating of the problem as it is found in the concrete life of faith. The advantage of the view presented here is that its problematic points are in the right place from the standpoint of revelation theology in the traditional Christian tao. Many difficulties with traditional speculative categories for Trinitarianism stem from improper location of the focal problems.

In summary of this section, let me state that the persons of the Trinity are taken to be eternal, relative, and connected with creation. They are eternal in the sense that they are ontologically prior to things that happen in time, since time is one of the things created. They are relative, or related, in such a way that their natures are determinate only in terms of each other. The Father is determinately the Father only with respect to the Son in the Spirit, and so on. This is the perichoresis of the ancient Fathers and the subsistent relation theory of Augustine rendered in terms of the speculative theory of creation. Because the persons are interdeterminate, their distinction is eternal from yet another point of view, and it is false to say of the Son that "there was when he was not."[30] The connection of the persons of the Trinity with the world is the crucial problem and must be pursued.

IV. Begetting and Creating

In ancient Trinitarian controversies it was seen from many quarters that an ordering of the persons is essential.[31] But it was also seen that, if the ordering of the persons is of a piece with the order between God and world, subordinationism, with its degenerate forms of divinity, is inescapable.[32] Therefore, two orders were acknowledged. The order of God and world was said to be a creator-created one. The order between the persons was said to be begettor-begotten for Father and Son and that of procession, "spiration," or generation, for the Spirit from both other persons. Theologians have long been hard pressed to make good these distinctions.

Creation is said to be the making of something out of nothing. Begetting is making something out of the begettor.[33] The trouble with the usual interpretation of this distinction is that the theory of begetting leads directly back into subordinationism. If the Son is made out of the substance of the Father, either he is everything the Father is, and is indistinguishable from the Father, or he has only some of the Father's substance and is less than the Father. The first alternative denies the distinction between persons, and the second is subordinationist. To provide for the distinction between the persons, the Father would have to give some determinate features to the Son that the Father did not already have. These features would then seem to be *ex nihilo*, and the distinction between creating and begetting begins to collapse. To provide for the equal divinity of Father and Son, the process of begetting the Son must not involve an alteration in Fatherly substance that makes the Son's part of it less than the Father's. Yet, as Aristotle pointed out, any change in the perfect is for the worse.[34] These are among the chief difficulties with the notion of begetting.

The difficulties stem from the Aristotelian notion of substance as that which has primary identity, a speculative scheme we have already implicitly rejected. Furthermore, it is apparent from what has been said in previous sections how our own theory of creation would resolve the problems of the relationship of the persons. The created domain, *as the normative terminus and expression of the creator's act*, can be said to be "begotten."

The difficulty to be faced in the view defended here is that of making a distinction between begetting and creating. The speculative theory is called a theory of creation because of the philosophical use of the notion of creation. What must be done now is to determine what the *theological* tradition meant by the created order and see if that can be rendered within the speculative theory as something subordinate, in the proper sense, to the begotten Son.

What the ancient fathers often meant by *creation* was something quite philosophical; it was dependent on the various speculative schemes prevalent at the time. In reply, I can only argue that our own speculative scheme is better on speculative grounds, and allude to the straightforward philosophical defense of it.[35]

The more strictly theological roots of the ancient creation doctrine were basically twofold. First was the testimony of scripture. The exegesis of scripture, however, usually depended on philosophical views, and scripture itself is not clear in making a distinction between creating and begetting.

The other root of the creation doctrine had more to do with theological implications of scripture. If the work of redemption, especially the Incarnation, is to be significant, the world that needs redeeming must have some independent status for God to work on. If redemption is to be significant for human beings, this "independent status" cannot be some opposing, evil, divine principle, as the Manichees claimed, but has to be of the household of the human. Further, if the created order is identical with the divine Son, the Incarnation is needless. But according to tradition, the Incarnation is a great move of grace, one not necessitated by the determinate character of creation. Thus, to protect the integrity of the Christian revelation in Christ, the church fathers had to emphasize the distinction between the begotten Son and the created, fallen world.

What is theologically necessary, then, is to have a world that at once can be fallen and redeemed.[36] Because the revelation is that redemption is actually accomplished in and by Jesus Christ, the world must be sufficiently distant from the Son to be changed by his incarnation, yet close enough that his incarnation can be its proper redemption and fulfillment. The crucial theological notions that must be reflected in the distinction between the merely created status of the mundane world and the begotten status of the Son are the Fall and redemption.

These are basically eschatological notions, however, including in the Incarnation the last judgment on things. Eschatology requires the doctrine of the Spirit, for it is only through the Spirit that the whole creation can participate in Christ and thus be the proper expression of the Father's creative act. We must suspect, therefore, that the notion of begetting is intrinsic to the notion of Spirit and cannot be contrasted with creating except in conjunction with Spirit. Thus the task of contrasting the order of the persons with the order in creation comes down to this: (1) to show how, in light of the creation theory, the world may be fallen and redeemed; and (2) to show how the redemption is accomplished by Father, Son, and Spirit. If some of the factors in the two orders coincide or appear to be the same things viewed from different contexts, no confusion exists as long as the proper theological motives of accounting for the Fall and redemption are kept uppermost. Again, this is to locate the speculative problem in the right place from the standpoint of the tao of faith and practice.

First, the theory of creation notes that every created, determinate thing is a harmony of one sort or another. Further, in its normativeness, the harmony in the determinations is the expression of the Father. Not every mode of harmony in determinations—for example, people—is always the richest possible under the circumstances; hence, people have moral responsibilities. That is, their actions are judgable according to the normative character of their results. The created world being the particular thing it is, determinations such as people have the capacity to live so as to alienate their actions and themselves from their created function of expressing the Father in normative structures. This is not merely a moral error, it is rejection of one's created status and the divine purpose of created existence, from which moral error may follow.[37] That people *are* fallen from their created status is the testimony of Christianity. Perhaps the entire created world is distorted by people's perversion into participation in the human fall. No created thing can cease to be an expression of the Father and still exist, since to exist at all, it must have a harmony in *some* mode. But it can exist in a mode of harmony that does not express the Father in an appropriate way. Since the creator is the source of *all* harmonies, even low grade, perverse, inappropriate, sinfully chosen harmonies, indeed the source of the harmony of sinful choosing, in a deep and dark sense the creator is the source of evil and is normatively present as demonic.

What about redemption? From what has already been said, it is apparent that redemption is the restoration of the created domain to a status of proper normative expression of the Father, the reestablishment of the created realm as glorification of the Father. *Glorification* is the theological word for the way in which determinate harmonies reflect the Father as their normative ground. How can the world be made to glorify the Father? The Christian answer is through participation in the Son, Jesus Christ. The upshot of participation in the Son is that the world enjoys its proper – as opposed to fallen – created status. Through participation, the created world can be said to be identical with the Son (the thesis the creation theory is committed to): The normative fulfillment of the world in Christ is the normative expression of the Father, that is, the Son (1 Cor. 12:4–6, 15:28; Eph. 1:16–23).

The matter must not remain on the general level, however, Humanity's fallen state is something both historical and particular, regardless of whether it is universally widespread, as it is according to Christianity. Something historical and particular must happen to accomplish the redemption and make the world's glorification of the Father a historical reality. Each determinate thing must glorify the Father in particular. Therefore, in the case of people, something particular for each person must be done to accomplish the redemptive glorification. For this, the tao turns to Christ and the Spirit.

Second, Jesus Christ is the redemptive incarnation of God the Son. This means, first, that Jesus was a human being; otherwise, he would not be incarnate. Since people are particular people, Jesus is a particular person.[38] Second, it means that Jesus is the perfect expression of the Father. He would not be a perfect expression of the Father, however, nor would he be the incarnation of the full reality of the Son were he not to accomplish the redemption of the whole world. Since Jesus Christ is fully God, he must be the full glorification of the Father that the Son of the Father is. Therefore, it is necessary for the divine identity of Jesus Christ that the whole world participate in the glory he gives the Father. Because Jesus Christ is also a human being, the world must participate in his human life, too.

The identity of people lies in what they do with their historical material, their selves, and their situation. Thus the identity of Jesus is to be determined in part by noting his historical situation. It is to be determined in large part by noting the personal things he did in that situation (his righteousnes, compassion, obedience, and so forth). Most importantly for Christians perhaps, it is to be determined by noting what he has done and is doing and what he promises for the world's redemption. Jesus – and this is a historical claim – was raised from the dead (Acts 2:32). He commissioned his followers as apostles (Matt. 28:18-20), ascended into heaven, and is present in history for the moment in the Holy Spirit (Rom. 8:9-11). That Spirit has worked in the Church, tempering it so that it became the body of Jesus Christ (1 Cor. 12) continuing his work. Spirit and Church together, therefore, continue the growing identity of Jesus; in large part, that identity still consists in promise. The metaphysics of redemption, however, is that the world properly glorifies God only in that it participates in Christ. It is the function of the Holy Spirit both to constitute Christ as the one in whom people participate and to move people so that they participate in Christ.

The reason why Christianity demands a historical Jesus should now be apparent. A picture of Jesus may be all that is necessary for the response people make to God's redemptive act. But salvation or redemption consists, over and above people's choices, in participation in the real person Jesus. Only in actual redemption or the completion of creation does Jesus have a divine identity. He is divine because he is the Word not only through which things were made but also through which they glorify the creator. He *is* the divine glory, the proper normative expression of the Father. Without participating in his concrete reality, there is no concrete glorification for other people. If there were only a picture, there might be an adequate human response to God's declaration of love; but the most adequate human response is not adequate to the task of redemption. That task requires God's cosmic activity. To say otherwise is to step into Pelagianism, to be blind to the cosmic drama (Col. 1:15-20).

Contemporary Christian theology not only arises out of the specifically Christian tradition but also needs to make its case in a community including Jews, Muslims, Hindus, Buddhists, Neo-Confucianists, and others. Whereas Jews and Muslims would object to any reference to a divine personage, Hinduism with its many avatars, Buddhism, particularly with its Mahayana conception of Buddha-Mind, and Neo-Confucianism with its doctrine of Principle, all advocate competitors to Jesus as Second Person of the Trinity. From a non-historical perspective, it would seem that theologians would have to choose one, none, or a soupy mixture. From an historical perspective, however, each tradition must be recognized and identified in terms of its own origins, and then the question of theological truth or religious validity must be raised in terms of our own historical situation which has its origins in many traditions. This book attempts to assemble a picture of our situation, and the final chapter addresses it directly. But as the initial chapter states, to conceive the theological situation in this pluralistic fashion is to relativize any special authority in the Christian (or any other) tradition. The focus of the present chapter is to employ the theory of creation to express Christian theology in stages prior to its historical relativization because the aim is to test the speculative theory against the integral origins of the Christian tao, as other chapters do for other traditions. Hence the direct concern with Christology.

The key to Christology is pneumatology. For the Christian tao, the divinity of Jesus in both his person and works consists in his being both the beginning and the end of creation, as well as its middle. He is the general Word that is the normative expression of the Father in every harmonious determination of being, the consummation of the world in which every determination enjoys its perfect status as a normative expression of the Father in glory. He is also one who, so far as his historical particularity goes, lived for about thirty years some two thousand years ago, now is in eternity, and for whom the world waits in its consummation. But the only way by which the whole world, from beginning to end, can have Jesus Christ as God-man Lord, seeing that his full reality is human as well as divine, is through spiritual participation. This participation is part of the very fiber of created being, and the Spirit is the divine creator's.

The doctrine of the Spirit is a conundrum in modern Christian theology. It is clear now that the Hegelian notion of *Spirit* does too much; it is also clear that the psychological interpretation of the Spirit as the cause of the "warm heart" does too little. There is a truth to both sides. With the Hegelians, we can acknowledge that Spirit has sufficient cosmological import to bring the whole created domain to perfection, if the Christian tao is authentic. With the evangelicals, we admit that this must be done through the personal moving of each individual soul. Without this individual quality, the historical reality of Jesus is lost, as it was in Hegelian thought. What is needed is a speculative scheme that satisfies the categorial demands of the doctrine of Spirit.

The argument of Chapter 3 is that the theory of creation defended here offers such a scheme. The Spirit act expresses the Father; what the expression is, is the Son; the Spirit proceeds from the Father as an act proceeds from an agent; it proceeds from the Son as an act's character proceeds from what it does. The Spirit is the Spirit of the Father and the Spirit of the Son, with *of* interpreted in its respective senses according to the relations of the persons in creation. The Spirit could not be the Father's Spirit without also being the Sons' Spirit, and vice versa, as is apparent in the discussion above.

It is a contingent fact asserted by Christianity about the created natures of things that they have their consummation in Jesus Christ. That makes participation of the world in Christ a *particular* work of God in the Spirit. Further, the only way by which a particular created thing can be what it is, is by the operation of the Spirit. Some elements of created being involve possession of general features; for example, it is part of the created nature of Socrates to possess humanity. Other features of individuals are themselves individual, individually created. Some determinations are what they are mainly because of cosmological causal relations with other things, while other determinations, such as people, have significant features that are not caused, at least in the cosmological sense. Scientific causality has to do with the being of things that are mutually determinate. The Holy Spirit is the divine ground of each determination, in both its caused and uncaused features, as Chapter 3 argues.

It is in their created being that determinations participate in the Son, from the most general to the most specific levels. Regarding redemptive participation in Jesus Christ, the relevant features of people are their minds, hearts, wills, and historical deeds. Although acknowledging that the activity of the Spirit is omnipresent, Christianity concentrates on its activity in enlightening the mind, quickening the heart, and directing the will. The revelation of God in Christ is complete only in "the consummation of last things in glory." It is the task of a complete pneumatology to trace how the activity of the Spirit, dealing individually and collectively with people, can accomplish such participation in Christ that God comes "into the full glory of his creation in us and in all men," to quote the famous prayer.

We come to the last problem: the unity of the persons of the trinity acting economically – that is, acting toward and in the world. The essential or immanent unity of the persons as mutually in each other has already been discussed. The implication for divine action in the world is that the essential unity is indissoluble. Nothing the Spirit does, even in providential activity, can fail to be the expression of the Father; it is the Father who acts in the Spirit. Further, nothing the Spirit does can fail to have the character of the Son, the normative expression of the Father.

Whether operating directly in Jesus Christ or in us to make us participate in Jesus Christ, the Spirit's activity constitutes the identity of Christ; for Christ is not Christ unless the whole world is in him. Therefore, Christians affirm the principle *opera Trinitatis ad extra indivisa.*

Trinitarian modalism must be rejected. The persons of the Trinity are not different modes of God's action in the world, nor are they modes of revelation. Every action and every revelatory thing must have the structure of Father sending Son through Spirit. While interpreting Scripture, we can admit what tradition calls the "appropriation" of certain things to certain of the persons. Dealing with Jesus Christ, Christians speak primarily of the Son. Dealing with participation in Christ, they speak primarily of the Spirit. Dealing with the grace in the gifts of both Son and Spirit, Christians speak mainly of the Father. Each appropriation, however, should be qualified with a nod toward the structural unity of each person with the others. Likewise, the strong claims of trinitarian monarchianism must be rejected. Indeed, the persons of the trinity are united in nature and action; the being of one entails the being of the others. But in the one unity, there are three persons; it is a mistake to say simply that God is one. It must also be said that the one God is Trinitarian. This is not tritheism, for three gods would have to be independent substances. The persons of the Trinity are not substances in the Aristotelian sense; they are mutually determined, though different, characters in the structure of divine creativity. Monarchianism commits the error of claiming that there is a unity in some god beyond the characters expressed in creation; but God gives divinity a unified character precisely in the Trinitarian function of creating.

The unifying notion in the Godhead is glory, since it is God's glory that is the ground for God's being called "divine." The notion of glory is essentially Trinitarian. God cannot be glorious without being glorified. The Son, and the whole world in him, glorifies the Father; but the Son would not be the glorification of the Father were he not the Father's normative expression. Otherwise, the glorification would be gratuitous. It is only through the Father's creative act making the Son a normative expression that the Son glorifies the Father. Therefore, Christians say the Son glorifies the Father through the Spirit act. Each person of the Trinity is said to have its own glory. The glory of the Father is to be glorified by the Son. The glory of the Son is to glorify the Father (John 13:31–32); the glory of the Spirit is to glorify the Father in the Son and the Son in the Father (2 Cor. 3:12–18). The glory of the Christian God is one complex, unified thing, and that one thing is indissolubly Trinitarian.

Although the claims of this chapter would in no way be uncontroversial among traditional Christian theologians, they do go a certain distance toward showing that the systematic, speculative theory of creation offers a cogent interpretation of a central conception of the Christian faith. The theory offers a better model for divine relations, for instance, than does the Aristotelian theory. But if the theory of divine creation is to be truly advantageous for singling out what is important in the Christian tao of faith and practice, it must be focused more precisely on the problem of freedom. The sovereignty of God and the freedom of created people have been held in tension throughout Christian history, and theological controversy has heated up to the boiling point when one side seems to be affirmed at the expense of the other. The concept of divine sovereignty comes from the Western God-as-king mythos; the conception of freedom comes in part from the theological tradition that says people become free insofar as God addresses them. Admitting, then, that this expression of the problem of freedom has a decidedly Western bias, how can we use it to specify the conception of God as creator? How can the concept of the creator lift up what is important in that problem?

Chapter Five
Can God Create People and Address Them Too?

T HE WESTERN PHILOSOPHICAL problem of whether God can create free persons has a special form for Christian theologians. Among the many kinds of freedom that might be claimed for people, theologians are most interested in the kind that involves a human response to God. For Christians, the important response is to God's revelation in Christ. The form of the problem of creation and the freedom of chief interest to Christian theologians, therefore, is whether these two doctrines are compatible:

1. That God is the sovereign creator of everything finite and contingent, including human beings and their responses.

2. That, through the gospel of Jesus Christ, God addresses people who may respond freely.

The doctrines seem incompatible. If we interpret the situation of God's address on the model of one person addressing others, it would seem that the human response ought to be the product of those addressed and not of the addressor. Otherwise, their response is not free. But in the case of divine creation, if God produces people and their responses (and those surely go together), it would seem that their responses are not free, which would make the entire logic of personal, divine address a pretense.

Both doctrines seem to be necessary interpretations of the Christian gospel, doctrines close to the heart of the uniqueness of Western religions when the locus of divine address is conceived broadly. Their apparent incompatibility has led to great tension, however, with serious attempts being made to soften one or the other side.

The doctrine of sovereign creation has been roundly attacked on two major fronts. Since the time of Kant, transcendental philosophy has tended to undermine the belief that anything like the classical notion of creation is meaningful. If intelligibility is constituted by the transcendental conditions of the possibility of human experience, it is difficult to see how it is intelligible to say that those conditions are themselves created. Yet the transcendence classically attributed to the creator, and the contingency of all finite conditions, seems to require saying this. Under pressure of this embarrassment for the classical doctrine of creation, the tradition of transcendental theology has shifted its concern to historical, experiential, and moral matters.[1]

More potent, perhaps because it is less hedged in by a single tradition, is the attack on creation launched by process philosophy in various guises. Inspired by William James[2] and Alfred North Whitehead,[3] such philosophical theologians as Charles Hartshorne[4] and Paul Weiss[5] have developed dialectically acute concepts of a finite God who interplays with the rest of nature, influencing it with unsurpassed power and wisdom for the better. Dogmatically sensitive theologians such as John B. Cobb, Jr.,[6] and Shubert Ogden[7] have directly related these concepts to Christian theology. The chief dogmatic argument in favor of a finite God is that such a God clearly can be represented as a person who may address people in the way Western religions seem to exhibit.

The doctrine that God addresses people through the gospel is less easily denied on dogmatic grounds that are supposed to be true to the Christian tao, but the doctrine can be played down by calling it a metaphorical expression of something much less humanlike. Instead of claiming that what is revealed in God's address is God doing what the address says God is doing, it can be argued that the address reveals the depth of Being more profoundly than does anything categorizable in terms of addresses to people. By the same token, people's response to the address is not really like their response to their fellows; rather, it is like the surge of Being, "sighing" in them.[8] This approach, characteristic of Tillich in some writings, is highly compatible with the doctrine of creation, but it takes the edge off (and interest out of) the problem of what is at stake in the way people ought or ought not to respond to the proclamation of the gospel.

In this, I do not wish to argue directly against those who would attack one or another of these doctrines. Rather, my aim is to elaborate a conception of the alleged commerce between God and people that exhibits compatible doctrines interpreted in terms of certain philosophical categories. To the extent that the aim is fulfilled, it illustrates the mediating function of philosophical theology between the Christian tao and the contemporary problem of freedom.[9]

I. That God Can

Suppose, as we did in Chapter 4, there are good philosophical reasons for saying that God creates everything determinate, including God's own determinate features. Within this general supposition it is a contingent possibility that some created things may serve as addresses to people. Just as some things function as food and others as shelter, ancestry, or biological components, some things can function as addresses. Thus, if some things function as addresses, those to whom the things are addressed must be capable of being addressed.

The philosophical fulcrum of this argument is the conception of things functioning with respect to each other. Everything with a nature is a determination of some sort, and every determination is determinate with respect to other determinations. Determinateness is a relational notion. What the particular kinds of determining interactions are is a matter for empirical investigation. It seems certain, however, that some things are determinate with respect to certain other things as effects related to causes. The kinds of causation themselves vary. The question here is whether people are determinations of the sort that can be determinate with respect to certain other things, as beings addressed are related to a divine address. This question has two major sides: First, can people respond as beings addressed? and second, can there be something in the created world that sensibly can be called God's address to them? (The latter question is considered in Section II.)

There seems to be no experiential problem in acknowledging that people are the kind of beings that can be addressed. The evidence of common experience is that they are indeed addressed, at least by each other, and that they respond to these personal addresses. Whatever it is that people do in responding to the address of each other, they can do in responding to the address of God. Response to an address usually involves cognitive interpretation and doing something more overt with regard to the address. Concerning God's address, the knowledge of it involves vast problems (most of which are not raised here). In the Christian tao, the actions called forth in response include obedience, praising God, repenting, becoming happy, and loving–in sum, glorifying God.

Both the cognitive and the overt response to being addressed must be free to be genuinely human. The very meaning of the concept of addressing, in fact, requires a free human response. We do not address "things"; we address people. If God creates addresses in the world, it is because there are people there whom God wants to address. If there were no people, God would likely do something different to make things in the world respond.

The problems of the kinds of freedom involved in human response have to do with the relationship of the moments of a person's temporal existence: (1) The freedom *to act overtly in expression of a wish* involves determining some distant future event by determining one's local and present state so as to trigger the regularities of natural processes that lead to the end desired. (2) The freedom *to choose between alternatives* requires both a vagueness in the future that may be made determinate by one's own action and a degree of independence from prior causal processes. (3) The freedom to make a choice *on the basis of standards* requires both the ontological possibility of determining one's present state on the basis of norms and the possibility of assessing alternative resolutions of a situation in terms of norms. (4) The freedom *to criticize the standards* requires not only the various cognitive factors involved in recognizing standards and their normative grounds, but also the possibility of reconstituting one's posture of acceptance or rejection from moment to moment, on the basis of new standards worked out in reflection. The freedom to act, the freedom to choose acts within alternatives, the freedom to choose on the basis of standards, and the freedom to criticize the standards are all freedoms involved in a free and creative response to being addressed. And the critical note in all these problems is that they turn on how agents are constituted relative to the series of moments in their moment-to-moment existence. If the antecedent moment determines completely the determinate character of the decisive moment, there is no freedom. On the other hand, if the decisive moment is cut off completely from antecedent and consequent determination, it cannot be a moment in the life of a continuous agent, nor can it be responsible for effects. Vast philosophical problems with this view of freedom are certain to be raised by determinists and existentialists; but they are theoretical demurrers lacking the prima facie plausibility of the experience we all have of being free in these ways.[10]

According to the arguments set forth in chapters 1–4, it is possible that God creates people who have all these dimensions of freedom, yet that God is the foundation of every determinate element people possess. Every determination included in a human being is part of the terminus of God's eternal act of creation. But the determinate character a person has, though given that person in its very being by God, relates the person to the other determinations with respect to which it is determinate. If the determinate character of something is *in*determinate with respect to an antecedent or consequence, though it must be determinate with respect to some other things to be determinate at all, it is still involved in a partially indeterminate causal process. However philosophers decide that indeterminateness is involved in freedom, free people can be indeterminate with respect to prior causes, constituting themselves in their own decisive moments while also depending on God for their self-constituting self. God simply creates people partially indeterminate and therefore free of certain causal features.

If creation were said to be only by way of secondary causes, so that God would not be immediately present to people but would give them their determinate characters by antecedent causes, there would be no freedom. Concerning the theory of creation I am suggesting, however, God as creator is immediately present to each created element. Secondary causes are employed only in the sense that, to create something determinate with respect to something else, that something else must also be created.

If people are in any way free – and they seem in experience to be – God creates them with the determinate character of constituting determinate development freely. Whatever freedom people need to respond to the personal addresses of each other, they also possess for responding to the addresses of God. Expressed another way, human responses are matters of establishing cosmological relations; whatever is cosmologically possible is ontologically possible. Any possible *what*, God can make an actual *that*.

II. How God Might Address

How are we to interpret those peculiar elements of God's creative act that might be his addresses to people?

The first thing to note is that in creating something, the meaning of which is an address of God to people, God constitutes God the addressor. To address someone is, ipso facto, to reveal in part what you are. Thus God's addresses to people are revelations of God; they reveal God's character as one who addresses people. That precise divine character is revealed in the precise character of the address. If God addressed Moses from the burning bush, it made God not only one who deigns to address outlaws like Moses but also a God who uses a burning bush to do so.

The gospel of Christianity is that God addresses people in Jesus Christ and in the kingdom that Christ brings.[11] The content of the gospel is the news of this address (we will return to this shortly). Further, the gospel claims that God the creator-father is perfectly revealed in this address, meaning that all God's nature that might under any circumstances be revealed is revealed in Christ and his kingdom. This is the import of the claim that Christ is the perfect and complete revelation of God. Whereas gnostic religions say that God partially and differently reveals the divine nature according to the recipient's preparation for understanding, the Christian incarnational claim is that God is wholly present, with no remainder, in the historical Jesus and that people understand this differently according to their different capacities.

The second thing to be said about how God addresses people is that, in doing so, God constitutes or creates people as beings addressed by God. Of course, God creates people to be whatever they in fact are; in my systematic hypothesis, their being derives wholly and immediately from the divine creative act. God, however, cannot create people with the specific determinate natures of the divinely addressed without also creating some addresses with respect to which they can be determinate. It is a contradiction to suppose that God could create divinely addressed people without also creating a world with a divine address in it.

To be addressed requires people to respond to some natural thing as a vehicle of address, including both interpretation of it as an address and doing something about it; therefore, the determinate natures of people addressed by God must involve a process of response to the address. Although God may make a sign at a given moment, no one can have the complete determinate nature of being constituted as a person addressed by God in only one moment. People are not addressed by God until they respond freely to the address, and that takes time and self-criticism. They may be confronted by what God does to address them, but they are not fully addressed until they respond. An address that falls on deaf ears is an address only in the intent of the addressor; it is not an actual address. It is, rather, only sounds or events. This is not to say that a sound or event has no meaning unless someone interprets it; what it does say is that sounds or events cannot be actual addresses unless they are interpreted as such.

For God to address people is to make them beings who are divinely addressed, but that can be done only if people respond freely, since they are not addressed actually unless they freely respond. Therefore, God cannot create an address without creating people who respond freely. If God can create *persons*, God can create persons who freely respond. A person's character, nature, or personality consists in part of self-initiated action. In this sense, God is sometimes said to be a person (*person* is not used here in the technical, trinitarian sense).

Many philosophical problems are involved in interpreting the extent to which the evidence of creation reveals God to have the character of what might be called a "personality"; but at least the *structure* of creating is there, and it is that structure that lies at the heart of being a person.

Humans differ from God in two interesting, important respects. First, God is creative in the sense of giving rise to the whole being and determinate nature of creative products; God's creation is eternal. People, however, create temporally; that is, they act in a present moment in such a way that a future moment has a determinate nature for which they are responsible. The way people resolve themselves in a present moment leads to future effects according to the general laws of nature. One resolves the indeterminateness of one's present moment in the form of throwing a rock at one's neighbor; the natural laws of ballistics and psychology lead to the effect of injury to the neighbor and to enmity between you and the neighbor. Where people's resolution is free – that is, where it is a genuine choice among alternatives made on the basis of criticized standards, the causation is creative. All in all, people *create* in the sense that they determine something of the determinate nature of their effects; God creates by producing the whole nature of effects.

The second contrast between divine and human creativity lies in the nature of the medium of creation. God has no medium of creation. Divine effects are produced immediately. God does not have to work through time, but creates it. God does not have to create through the limits of space, but creates that too. The reason the created world is temporal and spatial is that God made it that way, not that it was the medium in which God had to create. Space and time are among the terminal products of the creative act, not its media. God's products derive *all* their being from God's creation. They are the termini – or, collectively, the terminus – of the divine creative act. God cannot, so to speak, walk away and leave the creations standing. There is no "place" for God to go; without God's immediate presence as creator, the creations would cease to be. Human creators, on the other hand, are finite precisely in that their creation has multiple media. Furthermore, unlike God, whose expressed personality is from eternity in the eternal creative act, people never approach a situation for creative action without some given character. They always have a nature that, in many respects, is determined antecendently, even though it is indeterminate with respect to what it can be created to be by their action in a specific case. Also, people always have the range of their possibilities relatively limited in any given situation; that is what is meant by "being in a situation." God, on the other hand, creates the very structure of possibility. People always have a situation that determines alternatives that are better or worse. God creates the structure that makes some things better than others. People can walk away from the result, or product, of their actions; other people can interfere and thwart a person's creative aim. There is so much in the constitution of the world that is relatively independent of people that the stuff of their creativity changes, decays, and slips from their hands. People's control over the products they create is forever being compromised and threatened by the accommodations they must make to the stuff of their creation before it can be worked into shape. Nothing slips from the hands of God, however; there is no place for it to "slip" to. God creates the very ontological context of mutual relevance that makes human cosmological creation possible.

Although the analogy between divine creativity and human creativity and personal self-constitution is strong; the differences between them make it possible for the same thing to be created, both by God and by some person. God immediately gives rise to the entire being of the thing, including its character of being determined in part by the creativity of some person. The thing would not be what it is unless a person made it that way. God creates the thing and the person (the person's whole situation, for that matter). A person's contribution is to create something of the determinate character of the thing by making it mutually determinate with respect to things the person can control. If it is the case that a person's freedom lies in a critical determination of the future through a series of critical determinations of present moments, then that person, though created by God, can be free and can *create* in the full human sense of the word. People's freedom consists in a mutually critical cosmological relationship between moments of their lives. The entire series, as well as its external effects, can themselves be created by God in their total being.

When people create something in response to an address by God, the effect is one of creating something of themselves that is new. Not only do they become formally one-who-is-addressed-by-God but their particular response may alter many aspects of their previous character. For the Christian, this means that, in responding to God's address in Christ and his kingdom, one makes oneself a glorifier of God, something that usually is a change from one's previous business. The Christian's response includes not only acknowledgement that Christ is lord of the kingdom and that the kingdom is at hand (the interpretative part of the response), but it also includes becoming obedient to the Lord (the overt part of the response).

On the other hand, the response people make to an address of God's creation is itself divinely created, even though it is also the creative action of the people. The created thing that addreses people for God, the way a person's words are used to address other people, is not identical to the response; yet it would not have the determinate nature of being a divine address for people if they were not themselves determinate with respect to it as such in their response. Just as people, in order to be divinely addressed, must have a divine address to respond to, so the address to be itself must have people responding to it as such. Both the address and the responding people are what they are in being mutually determinate with respect to each other. This is precisely the character of determinate being – to be mutually determined with others – that is the mark of something divinely created. People could not respond to something, they could not determine themselves with respect to another something, unless they and the other thing are created. No thing can be determinately what it is without being with some other mutually determinate thing. A thing's very identity presupposes its combination with something else, which means, according to the argument of Chapter 3, that both must be created by an ontologically independent God. No determinate thing can create the being of any other determinate thing, since a determinate thing needs another determinate thing in order to be itself. Every determinate thing depends on God. People's creative freedom, however, consists in their ability to determine other things by determining themselves according to standards of which they have made themselves the critic. This means that people's creativity in response to God's address depends on God creating them as determinate free creators.

III. The Address and Life in the Spirit

The discussion so far has been quite metaphysical and therefore may not prove much from a theological point of view. Christian theologians are interested in understanding how God addresses people in Christ, what response people should make, and with what resources. The unique contribution of speculative metaphysical reflection to theology, is that it gives a general, abstractly precise representation of historically dogmatic claims, showing how the dogmatic content is possible (which is of great interest in the face of common doubts that it makes sense) and showing what its connections are with the rest of things.

Christianity's gospel is that God completely addresses mankind in Christ and that all divine addresses are to be related to, if not contained within, the address in Christ as properly understood. The identification of God's address with Jesus Christ must be taken seriously if we are to understand the Christian tao. There is, I think, a threefold identification. First, Jesus is the primary material vehicle of God's address; New Testament manuscripts and church tradition, for example, are secondary vehicles. Second, Jesus is the intent of God in addressing man. Third, Jesus Christ is the meaning, or true interpretation, of God's address. The meaning of the Gospel is in part assumed to be that people are actually reconciled to God; this is where the matter of free human response to God's address comes in. Let us elaborate these three identifications.

The First Identification

Concerning the material vehicle of God's address, it may be said that God addresses people through voices from on high – visions of seers, dreams, and the like. Christianity's claim is that God addresses through the person of Jesus Christ. This person had for some thirty years a historical life like other persons. Most of what we know of Jesus' personal identity comes from interpreting this life, including what he said. But the personal identity of Jesus stretches beyond the ordinary sense of his historical life, in two directions. His thirty-year-long life took at least the rough outlines of its identity from the tradition of Israel; Jesus was the Son of David. The identity Jesus had for the early Christians took even more than this from his historical antecedents. His identity was formed partly by the cosmic drama involving God and man; Jesus was the Second Adam. Even more, his identity as a person was partially formed because he was the Wisdom with which the world was created – the Word of God, the Logos. Today, this part of his identity is often put down to Hellenizing interpolations by the early church, but the Christian tao includes both Hellenic and Hebrew antecedents.

In the other direction, the personal identity of Christ is determined by eschatological elements. Jesus, who lived in an ordinary way for thirty years, is proclaimed by Christians to have risen from the dead and not, for the moment, to be present in the way he was formerly. Rather, he is transformed and now rules in heaven, which means that, however the creation ought to be in order to glorify God perfectly, Jesus is in that state now. He has a functional identity analogous to the one he had for thirty years on earth. That is, he is Lord. Meanwhile, people are not in such a state of perfect glorification, and Jesus Christ is present with them in Spirit. Spiritual presence is general in that it can be present to many people simultaneously in different circumstances. It can mediate the person of Jesus, especially in his authority as Lord, to a world that changes. It staggers the imagination to think of a person in the ordinary sense relating to Buddhists, medieval Christians, and contemporary technocrats altogether and in an equally intense way. Jesus, remember, was personally involved only with a small part of the Jewish community and its rulers. He was reluctant to deal even with the Gentile Canaanite woman (Matt. 15:21–28). According to Christianity, Christ's presence in Spirit is not so limited. The personal identity of Jesus Christ includes his presence with living people in Spirit after his death and resurrection. Whether this,strictly speaking, is a historical identity is a hard question to answer; but as the history of the world proceeds and the Spirit deals with different conditions, the identity of Christ grows. He once was the one who was present in the Spirit to the world of the Middle Ages. He was not then present in the Spirit to the world of the Enlightenment, but now he is present in the Spirit to people who prepare to leave the earth in rocket ships. Whereas it is uncertain where they will land, it is equally uncertain in what way Jesus Christ will be with them in Spirit. Interestingly, the identity of Jesus Christ consists partly in the fact that in him, at the end of time, the world will be be perfected so that it glorifies God with complete reconciliation. This Christians conclude from what Jesus said during his ordinary life; they at least believe what he promised. The person of Jesus is the one in whom mankind will all be reconciled in the glory of God; it is as much a part of his identity as his crucifixion and resurrection; indeed, according to the faith, it is their completion.

The personal identity of Jesus Christ is the material vehicle of God's address. Instead of verbal sounds or handwriting on the wall, the whole person of Jesus, from alpha to omega, is what God uses to address people, and it is what they must interpret.

The Second Identification

The second identification, that of Jesus Christ with God's *intent* to address people, follows from the first, plus the principle that God constitutes the divine nature in creative action. God is the Christ-sender and the revealer of God in Christ by actually sending Christ. The advent of Jesus Christ is God's constituting of himself as the one who reconciles people in Jesus Christ. It is not meaningful to speak of God intending to send the Christ *before* actually doing it. God's determining of determinate things is eternal. God's intention to send Christ as an address, and the real being of Christ in person, are the same thing. The Father's identity is that He is the one who addresses in Christ. As Jesus put it, "I and the Father are One."

In view of the Christian claim that Jesus Christ is the complete, sufficient address of God to men, how do Christians come to terms with all the other things that seem to reveal God? They do so either by saying that they do not reveal God at all or that they are all part of that whose full identity is the identity of Jesus in person. Thus, for Christians, there must be a sense in which all revelations of God are part of Christ, including the revelations of other religions.

If the person of Jesus Christ is identical with God's intent in addressing people, then it is not misleading to call Jesus the Word of God. There is no distinction, so the identification says, between God's unspoken Word and its spoken reality. If we bracket out for the moment the question of the content of God's address, perhaps we may call on the metaphor "Word of God" as used in chapter 4. The Word of God is whatever God does in creation that is normative, that expresses the Creator and makes the Creator the one who is expressed that way. Whatever there is that makes things the way they are because they ought to be made that way, or are that way, from the barest requirements of consistency to the elegance of the world so dear to poets in cell and galaxy, is the normative expression of the creator. All this is revelatory of God; it is part of the Word, the Wisdom and the Logos. What *is* the content of God's Word? What *is* ultimately normative for Creation? Christians say it is Jesus Christ. That was the way the author of *John* saw it when he began his gospel with a reminder of the Word of God and then proceeded to say what this Word is by telling the story of Jesus Christ.

How can Jesus Christ be all the things that are part of the Word of God – burning bushes and prophetic inspirations? In a genuinely cosmic sense, for Christianity to be true, Jesus must be the lord of creation. "In him," the world will be transformed so as to glorify God perfectly. The Word of God is God's glory. According to the Christian tao, every part of the Word, including the beautiful consistency of mathematical systems and the harmony of world peace, is a part of that glory. Whereas we have consistent mathematics, we have no harmonious world peace, or at least not very often. Estranged from God, people estrange themselves from each other and from nature and do not live up to what is normative for the world. By living in Jesus Christ, however, the estrangement can be overcome, and his coming again will bring God's full glory. The personal identity of Jesus Christ, including his coming again to perfect mankind and the world, is that of the Word through whom, finally, the creation will be brought to perfect normative expression.

In the beginning, said John, was the Word, with God, in and through which all things are created, the normative expression of the Creator. This Word became human flesh in Jesus Christ, John said, thus completing the creation. Two thousand years ago the decisive creative moves were made, and people live now in the time they work themselves out. In the end creation will be complete, in the sense that it will glorify God perfectly. But how do Christians understand this–that the Word became flesh in Jesus?

In creating a world with free human beings in it, God necessarily must create the conditions for the exercise of freedom, including the possibility of sin. At the same time, God created (and creates) people to be normative expressions of divinity, which apparently means that they should recognize that they are God's glory, not their own. By choosing sin, people make it necessary for their proper creation to involve a cosmic historical drama of reconciliation. People are not created as both a free expression and an adequate expression of God's Word until they are properly reconciled to God. And they must be reconciled in history, since that temporal dimension is where they can be free, given the kind of determinations they are. Because of his natural historical creativity, the first man Adam had his chance, as do we all. But because we freely sin, said Paul, creation is complete only in the last man Adam.

Put simply, within the Christian tao, Jesus Christ is the completion of the creation of people. Because God created free beings, they were created in the situation of history with the possibility of making estranging choices. People become genuinely human in their free response to what interests them. "Being persons," though, consists in being proper parts of God's creation, and that means, to create people, God must make them in such a way that they respond to the creation and its Creator. If the response is rejection of the world as expression of God's Word, then God must make people who respond to a special address that reconciles them. This address is Jesus Christ, say Christians, who, in his very being as the completer of creation, is the incarnation in human flesh of the Word that was with God in the beginning and is in the world as God's normative expression.

The present, difficult problem is to determine how the world participates in Jesus Christ so as to be redeemed and transformed to a pro-

per glorification of God. This brings the discussion to the third identification, that between Jesus Christ the person and the meaning and interpretation of God's address.

The Third Identification

The ultimate meaning of God's address in Jesus Christ is reconciliation
and perfection of the world. The proximate meanings are the responses
people make to Christ, both active and intellectual. All are genuine
meanings of God's address. Christians believe that God means what
Jesus accomplishes eschatologically. Ordinary people say something
other than their meaning because they speak words when they mean
something beyond words. God does not speak in that sense, however.
Although Jesus Christ has symbolic content for Bible readers to interpret, the symbol is identical to that which is symbolized. The
hermeneutical problem of the Christian tao is not one of defining a term;
rather, it is one of getting to know a person in that peculair sense in
which getting to know the person means participating in the person's
identity.

The proximate meaning of God's address in Jesus Christ is indeed
something apart from Christ, in that, whereas people have the meaning
in their heads and exhibit it in their books and policies, Jesus is in
heaven. But even the proximate meaning of Christ, although it is one
derived by a free human response in interpreting, is the product of God's
Spirit. The Spirit is the power of God creating in the created order. It
cannot be just any old creating power, it must be the power of creating
according to the norms of creation, according to the Word. The Spirit's
character must be the character of the Word, the normative expression
of the Creator in creation. For Christians, however, the exact, complete
character of the Word is Jesus Christ. Therefore, the character of the
Holy Spirit is that of Jesus Christ. By this is not meant mere personality.
The Spirit mediates the personality of the historical man Jesus of
Nazareth, and that is enough personality. Rather, the character of the
Spirit is that of God creating the world with human beings, bringing
them to reconciliation with their glory duty to God. But that is mere
fleshing out of the life of Jesus Christ!

The heart of the identity of Christ lies in people's participation in
him, and in that lies what the Christian tao takes to be true spiritual
freedom. The Holy Spirit is God acting in the world so as to evoke a free
response from people which consists in joining "the body of Christ." This
God does through the finite and fallible things of the world, for example,

writers, traditions, lovers, churches. Exactly how the Spirit works is a topic of great importance in historical theology today.

Whatever creative move persons make toward accepting participation in the life of Christ, it is a matter of their own choice. God is the creator of their very being, of their ability to choose. The responsibility is theirs because they set the determination of themselves in time; the glory is God's because God made them the ones who do this. Whatever move they make of their own will, such as rejecting life in Christ, or God's lordship over the world, or their own identity as creatures, that move is their responsibility, and for the same reason. God, however, still finds glory in whatever being people enjoy in estrangement, a glory not as bright as Christians say it will be made someday in Christ but a glory, nevertheless.

The conclusions we have reached are striking in that they justify the contention that the two doctrines initially stated are compatible only in the context of certain other theses.

The doctrine that God addresses people in a manner genuinely revelatory of divinity supposes that God constitutes the divine nature as the one so revealed in the actual revelation. The revelation must be God's nature revealed. Such a revelatory address is possible only when the material vehicle of the address is both the address's meaning and the divine nature intended to be revealed.

Revelation is addressed to people who are supposed to respond freely. The meaning of the address, therefore is, what people, interpreting it rightly, make of it. Unless people's interpretation is itself *part* of God being revealed and revealing, the interpretation people make is not itself the revelation conveyed in the address. What people make of Christ in their proximate and ultimate interpretations in large measure fixes the identity of Christ. Nothing less than participation in the revealed and revealing God is satisfactory for human response to a divine address. It seems to me that Christian doctrine appreciates the depth of this concept in a striking parallel to the way Mahayana Buddhism says everyone is Buddha.

People's responses must be free, and their participation in Christ must be one of *their* whole hearts. If people are to be free, they must be able to deal critically with their own response, and the only way to do this is to take part in what they are responding to, that is, by living with critical feedback in the content of God's address. The only way to take part in the reality of God's address and addressing is to be worked into the fabric of God's identity by God's own creative self-determination. In a general sense, God is the creator of the being of everything determinate.

Free, determinate beings, however, must be created in connection with other determinations, a response that elicits their freedom. People have the person of Christ to encounter and respond to, and they have the creative Spirit giving them a world to respond from, including their own natures. Although from the standpoint of freedom, it is possible for people to thwart God forever, the Gospel of Christ says this will not be so because the things for which people freely turn from reconciliation have been broken. As the whole of creation is contingent on God's choosing to create this sort of world, so freedom is contingent on God's creative pleasure. The Christian gospel is that God does address people fully in Jesus Christ and that, in response, people are their freest. It was recognition of the implications of this that led the early Christians to elaborate their doctrines of Christ in such a cosmic way as creative Word and Wisdom.

To articulate the connection of divine sovereignty and human freedom, God can be said to be Father, Son, and Spirit. The nature of the Father is that of creator, constituting and revealing itself in creative Word – divine Word, not just any old creative word. And according to the Christian tao, that Word is Jesus Christ; for, in nothing less than the person of Jesus can people participate so that God can be revealed. Further, the Spirit cannot make people participate in the Son unless people's freedom is maintained; any other kind of participation would not be the free interpretation of a divine address. Therefore, the divine creative work must be such as to bring people to critical interpretation and life. Unless God is triune in something resembling the way the theory of creation suggests, it is impossible for God to address people in a revelatory way while at the same time creating them in all their being. Unless God creates them in all their being, God cannot bring them to the only proper response to divine address: full participation. If God does bring people to participation in divine glory, they will, in the Christian phrase, become sons of God and fellow heirs with Christ.

The speculative theory of creation does not imply that the intellectual tradition of the Christian tao is true; it does, however, provide an abstract system of categories that indicates how Christian assertions are possible and what they might mean abstractly. This allows philosophical theologians to engage, seriously and with respect, the Christian tao of faith and practice. It also enables them to relate at least certain typical Christian claims to other concerns of culture, which can also be expressed as specifications of the system. Furthermore, in connection with the thesis of this book, the long history and vitality of the Christian tao lends plausibility to the theory of creation; for, if there were no serious tao of faith and practice that could be interpreted profoundly by the theory of creation, there would be no experiential need for abstract theory.

By focusing on the Christian tao, this and chapters 3 and 4 were setups for the theory of creation, because that theory arose out of theological reflection in the West. The more difficult case comes when we inquire whether the theory of creation makes plausible connection with taos of faith and practice other than Christianity and Western religions. From the abstract standpoint of the system, philosophical theologians must treat all religious traditions as though they were at least serious candidates for being true. Then the specification of each of them separately can allow for comparisons that will throw the question of truth back down from the system to the cases that can be made for each tao. That is the thesis of Chapter 6.

Chapter Six
The Empirical Cases of World Religions

THE ENCOUNTER OF CHRISTIANITY with the world's other religions has shaken Christian theology to its foundations. As if the blows of critical philosophy, positivism, and historicism had not been enough! Some thinkers have predicted the end of Christian theology and the development of a single ecumenical perspective toward which all religious traditions converge. This prediction seems plausible.

But Christian intellectuals have encountered serious alien philosophico-religious traditions before without losing integrity, and often the alternatives were more vital than Christianity's present competitors. One thinks of the encounter of the church fathers with Greek thought and piety and of the introduction of Islamic texts into medieval Latin Christendom. In these cases and others, Christianity did not just melt away like Sambo's tiger into a stack of pancakes and butter; its theology was transformed to handle the challenges of the alternatives but with enough continuity to sustain community ties. Wholly parallel remarks could be made about crisis and integrity in Judaism and Buddhism.

What I want to recall about these crises is that one of the chief tools of transformation was speculative philosophy – *metaphysics*, if that term can be allowed a generous interpretation. The first theme of this chapter is that speculative philosophy is at the center of a rational response to the present encounter of Christianity with the world's religions.

A second, and contrasting, theme should be introduced immediately. No religion, Christian or otherwise, has ever wished to claim that its main tenets are speculative constructs, even when they are intellectually expressed. The tenets are not constructs of *any* finite kind, however their expressions are constructed and culturally relative. Rather, religion's tenets are *given*. They come from experience.[1] The experience might be a matter of formal revelation, as in some kinds of Christianity and Islam, or it might be a historical experience, as in Judaism and some Indian religions. It might be pure individual experience conditioned by some discipline, as in Hindu and Buddhist sects and in much Christian mysticism (this was William James's primary conception of religious experience). Of all the major religions, only Confucianism derives its tenets from what it claims to be only the wisdom of a man; the *religious* elements of Confucianism are not so much in the Confucian intellectual tenets as in the sensibilities of respect and shame claimed to be primordial experiences.[2] *Neo*-Confucianism asserts plainly that its wisdom comes from heavenly principle. Theology is at base empirical. If any theological tradition ever meant to claim that some *religiously* important tenets were "truths of reason," it was an aberration from what seems the more general religious situation. My second theme is that the religiously important claims of theology are empirically grounded.

The key argument I shall use to develop these themes involves defending the truth of our speculative hypothesis about God and the world. The hypothesis itself is metaphysical; its ultimate justification as a *hypothesis* is, of course, empirical.[3] Furthermore, one of the virtues to be claimed for the hypothesis is that it is vague enough to be true no matter which or what parts of the major religions of the world are true. This puts it prima facie in a favorable position to provide the context in which conflicts between the world's religions can be discussed. The most helpful characteristic of the hypothesis, however, is that it exhibits how and why the religiously interesting aspects of the relation between God and the world are *contingent* facts. As contingent, they are to be known empirically in various other senses of empirical knowledge.

Briefly, the hypothesis is that God creates everything having a determinate character. This includes God's own character as creator. Apart from creating, God has no determinate character. What God creates of the world may, depending on one's cosmology, be divided into (1) metaphysical conditions for the rest of the world and (2) contingent facts which might have been other than they are under the same metaphysical conditions. Both are contingent, though, even metaphysical conditions. God's own character includes not only being a creator but being *the* creator of *this* world, with its metaphysical and cosmological features. God is also creator of this historically unique world, if indeed this is religiously important, as it is for Western religions. Thus, the religiously important aspects of God are to be gleaned from examining what God has made.

In this chapter I want to make a case for the hypothesis by reference to the world's religions. In the discussion immediately following, I cite "evidence" for a hypothesis that will mean one or both of two things. Minimally, I hope to show that the main claims of the various religions are special instances of the vague hypothesis; although the religions' claims may conflict with each other, they all illustrate the vague hypothesis. Maximally, I hope to show that the vague hypothesis illuminates the religious claims themselves, particularly, that it resolves conflicts between claims by showing that on a higher lever they are either compatible or identical. For claims that respond to the maximal hope, the encounter of Christianity with the world's religions is pure profit, since the common experience is enriched by different traditions. Where the minimal hope alone is realized, we must look to experience to determine which, if any, of the conflicting taos is best. The strategy in presenting evidence is to deal with notorious "problems" for hypotheses such as the above – for instance, the problem of calling Buddhistic "emptiness" divine.

After development of the speculative hypothesis, we discuss the senses in which the hypothesis supports the empirical basis of theology and examine the importance of speculative philosophy in preserving experiential concreteness in religions and life.

I. The Speculative Hypothesis

For our present purposes, the speculative hypothesis can be posited in the form of three propositions: all determinate things are created by an indeterminate ground; the indeterminate creative ground of the world is God; and God's character is derived from the divine creative act.

All determinate things are created by an indeterminate ground.

Explication. To be determined is to have an identity different from the identity of something else. The proposition thus states that everything with an identity is created. Creation does not mean the *causal* determination of one thing by another. Cosmological causation occurs between determinate things. Rather, creation is the granting of reality to all determinate things from outside the system, a point determined only by the act of creating. Such ontological "causation" does not merely give existence to things whose natures are determined by cosmological causation, it grants reality to the entire society of determinate things. The dialectical defense of the proposition, in fact, takes the form in Chapter 3 of showing that there could not be even one determinate thing unless it exists together with other determinate things, that anything which could be related to the determinate thing must be created with it.

The togetherness of the created order is not temporal simultaneity but the mutual relative determination of related things. Time itself is something created. The creator cannot be determinate; if it were, it and its creation would have to be created by yet another creator; and so on.

Evidence. In religious terms, this proposition expresses the doctrine of creation *ex nihilo.*

The first creation story in Genesis 1–2:4 is central to both Judaism and Christianity. This centrality is familiar enough that it need not be spelled out. Of course, there is no one consistent interpretation of the creation story. It is especially controversial to say that the creator is indeterminate and that everything determinate, including what the Augustinian tradition called the "intelligibles," is created.[4] But even in the interpretations giving a determinate antecedent character to the creator, the character counts for something religiously only because of the creative "word."

Hinduism is even more internally diverse than is the Judaeo-Christian tradition. Analogues to creation *ex nihilo* can be found throughout, however. The ancient creation hymn from the *Ṛg Veda*, for instance, claims that before creation there was neither being nor nonbeing. I interpret this to mean that there was nothing determinate, one way or another.[5] The hymn closes with the thought that the origin of creation is mysterious; perhaps it is understood from the vantage point of highest heaven, but then perhaps not. The later Upaniṣadic tradition distinguished the world of appearance from the qualityless Brahman on whom the appearances depended.[6] Even the character of Brahman as God was a matter of appearance. "Appearance," of course, does not mean mere illusion but evanescence, insubstantiality. Appearance, the realm of *māyā,* is the *play* of the Gods in more popular expressions.[7]

Early Buddhism paid less attention to cosmology and cosmogony than to the spiritual life, but later developments of Mahayana Buddhism clearly affirm that the world of characters or *dharmas* is ontologically nonexistent. What this usually means is that everything determinate is dependent on something else, and ultimately there is nothing substantial to depend on.[8] The final ontological truth is that everything is emptiness. Although we live in the world of *dharmas,* our home is in Emptiness; and the Mahayana moral of the Emptiness doctrine is that there is nothing more than the contingent world of *dharmas. Nirvāna* is *samsāra.*[9]

Three caveats regarding this interpretation follow:

1. The Western doctrine of creation is often taken to mean that the created world is given existence of its own, distinct from, if not over and against, God. This interpretation makes it embarrassing to cite, as I have, doctrines of an "apparent" world dependent on a qualityless ground as examples of creation. But the metaphysical status of the created world per se is not at issue here. The issue is whether the determinateness of the world is dependent on an indeterminate ground. The examples I have cited, and many others, illustrate this thesis. I suspect also that a careful interpretation of what is meant in the Indian and Chinese doctrines of the world as appearance would reveal less difference from Western conceptions than the language might indicate.[10] At any rate, my claim is that the concept of the world as created or contingent on a source other than itself is more general, though it is illustrated by the Western conceptions of the existential status of the world.

2. A similar qualification should be given to the Western concept of creation: Creation should be approached from the standpoint of the world. Although some of the mythological elements in Hinduism and Buddhism refer to creation of the world in a sense plainly analogous to Western conceptions of creation, more sophisticated expressions do not. For instance, some doctrines merely hold that the world is insubstantial, that beyond the world is emptiness. Others say the world is an appearance *of* Brahman or the Buddha nature and that the relation of qualityless ground to its appearance is not necessarily like that of an agent to what the agent creates. Indeed, the term *creation* may well have been preempted by use in connection with the term *agent*. But the speculative theory presented here does not limit "creation" that way. Creation may be by an agent or it may be the arising of the world from nothing. I use the term *ground* in an attempt to be neutral at this stage. One of the main points to be made later is that the question of what kind of ground creates the world is an empirical one. Lest they think this makes undue compromises with language in order to benefit from Eastern theology, readers should remember that the mystical tradition in the West, perhaps exemplified best by Jacob Böhme, asserts that the world is created from the depths of nonbeing.[11] The term *ground* was made an essential element of establishment Christian theology by Tillich. I mean to have creation understood from the point of view of the created things, not the creator.

3. One final qualification to the citation of evidence should be expressed.

It might be claimed that some forms of Hindu or Mahayana Buddhism believe the world is insubstantial or "nonexistent," that its defective reality is contingent on nothing. In this belief, ultimate reality is nothing, and proximate reality *appearing* to be something is *only* apparent. It would not be consistent with this belief to say that the world depends for its merely apparent reality on some creative ground. I am not persuaded that this belief is held as an empirical point by any religious group. Most forms of Hinduism and Buddhism intend to claim that the things of this world are defective merely in their durability, their basic unity, their self-sufficiency, or their causal basis. Let us consider two strong candidates for exception to this claim.

Advaita Vedanta is often interpreted as holding that all determinate differences are merely apparent and that at base all is indeterminately one. Therefore, there are no appearances to be contingent on a ground. The conclusion denying appearances does not conform to the texts, however. The *Vedānta Sutra* claims Brahman is that from which the origin, subsistence and dissolution of the world proceed.[12] Commenting on this, Samkara says plainly that Brahman is the cause of the world. He distinguishes, however, between causes within the world *which can be objects of the senses* and Brahman which *cannot* be an object of the senses. The conclusion he draws is that the relation between the world and Brahman is not an empirical one because Brahman is not empirical but known from scripture.[13] I would conclude, in turn, that this can be an example of the more general thesis that everything determinate is created (that is, caused by Brahman) and that the creative ground is indeterminate (that is, not an object of the senses).

A second position seemingly denying the dependency of the world is the Madhyamika Buddhist doctrine that a thing cannot be said to exist; nor can it be said not to exist. It cannot be said both to exist and not to exist, and it cannot be said neither to exist nor not to exist.[14] The conclusion is that the world is inconceivable and that it makes no sense even to deny its existence. But this logical dialectic is not itself a religious or theological view of the origin of the world; it is, in fact, about intelligibility. It is also preparatory to the religious experience of emptiness as interpreted by Nagarjuna to mean that *nirvāna* is identical to *samsāra*. According to this position, it is unintelligible to talk about causation at all, not to mention ontological causation. If, however, someone were to find a way that *is* intelligible, Madhyamika Buddhism would not propose the thesis that the world is not created.

I have pushed the discussion of creation about as far as I can without turning to more explicit consideration of the nature of the creative ground. What is an indeterminate ground? This brings us to the second proposition.

The indeterminate creative ground of the world is God.

This proposition has two controversial elements. The first is that the creative ground is indeterminate, a point mentioned but left undeveloped in the discussion of the first proposition.[15] The second is that the ground is divine, worthy of being called God or given a religious interpretation.

Explication. According to the concept of creation developed above, the creative ground must be indeterminate. If it were determinate, the relation between it and what it creates would need a ground prior to the ground in the relation, leading to infinite regress. Taken at face value, the statement that the ground is indeterminate might seem to be a nonstatement. To say anything about a subject, even that it is indeterminate, is to assert a determinate character of it; it would seem that this contradicts the very claim of indeterminateness.[16]

In light of this criticism, it is necessary, of course, to spell out qualifications. Let me mention two.

1. Both the intellectual and religious contexts in which it makes sense to say "the ground of the created order is indeterminate" involve progression through stages of reflection about the character and contingency of the world. Intellectually, the dialectic moves back from ordinary experience, seeking more nearly ultimate causes or explanations of intelligibility. Religiously, the meditation seeks feelings or appreciations of more nearly ultimate origins and foundations of transitory experience. Because the quest moves up an ordered series of one-way dependencies, the terminus is always viewed in light of its relation to the series. But because the order of movement is from the more dependent to the less, the terminus, by definition, must be seen as that which is in no way dependent. The series depends on the terminus, not the other way around. Thus, if dependence derives from determinateness, the ultimate ground on which all else is dependent but which is not itself dependent, must be indeterminate. This fact itself derives from *the order of dependent relations*, not from any determinate character in the ultimate ground.

The ground, however, is not indeterminate in every respect. With respect to its relation to its dependencies, it has the determinate character of being ground or creator. The cash value of the *ordered* relationship of dependence is that the ground could not be *ultimate* ground if *that* determinate character were in any way derivative from its independent *nature* and not from its *relations* with dependents. To say the ground *creates* the dependents, and with them its own relational character as creator, is not to say anything about a prior nature in the creator, only about the creative act. My point here is that it is improper to consider the meaning of such a statement as "the creative ground is indeterminate" outside the context of the intellectual or religious quest for origins. *In* this context, it is clear why, in one sense, the ground must be indeterminate and in another it is determinately related to its dependents as their creator.

2. The second qualification is that the logic of the dependency relationship must be spelled out. In itself, apart from created things, the ground is indeterminate because all determination is created; in relation to created things, the ground is determinate as creator. To be indeterminate is to be nothing. Apart from the creation relationship, therefore, the ground can be called *nonbeing* as well as *being, emptiness* as well as *pure act.* But the ground is *not* "apart" from the creation relationship. Because there is a created order, the ground *is* creator, and that is not nothing. In speaking of the ground in relationship to the world, it is false to say that it is indeterminate except in the sense that relationship itself springs from an indeterminate source. So, whether the ground is to be called "indeterminate" or "determinate" is a function of whether it is being considered as (a) the condition for the relationship between it and what it relates, or (b) implicated in that relationship.

Explication of the second element of the proposition – namely, that the ground of creation is divine and to be called God – is fairly simple. Something is worthy of worship and may be called God if it is apprehended as the ultimate condition of the world. "Ultimate *condition*" means that which affects, causes, or sets the context for everything else. "*Ultimate* condition" means that which itself is conditioned by nothing else. The creative ground is the ultimate condition of the world.

Evidence. It is commonly believed that Western theology – including Judaism, Christianity, and Islam – interprets God as definite, personal, and active in history; whereas Eastern theology – including Hinduism, Buddhism, and taoism – interprets God as indeterminate, empty, and removed. Some have even suggested that the Eastern God should not be called God precisely because that God is nothing. But I believe this historical observation is misleading. The different emphases of Eastern and Western theologies are better understood with a model derived from the speculative theory.

Consider the Upanisadic distinction between qualityless (*nirguna*) Brahman and qualitied (*saguna*) Brahman. The former is the utterly incomprehensible absolute. The latter is Brahman in relation to the world it creates and is often personified as the God Isvara. This corresponds to my distinction between the ground of the created order considered out of relation to that order and the ground considered as implicated in it through creating. The Hindu way of making the point, however, separates the two sides with different names, admitting the relation between them.

I suggest that this is a dominant orientation in much Eastern theology. Western theology, by contrast, deals with the two sides together, distinguishing them only when forced to do so by logic or a religious need for mystical, pure transcendence.

The logic of the *Tao Te Ching*, especially in the first stanza, exhibits the Eastern orientation. Distinguishing being and nonbeing, Lao tzu notes that this is a determinate relation and that they depend on each other. Therefore, both are produced by a nameless ground.[17] Mahayana Buddhism, in turn, also maintains a strong contrast between the emptiness of the absolute reality and the salvific character of its apprehension by persons. Consider the distinction between the *dharmakāya*, on one hand, and the *sambhogakāya* and *nirmānakaya*, on the other. The first is the indeterminate essence of pure being about which nothing can be said; the second and third are spiritual and earthly realities about which much can be said. The latter two are manifestations of the first. (The relationship between them is such, however, that the pure Buddhahood of the *dharmkāya* is loving, and its love is located in the *sambhoga-* and *nirmānakayas*. Therefore the distinction between the abysmal transcendence and the relative transcendence is less sharp in Mahayana Buddhism than in taoism or the Upanisads.) That is why Buddhism is often said to be the closest of the Eastern religions in emphasizing the remoteness of the absolute to the extent that religious piety populates the relative transcendence with a pantheon of gods and mythological figures.[18] There is no fear of idolatry because the transcendence and ultimacy of divinity itself are protected by remoteness from any transcendence implicated in the world.

Western religions, by contrast, emphasize the *connection* rather than the distinction between absolute and relative sides of divinity. On one hand, they fear the idolatry resulting from merely relative transcendence of the creator. On the other hand, they are suspicious of otherworldly mysticism. The model of God as an individual agent has been attractive in the West in part because it seems to display the *connection* between (1) internal action *ab initio* and (2) external relations in which the action is conditioned determinately. Nevertheless, when setting limits to the analogy of God with an individual agent, Western theologians have recognized the dialectic distinguishing the indeterminate transcendence from relative and determinate transcendence. Christian trinitarian controversies have wrestled with this. Even Thomas Aquinas, for whom the Trinity was a mystery, philosophically speaking, called God "Pure Act." *Actus purus* is a far cry from any ordinary individual agent; it is much closer to the Eastern Brahman shining forth in the glories of the world.[19]

The strains in Western religion best paralleling the Eastern distinction of the sides of God have often been on the fringes of orthodoxy: Sufism, cabalistic Judaism, medieval German mysticism. But, although orthodoxy has been wary of radical breaks between worldly religion and the mysticism of complete transcendence, it has also been unwilling to deny those two sides.

The conclusion I want to draw from this part of the discussion is that religions of both East and West acknowledge the essential integrity of a distinction between (a) God as creator of the world and thereby determinately related to it, and (b) God as indeterminate *in se*, transcending any relation to the world. Moreover, whereas the Eastern religions tend to emphasize the difference between the two sides, Western religions emphasize their connection.

Basic agreement in metaphysical matters is more to be expected than not, logic being less culturally relative than most things. Experience of the world, however, and therefore the flavor of salvific activity, marks a more significant difference between Eastern and Westen orientations. The religious quest in the East has often meant an attempt to transcend the vicissitudes of the world. It follows the path of the dialectic of dependence traced above. As a result, the last step of appreciation of the ultimate condition is taken as most important; God on the side of ultimate indeterminateness is religiously more significant. Whereas this path has also been followed in the West, there the emphasis has been on God's reverse movement from aseity to involvement with the world. God acts, makes covenants, reveals divinity, saves. God's action – and therefore the divine nature as constituted by God's relating to the world – is often religiously more significant for the West. This Western bias finds its closest Eastern parallel in the Buddha's love in Mahayana Buddhism.

There is also an analogue, albeit greatly intellectualized, in the doctrine of principle in Neo-Confucianism.

I do not mean to slide over the difficult problem of whether the absoluteness of "atheistic Buddhism" can be called divine or be interpreted as a religious category. It is difficult to locate exactly where this problem lies. It does not lie with the kind of Mahayana Buddhism I have been describing, for there the emptiness is the Pure Buddha who, in connection with his fulgurations in the world, is very worshipful indeed. Nor does the problem lie with the orthodox Theravada Buddhists who eschew any cosmological speculation, for they would *not deny any claim* about God; they would resist only the suggestion that the Buddha be deified. The problem may lie, with Zen Buddhism or with forms of Theravada Buddhism emphasizing the ultimacy of suchness. For these religious outlooks, religious life involves attaining and organizing one's life around the insight that things are simply their presence to themselves, and nothing more. There is no ultimate, transcendent meaning to life or the cosmos or any interesting origin.

I admit that this is the most difficult religious style to catalogue as an instance of our speculative hypothesis. If our hypothesis is somewhat weakened, however, the cataloguing is less difficult. Suppose we say all diversity is a *manifestation* of ultimate reality. Then we would latch onto the fact that suchness manifests itself in all determinate forms. Suchness itself is indeterminate. The determinations of the world are all such as they are, but their reality consists not in the different identities but in the fact that each is such as it is. Suchness does not create or cause manifestations, but it is the passive condition for their existence. More importantly, the suchness is the ultimate condition of things, which, when apprehended, inspires a person to religious awe and peace.[20]

With this last qualification of the evidence for our hypothesis, let us pass to the third proposition.

God's character is derived from the divine creative act.

Explication. This proposition has two main specifications. *First,* God has the character of being creator as such. The religiously interesting elements of this character have to do with mystical experience and the appreciation of worthiness and supremacy. Most of the major religions of the world are in fair agreement about this character and this kind of religious experience, however widely they may disagree over what symbols are appropriate and what conclusions can be drawn. *Second,* God has the character of being creator *of this world.* All divine actions, revelations, and personality traits depend on how one interprets the general character of the world and its historical events. The major religions are in fairly profound *disagreement* about this aspect of the divine character. The first aspect of God can be called an ontological character, the second a cosmological character. In most religions, the salvific as well as the theological, question deals with both aspects.

Evidence. The religious experience of God's ontological character has been well described by Rudolf Otto in his *The Idea of the Holy*. There, Otto treats the "creature feeling" in the apprehension of the numinous before treating the character of *mysterium tremendum*. I take it that God's ontological character as creator is religiously experienced in terms of the dual meaning of transcendence discussed in the last section. People experience God by feeling themselves to be dependent and God not to be. The experience of God as having aseity distinguishes the divine as "Wholly Other," to use Otto's phrase. Otto draws his evidence for this religious experience from the major world religions, and I do not need to rehearse it here.

1. The issue for this proposition is whether the *ontological* character of God is experienced as *derivative from the divine creative act*, not whether the experience of God as numinous means the experience of God as creator. There seems to be a prima facie logical reason for denying the proposition. The numinal character of God is aseity, not God as creating. Therefore, how does it make sense to say that the numinal character derives from the creative act?

On this logical level, there is a clear answer. God's aseity, supremacy, and numinous quality all depend on a contrast with relations, and that contrast derives from the creative act. God could not intelligibly be said to have independence were the creator not independent of the world. This is not merely a distinction of reason. God would *be* neither within a divine nature nor relative to another if there were no others around. Because God is in fact relative to the world as creator, and because this relativity requires ontological independence on God's part, God has both aseity and relativity, by derivation from the creative act. Similarly with supremacy: God is not supreme unless there is a world to be supreme over. If one adopted the Aristotelian concept of creation in which God has the potential to create without creating, God's supremacy would still depend on relativity, but now to potential creatures. God's numinous quality, directly apprehended in religious experience, is a quality of revelation. God is numinous within a certain context and to properly equipped apprehenders. The *reason why* God is numinous is that God is a transcendent creator; that is what is apprehended in ontological religious experience. If there were no creative act, God would not be a creator, and would have no transcendence to manifest.

Is there experiential as well as logical ground supporting this?

In Western religions, where "creator" language is at home, it can be claimed that God makes God a creator and that God has no character except that which is revealed in creative self-manifestations. In ancient Judaism, God's character stems from divine deeds—in fact, from how God acts over against the local competitors. In more sophisticated forms this doctrine became that of God's creatorship as such, reaching fine expression in Job's whirlwind. In Christianity, the claim of incarnation raised the question of what God's role is, apart from relation to the world. The Trinitarian controversies reflect the deep experience of Christians. I think their result was a doctrine of God as *essentially* triune, and this in reference to the created order. The rejection of both monarchianism and economic trinitarianism marked the denial that God has a deeper nature apart from the Trinity, of which Christ is a part. The rejection of subordinationism marked a denial that Christ, obviously an element of creation, is less an essential part of the divine nature than Father or Spirit.

In Eastern religions, it makes little sense to wonder what the ultimate condition might be apart from the world of conditioned things. It is quite clear, however, that the absolute side of God, the qualityless Brahman or the *dharmakāya*, cannot be said to have any character whatsoever except insofar as that character stands in contrast to the qualitied side. Therefore, God's ontological character depends on the contrast, and the contrast itself is a determinate (and merely apparent) character.

2. The *cosmological* character of God stems directly from the way in which God is reflected in the world. The interpretation of this depends, in turn, on the way the world is interpreted as being reflective of God. By way of evidence, it is enough to cite some correlations between interpretations of the world and the concept of God. For Western scholars, the first correlation that comes to mind is that of the war god Yahweh with the nomadic Hebrews, in contrast to the fertility gods of the agricultural inhabitants of Canaan.[21]

In a comparison of Eastern and Western religions, the difference in time sense is usually cited as significant. The Western image of time is linear and the Eastern (at least Indian and Chinese) is not.[22] Thus, whereas gods are personified in both traditions, only in the Western is there an emphasis on a God having a single career. The God of Western religions has a unique career dealing with the world, and this means that each event in the world, because each is uniquely relative to God, has an irreplaceable quality about it. In Eastern religions, God can assume many forms, have many incarnations, and be fairly indifferent to when and where the incarnations occur.

Another contrast is in the ontological importance accorded time; the Western tradition gives it great ontological importance, the Eastern less. Whereas both traditions admit that the fundamental divinity is somehow above time (however much divinity may enter it), the Western divinity must *essentially* be able to relate to time. The Eastern divinity can be essentially indifferent to time. This difference reinforces the Western preference for a personal model, since a person can assume a position in time by deliberate acts. It also reinforces the Eastern preference for a non-personal model at the ultimate level, since a personal model would *have to* assume a stance toward temporal events.

This completes what I want to say in expressing general empirical evidence for the speculative hypothesis of God. Of course, much more can be said; if the evidence is to be coercive, much more should be said. I am especially aware of the dangers of the lack of qualification implicit in talking about religious "traditions" as such. Comparing Eastern with Western religions is even more treacherous. In every religious tradition there are elements of every other tradition; some examples are given above. The attempt has been made, however, to characterize religious traditions by their dominant strands. While admitting the inevitable distortions in such attempts, I believe the above discussion shows how the major world religions lend the empirical weight of their funded experience to the speculative hypothesis of God the creator.

II. The Empirical Task of Theology

The conclusion to be drawn from the speculative hypothesis is that theology is empirical in a variety of senses. Now I want to spell these out.

1. The speculative hypothesis is empirical

The ultimate test of any hypothesis is empirical, and metaphysical ones are no exception. There are, of course, nonempirical processes in the formulation and expression of hypotheses. A hypothesis is discovered or invented by an act of imagination that has no rules.[23] Its internal articulation, clarification, and empirical predictions are formed by logical, not empirical, considerations. Whether the hypothesis is *true* depends on whether it interprets experience well.

One difference between philosophical and scientific hypotheses is that philosophical hypotheses have no "critical experiments." They are so general that empirical probations at best make them only more or less plausible. A philosophical hypothesis is tested primarily by being lived with and judged according to whether it enlightens and fructifies experience. Further, the difference between the vagueness of philosophical hypotheses and the particular relativity of the cultural forms in which their confirming or disconfirming instances are found is so great that it is difficult to determine what is important and what is not. At least philosophers are adept at defending their hypothesis against apparently disconfirming evidence by saying "I really did not mean that." If the cosmonaut sent to find God reported "She's Black," the Yahweh hypothesis, no doubt, could be altered to accommodate that evidence.

A speculative theory about God as creator contains four general areas of empirical reference. The first is that the theory must be plausible in general experience, that is, experience broader than mere religion. In the long run, the experience not of one man but of an entire society or tradition reveals whether a theory is worth much in terms of cutting at the natural joints of life.

The second area of empirical reference concerns justification of the theory of God as a legitimate form of knowledge. Ultimately, the only satisfactory claim that a kind of knowledge is possible and respectable is an empirical demonstration of instances. In philosophy, this demonstration usually comes down to showing that something called by another name is actually the kind of knowledge alleged in the case. Tillich's discussion of ultimate concern is a well-known example with respect to knowledge of God as the ground of being.

The third empirical reference important to philosophical theology is the field of religious phenomena. By this, I do not mean the historical comparison of structured and integrated religious traditions. Rather, I mean more universal phenomena which enter into different connections in different contexts—for example, prayer; mysticism; priesthood; birth, death, and initiation rituals; and concepts of "the religious problem" (namely, sin, suffering, transience) and of "The Religious Solution" (namely, salvation, release, dissolution into the ultimate). Any hypothesis about God must be able to make sense of these fairly pervasive phenomena without at the same time explaining them away.

The fourth empirical reference is making a claim for universality with respect to comparative religions. That is what I attempt to sketch above for my hypothesis of God the creator. All these areas of empirical reference are empirical in unusual senses. Even the appeal to phenomenology and the history of religions touches not unwashed facts but phenomenological and historical classifications of facts. All are empirical, however, in the sense that the theory is brought to the bar of given evidence, evidence not constructed by the stipulatory powers of the hypothesis itself or by the purely formal truths of logical intuition.

2. The particular character of God as determined by divine creation is empirical.

One of the strongest elements of plausibility in the divine-creator hypothesis as it is developed above is that it is vague concerning the more concrete ideas about God over which religions disagree. As far as the hypothesis is concerned, God could be Yahweh, the Trinity, Allah, Brahman, the ontological Buddha, Suchness, or Nothing. At this level of abstraction, the hypothesis directly addresses a profound experience of divine transcendence and mystery. But some interesting religious claims are more concrete and conflicting between religions.

The question whether God is ultimately personal or impersonal is a vitally important one. While admitting that *person* is only an analogy, how seriously one takes the analogy determines the significance of prayer, historical revelations, and a variety of other religious elements that make sense only in terms of a personal God. The issue is an empirical one. We distinguish impersonal movements from personal actions by peculiar patterns and styles of behavior; the question of robots illustrates the distinction by being a borderline case. Is this world that God created one exhibiting the marks of a personal product?

Of equal importance with the "person" question is the issue of historical revelation. The "general" character of God is often discussed under the rubric "general revelation," that is, pervasive traits of the world revealing a character to God. But some religions claim "special revelations," particular historical events or histories (as of the Hebrew people), which are sometimes said to be more important than general revelations. Christianity makes an extraordinarily strong claim for the historical revelation of Christ – namely, that Christ was wholly God, incarnate and uniquely determinative of the meaning of history. Islam makes nearly as strong a claim of its reception by Mohammed. Judaism makes a more diffuse but still strong claim in its belief that the history of God's relationship with the Hebrews uniquely reveals God's personal character; God is not only a person (analogously) but he has a definite personality. Hinduism and Buddhism, insofar as they claim historical events to be revelatory, at most, say that God is *illustrated* in them, not constituted by them.

Special revelations are eminently empirical questions. One can say one "accepts" a cluster of events as revelatory "on faith." One can even carry out a "dogmatic" theology through the explication of beliefs premised on faith. But to do so would be to ignore the seriousness of the question of *truth*. A historical element alleged to be revelatory is a claim of empirical fact and must be tested accordingly.

The empirical testing of such claims is extraordinarily complex. There are problems enough with the ordinary historical reporting of events. But the revelatory claims usually also assert that some *effect* is made by the revelation, some new power of change in history. Encounter with the events through historical rendering is often said to have a self-authenticating quality, constituting a particular tao of faith and practice. People's response to revelations is surely as much a function of their readiness and of historical condition as it is of any coerciveness in the revelatory report. Wiliam James may have been right in holding that some kind of evidence demands prior faith to be grasped. These factors combine to make empirical justifications extremely tenuous; just about any claim can be explained away or made a function of something irrelevant.

On the other hand, a certain massiveness of evidence cannot be ignored. The spiritual regeneration of Christian experience is not falsified by other religons, or so it seems to me. The Jews are still a united people despite dispersions that have destroyed the folk integrity of competing groups. The people of Allah once conquered a large portion of the civilized world, and they are still the fastest-growing religious group.

The most plausible, logical, promising move in a situation such as this is to find some syncretistic scheme for integrating the strengths of the world's great religions. This has been attempted from various angles, from Schleiermacher to Panikkar. Whether it can succeed, however, is an empirical question. There is no intellectual integrity in asserting the preeminence of one tradition over the others without a thorough empirical investigation. Nor can we claim that they are compatible until we discover that they are, in fact, compatible.

III. Practical Conclusions

The comments in Section II concern theoretical conclusions to be drawn about empirical theology from the premise of the speculative hypothesis. The comments that follow are more practical.

A fundamental critical question must be raised about the entire procedure discussed above. Christianity may well be in the throes of a spiritual confrontation with the world's other major religions. But at least the encounter is concrete and vital, not a matter of mere theory. Why, then, should anyone take seriously the suggestion that speculative philosophy has a contribution to make? In fact, did we not abandon serious speculative philosophy long before we abandoned the cultural chauvinism that protected us from non-Western ideas? I want to offer three answers to this criticism.

First, reflection on the speculative level itself is part of concrete experience. To pit thought against life is to leave the evolution of the human mind an inexplicable mystery.

Second, culture legitimately becomes bored with such endeavors as metaphysics when they turn in on themselves and become academic. This is a serious problem: when metaphysics fails to enlighten concrete life, it is judged to have no experiential meaning; but when a cultural tradition no longer can look only to itself, when it must orient itself to other traditions appearing on the scene as live options to be handed over, then metaphysics once again becomes a vital, imperative need. Intercultural encounter calls into question the basic images and themes of each culture, and a new set of images and themes is required. But the only control people have over the formation of such fundamental contours of culture is through very general speculation – metaphysics. Only through speculative philosophy is it possible to give a *critical* account of what is threatened and what reinforced in an intercultural encounter. Only speculative philosophy allows both one's own culture and others to be compared. Only speculative philosophy allows cultural conflict to move from counterassertion (perhaps with bludgeons or bombs) to the adducement of reasons from a common perspective. Speculative philosophy is the hope of reason in the face of conflict which without the speculative perspective, is ultimate.

Third, speculative philosophy about God works. The growing concern for comparative cultural studies and Eastern religions has fed an increasing interest in speculative philosophy. Even if one has no taste for the hypothesis of God the creator, the school of speculative theology deriving from Whitehead is thriving, as are reinvigorated strands of Thomism, existentialism, and idealism. Our empirical studies of cultures are now sophisticated enough for us to criticize and nourish these approaches to speculative philosophy from the standpoint of a variety of cultures.

From the perspective of the arguments presented in this chapter, a tentative evaluation can be made of major trends in recent philosophical theology. Contrary to what liberals have said, the scholastic tradition of philosophical or natural theology is the authentic progenitor of the speculative contribution to theology today. It should therefore be encouraged in its contemporary successors, primarily process theology and its neighboring foes (I count the theory of God the creator as a neighboring foe of process thought).

Contrary to what conservatives have said, the empirical emphasis of Protestant liberalism and, more recently, "spirit" theologies in Roman Catholicism are fundamentally correct. The empirical approaches to theology cover a wide range – Schleiermacher, Strauss, Bauer, Schweitzer, Ritschl, Harnack, Rauschenbusch, Bultmann, Tillich, and John E. Smith, just to name some well-known Protestant liberals. They are not of equal value, but they are right in the belief that the intellectual integrity of religion rests with experience, be the experience feeling, tests, history, morals, cultural *Zeitgeist*, or existential concern. I would say that what this tradition needs now is a strong acculturation to non-Christian religions, a point Tillich made with force in his late work *Christianity and the Encounter of World Religions*.[24] Western *society* is absorbing non-Christian cultures while "merely" Christian theology is fast becoming obsolete, as Chapter 1 argues it should.

The encounter of Christianity with the world's other major religions is not a problem for Christianity alone; it is a problem for other religions as well. It is equally a problem for those people dissociated from all organized religions but seeking cultural means to express their religious sensibilities. In all these cases, steadfast pursuit of speculative heights is the best procedure for guaranteeing faithfulness to concrete experience. The following chapters attempt to press this point.

Chapter Seven
The Notion of Creation in Chinese Thought

T HE IDEA OF CREATION *ex nihilo*, of the arising of being from nothing, is usually thought to be more characteristic of Western thinking than of Chinese. This is especially true when the idea is interpreted in terms of a divine individual who does the creating. Careful thinkers in the Western tradition of creation *ex nihilo* have rarely maintained, however, that the Creator is an individual in the sense that created things are individuals; the *via negative* and the *analogia entis* are central to the creation tradition in Christian theology. Furthermore, Western mystical traditions have emphasized the validity of saying that God transcends being and is "nothing," that is, God is intrinsically indeterminate.

Chinese thinking, in its turn, exhibits concepts with some appearance of being close to Western notions of creation *ex nihilo*. In ancient taoism, the nameless tao gives rise to the tao that can be named.[1] In Chou Tun-i's Neo-Confucianism, distinction arises through the generation of yang and yin by the Great Ultimate, either of which is or derives from the Ultimate of Non-Being.[2] In some forms of Buddhism, the emptiness of things has an ontological character relative to the discriminated aspect of things, and the emptiness is the greater truth, so great, in fact, that its assertion transcends the distinction between truth and falsity.[3]

Aside from an initial orientation, however, wholesale advertisement of family resemblances between China and the West sets thought back rather than advancing it. I want now to qualify the parallels drawn in Chapter 6. There is not one idea of creation in the West, there are many; and at most, one can be closest to the truth. My aim in this chapter is to rearticulate the hypothesis about creation *ex nihilo* already introduced; this is not the only, or even the dominant, idea of creation in the West. Then I shall examine certain aspects of ancient taoism and Confucianism to determine not whether they agree or disagree but how they are responsive to the same issues as my hypothesis about creation. The concern is more with parallel sensitivities to dimensions of experience than with parallel or divergent theories; the concern with experiential sensitivities underlies an appreciation of the need for theoretical demythologising.

I. Creation *Ex Nihilo*

The radical character of the creation hypothesis is expressed in its claim that determinate beings come from nothing. In this hypothesis, all determinateness is contingent on being created. About the "nothing" from which beings come, nothing can be said except in the context of its relations with the beings that come from it. In itself, it is not God, worshipful or holy; in itself it is not creator or ground of beings. In itself, it cannot be said to exist or not to exist. In itself, it cannot be spoken of at all, because speaking or thinking presupposes that there is no "nothing" which is in itself but rather the "something" of speech or thought. If there is something determinate, then it is not the case that there is nothing in itself. Because there is "something," there is no unqualified "nothing."

Given the minimal fact we can think, or that any distinctions of any sort exist, there is reality to some determinate world. The nothing from which this determinate world arises is therefore a creative nothing, not mere nothing in itself. It is because of its relation to the determinate world that the "source" has a character, namely, the character deriving from its being the source of this world. This point is implicitly acknowledged in the negativity of words such as *no*thing, *a*sat, vacuity, emptiness, name*less* tao. It is explicitly acknowledged in calling the "source" God or creator.

The bite of the creation hypothesis comes in the sense in which it claims that the creator is the source of the world. I shall express this in four related points.

1. Anything determinate is contingent and positive. To be determinate is to be complex, for a determinate thing is determinate with respect to some other determinate things, and as argued in Chapter 3 this requires (1) features relating it to those other things, and (2) features contrasting it with them. Although the complex nature of a determinate thing might be a harmony in which the component features "fit together," the question remains: Why is there such a thing as harmony so that things fit? Harmony apart from harmonized things is vacuous. Therefore, harmonious determinate things are contingent on a ground, or they would not exist at all. This may be called "ontological contingency," in contrast to the "cosmological contingency" of a determinate thing on other determinate things with respect to which it defines its own determinate nature. Cosmological contingency itself, having to do with the interrelations and harmonies of determinate things, is ontologically contingent. Similarly, cosmological causation is causation between determinate or partially determinate things in the world, whereas ontological causation is the causation of the world by what itself cannot be determinate.

The contingency of determinate things also marks their positivity. They are positive in the modern logical sense that they could have been other than they are and that they are "positively" what they are. Although this does not entail that the creator has a "will" in anything like the sense applied to human beings, it does entail that the creating is a decisive process, eliminating alternatives. However, to phrase the positivity of determinate being merely in terms of the elimination of alternate logical possibilities may obscure its most important feature, namely, that the thing *is* real. It fills its existential or logical or emotional space. If it can be experienced (and we can neglect the things that cannot be) it is a positive contribution to experience, indeed, a datum out of which experience is made.

The creation of something determinate, therefore, is the making of a positive reality where otherwise there would be nothing. In fact, positivity is ontologically prior to the situation of a contingent thing being the result of a logical elimination. For, the rationality of a logical array of possibilities is itself contingent and positive.

2. Anything determinate is good to a degree. The argument for goodness has the following form. Any harmony is a way of having the components of the harmony together. Each component has its own value (for a reason shortly to be mentioned); having the components together is an additional value to having them apart. Even if there is no risk of losing the components were they not sustained together, since the harmony is a new entity over and above the separate components, it has the value of presenting them together. Each component is good for the same reason that the harmony containing it is good, namely, that each is itself a harmony of components. That having things together is by itself good is illustrated in the fact that at least some things allow of alternate ways of being harmonized. Sometimes we can judge which ways are better. The better ways, even if they are mere possibilities, are norms. In the long run, this argument appeals to experience: to experience something at the most basic level prior to abstraction and analysis is to experience it as a positive good. Things differ, of course, in their worth, depending largely on the causal relations and how they act as environments for each other, because these factors determine the ways by which things can be harmonized. Part of the positivity of contingent determinations of being is that they are positively valuable.

The creator, therefore, is the source of value. As source, the creator cannot be called good or valuable in itself, since only determinate, harmonious things are valuable, and all those are created. But like Plato's form of the good, the creator creates in such a way that any determinate product is a measure or harmony embodying whatever it is that makes harmonious things harmonize. The creator may be called "harmony itself," but this is vacuous since, in itself, the creator is not determinate and thus not harmonized. In fact, the creator can be called the ground of harmony, or harmony itself, only by reference to the harmonious things created.

  3. The determinate things of the world have complete integrity within the scope of the world. Nothing in their natures need be referred to the creator for explanation except for the existence of determinate things as such. The determinate nature of a thing is a function of two kinds of features. First, it is a function of all the other determinate things that provide cosmological, causal conditions for it. These are past states and environing conditions, if we are speaking of existential realities. Second, it is also a function of whatever factors enter to integrate the impingements of the external conditions so that the thing can be a harmony in its own right. In our world, there may not be many different ways by which a thing can harmonize the causal conditions to which it must conform. But even if there is only one way that the conditions allow, so that complete scientific determinism is true, there is still the existential activity positing the thing as harmonious. From the standpoint of the external conditons with respect to which an emerging thing must be determinate, its own emergence as a harmony in its own right is spontaneous. The spontaneity might mean that some of the determinate character is supplied in the emergence – character spontaneity; or it might mean only that the predetermined character is realized in a positive way here – "existential spontaneity." That a thing is determinate does not mean it is determinate in all respects; present things, for instance, can be partially indeterminate regarding the future.

To speak of the existential character of things is to assume more than a metaphysics of creation; it is also to assume a cosmology articulating what it is (1) to exist, (2) to cause in a cosmological sense, and (3) to "emerge." The point in the last paragraph can be put in explicitly cosmological terms. The integrity of existing things consists (1) in the fact that the basic entities are units of creative emergence that derive from the conditions presented by the background out of which they emerge, plus (2) their own spontaneous activity of ordering these conditions into the new emerged entity. The spontaneous activity is each thing's innermost being; the determinate character with which each entity emerges is to be accounted for in terms of either the conditions out of which it arises or its own self-determining activity. At the same time each entity is divinely created, in the following sense. Its own spontaneity is the creator creating, integrating previously created entities (the prior conditions) which themselves were created through their own spontaneity, integrating yet prior entities, and so on. Therefore, the creator is the source of each entity through creating both its subjective activity and the conditions with which it creates. Reference to divine creation, however, is never helpful in answering the question why an entity is this way rather than that, for the question always refers to determining conditions or to the specifics of the entity's own spontaneity. A thing's integrity is therefore compatible with the creation of everything *ex nihilo* because of the difference between these two questions: Why is this thing the way it is? Why is there this thing? The first question is answered exclusively by referring cosmologically to the determinate things within the world, including the creative spontaneity in each thing. The second is answered by giving an ontological creationist account of how there are real determinate things.

4. The last point to be made here concerns the emotional quality of life as interpreted by the creation theory. If the creation theory is true, one would expect that an awareness of the world would necessarily require appreciation. To apprehend the created world is to employ its values as elements in one's own experience. Appreciation can range from aesthetic delight through satisfaction of felt needs to deeply committed love. But value appreciation is a fundamental element of awareness, not "cool" mirroring. The theological implication of this statement is that relations between people "naturally" would be empathetic love because of the dual sense of divine presence. On one hand, one would perceive another person as equally with oneself the "offspring" of God; we are all "children of the same father" in this sense. On the other hand, precisely because our determinate reality involves mutual distinction from each other, one would perceive another person as existentially different from oneself, to be respected with deference rather than assumed into mutual union.

With these points about creation *ex nihilo* in mind, let us raise certain questions regarding taoism and Confucianism.

II. Taoism

Ancient taoism seems to have no theory directly corresponding with, or serving as an alternative to, a theory of creation *ex nihilo*. N. J. Girardot has reviewed the scholarly literature regarding a creationist mythology in China, attempting to prove that the interest of nineteenth-century missionary scholars in finding a Christianlike creation mythology, paradoxically, has led to a strong bias not to find such a mythology.[4] Even if his positive suggestions of a creationist mythology were unconditionally true, they would proffer only the late (ca. third century C.E.) legend of P'an-ku, the creating giant and the *hun-tun* idea of primordial chaos, the cosmic egg. Creation *ex nihilo*, by contrast, asserts that the world is created not out of a preexistent egg or fecund chaos but from nothing. This point distinguishes creation *ex nihilo* from various Western creationist theories, as well as from the Taoist. For instance, under the influence of personalist and process philosophers, some thinkers regard the Genesis creation myth as God's bringing order out of a primordial chaos with a divine word; this is not a creation *ex nihilo* view. It should be noted, however, that the issue we are discussing is one of theory, not (primarily) of imagery or mythology. One cannot argue that a myth such as the one in Genesis is better interpreted by a finite-creationist theory than by a creation *ex nihilo* theory without an assessment of the dialectical claims of the theories. Similarly, one cannot argue that the lack of a creationist mythology entails that the taoist outlook is incompatible experientially with the implictaions of a theory of creation *ex nihilo*.

Ellen Marie Chen argues that there is a taoist ontology expressed in the *Tao Te Ching* and elsewhere according to which being emerges from nothing, as vapor from the air, that it flowers into the ten thousand things, then, reaching its limit, returns to the original nothing.[5] Although this analysis allows her to express marvelously subtle interpretations of difficult passages and, particularly, to explain the emphasis on the feminine in taoism, the ontology is ambiguous with regard to the question of creation *ex nihilo*. Does the movement from nothing to being (in its three stages) back to nothing take place within the process of time – a cosmological generation and return – or does temporal process itself arise with the emergence of being (at one of its stages)? The metaphors are temporalistic. I suspect that it would be *reading in* a creation *ex nihilo* theory of interpret the movement from nothing to being and from being to nothing as transcending temporal process, as an ontological "movement" rather than a cosmological one.[6]

I follow instead the interpretation of Sung-peng Hsu which arises from consideration of a dialectical problem.[7] If the tao is an ultimate reality such that nothing can depart from it and such that every movement illustrates it, how is it possible for there to be unspontaneous, forced actions? How is it possible that the tao could be lost in human affairs? In response to this problem Hsu proposes that two kinds of change are discussed in the *Tao Te Ching*, spontaneous changes and unspontaneous changes. Only the former kind is in proper accord with the tao, although the latter presupposes the tao. Arguing on the basis of various texts, Hsu shows that unspontaneous changes are characterized by a competitive polarity and oscillation between yin and yang. Human action is unspontaneous when the yang elements neglect the intrinsic limitations imposed by their grounding in the yin elements and assert themselves independently, competing with other yang elements. Spontaneous changes, by contrast, always involve a harmonious relation between yin and yang elements; there is an ordered relation between them: yin is the source of yang. To be harmonious, yang elements can extend themselves as far as possible without separating from their yin source; then they sink back into the yin. I believe Hsu would not say that the yin produces yang which, in turn, produces yin, but that yang arises from yin and then returns to it; yin is to yang as nonbeing is to being.

From the perspective of creation *ex nihilo*, the relation between yin and yang is strictly a cosmological relation. That is, the nonbeing of yin is *not* the *nihil* from which being is created. But the yin-yang relation expresses a very important characteristic of what does get created on the creation *ex nihilo* view, interpreted with a process cosmology.[8] At every moment in which something comes into being, all of the previously realized past states of affairs constitute both the material and the limiting conditions out of which the novel being emerges. No element can characterize the emerging entity that does not derive in one way or another from the past. Furthermore, the past mediates the forces of nature shaping the emerging entity and sets the environing conditions that must tolerate the new being. The past thus enters into an emerging entity through the entity *feeling* the past conditions. What it means to emerge is that the new entity constitutes itself a subject that has the feelings, and this self-constitution is spontaneity. Throughout the spontaneous self-constitution, however, the entity must *conform* to its past conditions.

Past conditions as felt are the yin elements. To the extent that conformation to the past elements dominates the experience, the yin elements are dominant. No change occurs without spontaneity. But the extreme of yin would be when the change is repetition of what was there before, or rather, not repetition but the continuity of inertia. On the other hand, spontaneity might well involve a radically new direction, a new assemblage of old forms, a unique and decisive departure from inertia, as when the master of t'ai chi ch'uan transforms his or her opponent's victorious charge into an ignominious tumble. The novelty in this spontaneity is indeed spontaneous in Hsu's good sense, insofar as the new being fully embraces the past and the yin elements and transforms them. The novelty is derived from their ability to embrace in unexpected ways.

The spontaneous process of emergence also has the capacity to reject and ignore past elements, to shear off forces rather than conform to them. The new being is thus somewhat alienated from its environment and must "compete" for a place in the environment.[9] This is what Hsu calls "unspontaneous" change, yang gone wild. It does not call forth principles lacking in spontaneous change but rather organizes itself so as to be disharmonious with its yin source. In the end, of course, the environment wins, as water wears down even the hardest rock. In human experience, when conformation to the environment involves serious excising of important factors, a person's own integrity must grow rigid and relatively self-contained if the person is to be sustained. Instead of turning the environment to advantage, as the t'ai chi ch'uan master uses the opponent's strength, the person must set the limited force of the environment conformed to against the rest of the environment.

From the perspective of creation *ex nihilo*, the spontaneous activity of emergence or change reflects the ontological grounding of the change in the creator. Since, however, the change must conform in at least some ways to the past, the new entity is related in *some* ways to previous instances of divine creation. The degree to which current spontaneity conforms to products of past spontaneity reflects the degree of harmony within the created order. Although the interplay of yin and yang within change is a matter of cosmological relations, the ontological significance of this is that the integrity of the created world is harmonious. Where a new entity emerges in such a way as to partially alienate itself from its background, the created order is not as harmonious as it could be; but it is still harmonious. The spiritual significance of this is a feeling for the continuity and harmony of nature.

Now, it might be thought that creation *ex nihilo* makes more essential reference to the yang, male elements, since the immediate presence of the creator is in the spontaneity of the emergence. This would accord with the popular view that divine creation is a malelike activity, the Sky God's work in contrast to that of the Earth Mother. Cosmologically, however, the spontaneity is an activity of working the previously given elements into a new entity. The yin elements of feeling the past, and the yang elements of creating a new being from them, are strictly correlative. The ontological creator makes the present and past in strict correlation; the present cannot be determinate without the past. The creator's creating is temporal only from the standpoint of the creatures. The new being is created through present spontaneity relative to its own presence; the dated spontaneity of earlier things is past relative to the present, though it was present relative to the presence of those things. From the standpoint of the creator, since all the creatures are determined relative to each other, and temporal determinations of earlier and later are all products of creation, spontaneity is entirely immediate, whatever its dates relative to finite times.

From the vantage point of creation *ex nihilo*, the priority of the yin elements in taoism has no ontological significance. That priority expresses only the point that the past is the matrix out of which the present arises. From the ontological standpoint of creation, we may then ask critical questions of the taoist position. Admitting that the present entity or change emerges from the past, and that any present spontaneity introduces disharmony if it shears off its resources from the totality to which it might conform, *is this always bad*? Might there not be some elements of potential conformation that *ought to be rejected*? Should not some things be forgotten? Even if it were possible always to exhibit some harmony that rejects nothing important in the world, is that what *should* be done? What justifies the taoist priority of inclusive harmony over intensive, limited harmonies? Merely to point out that competitive, or what Hsu calls unspontaneous, action departs from the maternal yin elements is a tautology. Why should loyalty to the mother matrix come before loyalty to male-assertive elements?

What kind of questions are these? They seem to be value questions asking for justifications. As Lao tzu pointed out, when questions such as these arise, we have already departed from the tao in the sense of pushing spontaneity beyond inclusive harmony with the yin source. Indeed, so we have. To point this out is not to say it is wrong. The crucial question is whether we can find a context for raising the foundational issue whether the inclusive harmony of taoism is a norm requiring no justification. We cannot fairly ask this question, however, if its form presupposes a norm for justification that, in principle, eliminates the taoist contention. To explore the alternative, we turn to Confucianism, a view which in general accepts the taoist theory of the bearing of yin and yang elements on change but gives more emphasis to the yang elements.

III. Confucianism

Confucius, Mencius, Hsun tsu, and their followers focused attention on affairs of human scale rather than cosmic scale. The view of cosmos in the *I Ching* was the common heritage of all the Chinese schools, but the Confucians parsed this in terms of the trinity of heaven, earth, and the human, emphasizing the last.

What strikes Westerners as most distinctive about Confucian human ontology are the concepts of ritual (li) and humaneness (*jen*). The latter, being elitist, can hardly be a norm for being human as such, while the former seems downright artificial. Yet I believe those concepts make shrewd sense in light of the problem perceived by the Confucians over against the taoists (and Moists).

As in so many things, Hsun tzu is the most forthright Confucianist. In his essay "The Regulations of a Kind," he says:

> Men, once born, must organize themselves into a society. But if they form a society without hierarchical divisions, then there will be quarreling. Where there is quarreling, there will be chaos; where there is chaos, there will be fragmentation; and where there is fragmentation, men will find themselves too weak to conquer other beings. Thus they will be unable to dwell in security in their houses and halls. This is why I say that ritual principles must not be neglected even for a moment.[10]

Also,

> Heaven and earth are the beginning of life; ritual principles are the beginning of order, and the gentleman is the beginning of ritual principles .... Therefore, Heaven and earth produce the gentleman and the gentleman brings order to Heaven and earth.[11]

The underlying assumption of this view is that human beings, merely as the products of nature, are roughly equal in strengths and interests and lack specific principles of social organization.

The taoists accepted this assumption and embraced its immediate consequences: (1) that human beings are true to their sources when they rest in the natural matrix from which they spring, constantly returning to it; (2) that specific principles of social organization or human righteousness introduce a break with nature; and (3) that an authentic, natural person would tend to be (a) egalitarian, (b) morally superior to specific social principles which would have to be "merely" artificial, and

(c) capable of exercising authoritative power by charismatic appeals to natural impulses in people.

The Moists accepted this assumption as well and attempted to build a social ethic on egalitarian principles. But if there is a social ethic beyond spontaneous conformation to the tao, what is it based on? The Moists appealed vaguely to the status of things as the universal creatures of the creator but with what must have seemed like a regressive, superstitious cosmology.

The Confucianists accepted the assumption but sharply limited it: human beings are not *merely* the products of nature but bring their own ontologically real dimension, that of ordering values. Hsun tzu pointed out that social chaos results if there are no ritual principles establishing hierarchy or authority relations. His is not a utilitarian argument, however, as that point would be if made by the Moists. Rather, as for the other Confucianists, for Hsun tzu, ritual principles as a type are objective moral norms ontologically constitutive of the universe. Ritual principles are indeed artificial and conventional; remember Confucius' serious discussion of who is allowed to step on the door jamb. It is precisely through the ritual observance of some such conventions, though, that authentic harmonies of social human nature are made possible. Human fulfillment requires ontological acknowledgment of social order. It isn't exactly that the values of human life are transcendent entities for which rituals are mere enabling instruments; on the contrary, it is precisely in the ritual *exercise* of the conventions that human values exist. The value of the conventions is not merely one of keeping order where otherwise there would be chaos; rather, the order kept is itself part of the special value of human existence.

Herbert Fingarette points out the subtle relation between the ritual principles and "humanity":

> Thus *li* and *jen* are two aspects of the same thing. Each points to an aspect of the action of man in his distinctively human role. *Li* directs our attention to the traditional social pattern of conduct and relationships; *jen* directs our attention to the person as the one who pursues that pattern of conduct and thus maintains those relationships. *Li* also refers to the particular act in its status as exemplification of invariant norm; *jen* refers to the act as expressive of an orientation of the person, as expressing his commitment to act as prescribed by *li*. *Li* refers to the act as overt and distinguishable pattern of sequential behavior; *jen* refers to the act as the single, indivisible gesture of an actor, as his, and as particular and individual by reference to the unique individual who performs the act and to the unique context of the particular action.[12]

Ritual actions take time and arduous training to learn. It is possible to treat these actions as mere motions and go through them without having one's heart in them; when that happens, the rituals are artificial. It is also possible to be fully present in the rituals, where one's inner heart is expressed through them. As Fingarette puts it, the rituals then articulate the vector force of one's personality. They are the medium by which a person is present to the world. Shaking hands with a friend is *li*. Putting your heart into the handshake is *jen*.[13]

The ontological importance of the ritual-humanity norm for human affairs is that value is given to the creativity of the present moment which is not reducible, as it is in taoism, to the causal relation between yang creativity and yin matrix. Not that the Confucianists would deny the taoist account of the causal connections of yin and yang, but they would say that the true norm for life is not the integrity of that causal relation (though it ought not be perverted) but the realization of human harmony with personal investment in it. This has two elements. The ritual element is that harmonies of special human value can be created by people behaving in ways mutually adopted by convention. Though they are enabled by the resources of yin, these harmonies are not derived from the authenticity of the yin-yang relation in individuals' behavior; rather, they are sui generis, or better, are made by human art. Though artificial, their worth is immediately apprehended. It begs the question to attempt to derive them from what is "natural" about causation. The humanity element is that the spontaneity in the emergent process of human experience has the ritual (or human excellence) as a norm. Whereas, for taoism, spontaneity either had no norms but rather freshness or extrinsically set goals (as in the legalist wing of taoism), assuming that spontaneity remained within returning distance to the yin source, for Confucianism human values constitute a special norm.

With reference to the theory of creation *ex nihilo*, Confucianism, no more than taoism, has an explicit creation theme. But it does give expression to two elements in the creation theory lacking in taoism – that harmonies are valuable and that appreciation of this value is a norm for human experience. In concert with the creation theory, which finds special importance in the present because of the emergence of valuable harmonies, Confucianism emphasizes being "present" in the harmonies resulting from present action. Whereas taoism emphasizes that present spontaneity finds its determinate conditions in the past with past loci of spontaneity, not denying this Confucianism focuses attention on special obligations to create the human world with its unique values. Fidelity to human norms thus supplants authenticity regarding origins. Origins, of course, remain extraordinarily important; witness the emphasis on filial piety and the ancestor cult. In Confucianism, however, the emphasis shifts from conformation to utilization of the past; achieving true filial piety is the present making of a man. Ancestors are cultivated to secure their present cooperation. The Confucian tao is made partly by man, the result of yang spontaneity as much as the source and limit. With regard to emphasis, the center of balance in Confucianism shifts from yin to yang, with a resultant emphasis on action and maleness. Confucianism is a splendid illustration of the positivity and value of determinate being.

It is easy to caricature the shift from yin to yang in moving from taoism to Confucianism. We must not forget that Lao tzu was a social theorist as much as Confucius, not a nature romantic. Like the Confucian "gentlemen," taoist sages were supposed to be rulers, at least in Lao tzu's view. We must also not forget that the Confucian emphasis on action and maleness did not extend to aggression or assertiveness. The natural harmony of yin and yang is as important for the Confucianists as it is for the taoists. But the Confucian social order, and the implied or expressed cosmology, gives greater weight than the taoist to the autonomy of spontaneous, yang elements.

Because ritual can be "run through" without humanity, it risks becoming a hollow shell. Furthermore, the Confucian social order of authority relations, hierarchical as it is, easily degenerates into social dominance rather than the intended mutual fulfillment of persons according to their station. Thus, from the beginning, Confucianism has been liable to critical attacks by taoists and others. Elevation of human values gone sour isn't just failure, it is an artificial corruption of the natural. Is there any human impulse or trait that may serve as a potential fulcrum for moving people to genuine ritual and humaneness? Are we left only with moral appeals? In the case of evil, should we keep to our own virtue and lose, or use stratagems to maintain the social force of the right?

From the beginning, the critical question, for Confucianism has been whether it can keep attention focused on the disparity between the *ideals* of the gentleman and the good society, on one hand, and *realities*, on the other. Despite the extensive literature, particularly on Ming Neo-Confucianism, about the difficulties of becoming an ideal person, there has been a tendency to suppose that if one is rightly aimed at the moral good, one may assume the dignity, manners, and perquisites of someone who has reached it. This is not merely a moral mistake made through the seductiveness of an image of oneself as virtuous, but a mistake in experiencing the ontology of creation *ex nihilo*.

In the old anthropormorphic representations of God, what God wills

God gets. There is no medium, for instance, in which God could be frustrated or *only* "want" to be virtuous. In the creation theory, ontological creation is immediate and spontaneous; though one cannot easily attribute a "will" to God, it is clearly impossible to attribute unfulfilled ambitions to God. By contrast, human action always involves the medium of the cosmos through which one acts. Frustrations may arise either from a recalcitrance on the part of the world or from uncooperative elements in the actor's personality. Proper ontological perception is accompanied by a humility about the gulf between human intent and accomplishment, a recognition of the finitude of cosmological action.

Whereas Judaic and Christian traditions have long wrestled with the problem of "pride," of denial of the difference between God's ontological creation and human cosmological causation, it is not clear that the Confucian tradition has been equally sensitive.

Two major questions emerge in this chapter. The first, for the taoist tradition, is whether emphasis on natural harmony can be justified. Since the taoist tradition, in a sense, rejects this question, it was necessary to formulate a position that maintains the basic categories of the yin-yang process while shifting the emphasis to novelty in the present, which must be measured by norms. I believe that the Confucian tradition can be construed as such a position and that much of its critical force over against taoism consists in its forcing of this question.

The second question, this for the Confucian tradition, is whether the difference between the *appearance* of morality in ritual and the *reality* of morality in ritual, plus humanity, can be made sufficiently prominent to forestall arrogant pride. Confucianism is not intrinsically in danger of slipping toward taoist naturalism; its temptation is to confuse the order of a society that makes human value possible with a mere order of social domination.

In their cultural manifestations over the centuries, both taoism and Confucianism have had difficulty with these points. Taoism frequently has gone beyond the flirting stage with antinomian magic. Confucianism has been the official philosophy of harsh, repressive social orders. I am suggesting that there are certain elements of experience to which the theory of creation *ex nihilo* calls attention, and about which taoism and Confucianism need to say more. Have they creative answers to these two questions?

With these questions, the character of our study of various taos of faith and practice has changed. No longer is our concern to determine merely whether they can instantiate the categories of the creation theory; rather, we have found that the creation theory itself points up dimensions of experience those taos ought to address. Therefore, we have engaged in subtle theological probing. As these theories unfold, is it apparent how they deal with the issues creation theory suggests they deal with? To engage in this kind of questioning, we recall the elements of process cosmology introduced in Chapter 3, those having to do with causation and with being an actual event or occasion. Chapters 8 and 9, in particular, combine process cosmology and a specific Chinese tao of faith and practice in discussions which conclude that they should formulate their abstract principles in line with the theory of creation.

Chapter Eight
Process and the Neo-Confucian Cosmos

I T IS SOMETIMES SAID that Neo-Confucianism combines the meta-physical naturalism of taoism and the process psychology of Buddhism with the moral concerns of Confucianism. To the extent that this is so, process philosophy may have something to learn from it, for it is often remarked as a weakness of the process tradition in the United States that it has not developed a substantial ethical and political theory. Though an outgrowth of Western philosophy, process philosophy has many affinities with the Chinese tradition. As Chapter 9 details, process philosophy agrees with Buddhism in a rough denial of an underlying substantial substratum for enduring objects.[1] The taoist strand of Chinese thought has an even more basic affinity with process philosophy in its insistence that a naturalistic cosmology underlies and provides the limits for understanding persons and society, as suggested in Chapter 7.[2] Insofar as it embodies those elements of the Chinese tradition which most closely parallel process philosophy, Neo-Confucianism is an important mirror reflecting the achievements and limitations of our most adventuresome contemporary systematic thought. The aim of this chapter is to use each side to raise questions relevant to the other.

Wang Yang-ming (1472–1529), the great Ming dynasty Neo-Confucian, is an excellent case study, not only because he was the culmination of the most creative period of Neo-Confucianism and a gen-uinely original thinker, but also because early in his life Wang struggled to get along with only the taoist and Buddhist strains of thought, and was driven almost against his will to the active ethical orientation of Confucianism. Here, more than in most other thinkers, we find the special reasons for Neo-Confucianism. The method of this chapter is not to provide a new critical interpretation of Wang in terms of the Chinese tradition itself but rather to use certain conceptions of process philosophy to show the depth and subtlety of his thought.[3] The basic categories of process philosophy are introduced in Chapter 3; they are presented in this chapter in more sophisticated terms and again in Chapter 9.

Since the ultimate purpose of the discussion is to develop a viable philosophical theology, it will be necessary to ask whether Wang's thought is true and valuable. Similarly, we cannot take process philosophy as authoritative but must criticize it too. Consequently, what follows is not merely a comparison or setting of parallels but also an inquiry into whether parallel themes are valid. The inquiry leads to the ontological theory of creation. It is necessary to belabor the point about critical analysis because most scholarship in field is merely expository.[4] Yet the purpose of "finding ancestors" is to give depth and subtlety to one's own creative work. As Whitehead would say, "massive inheritance" of stable, complex structure is the prerequisite of high-level order.

I. Manifesting the Clear Character

In 1527 Wang Yang-ming wrote his "Inquiry on the *Great Learning*," a succinct summary of the main themes he had been developing throughout his life.[5] Its structure is a commentary on each of the famous "three items" in the Confucian classic, the *Great Learning*, ("manifesting the clear character," "loving the people," "abiding in the highest good") and then a discussion of the meaning and significance of the order of the "eight steps" for attaining the "three items." The first part of the structure allowed Wang to give an epitome of his metaphysical views and the second provided the occasion for defending his views against the prevailing theory of Chu Hsi (1130–1200), an earlier Neo-Confucianist.[6]

The first "item" is that the education of a great person (or perhaps the text means only the education of an adult) consists in "manifesting the clear character." Whereas, for ancient Confucianism this probably referred mainly to the moral virtue of sincerity, for the Neo-Confucianists it was an ontological statement about human nature and its foundation in the nature of things.

Wang began his exposition of this item with the assertion that "the great man regards Heaven, Earth, and the myriad things as one body."[7] In this claim, Wang was indeed asserting diversity in the universe; he did not claim, with Parmenides and Bradley, that being is one and diversity is somehow illusory. More to the historical point, Wang was not in any sense asserting a Buddhist or Hindu version of diversity as illusion. Rather, he was asserting that for the great person, heaven, earth and the myriad things – a longhand reference to the universe – are connected just as the parts of the body are connected.

The metaphor of the body can be interpreted in two ways. The first involves construing the body as an objective physical machine with interrelated and coordinated moving parts. Used as a metaphor for the connexity of the world, this conception of body suggests that the world is a totally integrated physical whole, perhaps a machine. But this is a Cartesian construing of the notion of body, and not very congenial to the Chinese tradition.

The second interpretation construes body in a more personal, or "embodied," sense, for instance as Husserl and Merleau-Ponty spoke of the "lived body" for which the objectified physical aspects are but abstractions. On this construction, Wang's point would be that, for the great person, the whole world is a body, that the difference between the individual's personal body and the rest of the universe is trivial and that the individual's feeling for the rest of the universe is of the sort most people have only for their personal bodies. From the standpoint of process philosophy, this point can be made without explicit use of the notion of *body*. The world is a world only for a prehender, an occasion arrived at by feeling past occasions. All the physical connections between things are orders of prehensions or feelings. Whitehead interpreted the human body as a special case of the human world – in a sense, reversing Wang's metaphor. The similarity between them, however, I suggest, is in the kinds of connection each uses to interpret the relation of things to knowers, connections generalized from cognitive activities. Both Neo-Confucianism and process philosophy interpret these cognitive activities as natural processes basic to cosmology.

Wang said, "the great man *regards* [italics mine] Heaven, Earth and the myriad things as one body." Does this mean that, in themselves, they are not one body but are so only when regarded by a particular kind of point of view? Not at all. Wang also said, "that the great man can regard Heaven, Earth, and the myriad things as one body is not because he deliberately wants to do so, but because it is natural to the humane nature of his mind that he do so."[8] This means, first, that the great person's view is not a special categoreal scheme or perspective that is one among others and that can be adopted. It is not like William James's suggestion that we should see things optimistically. The second implication of the statement is that the view of the things as one body is a function of the "human nature" that underlies a person's particular mind. Even inferior people have this human nature and see things as one body, except that they quickly cover it up with selfish desires. Wang quotes Mencius on the primordial quality of feelings of commiseration.[9] We will return shortly to why inferior people go wrong.

Before that, however, it is necessary to reflect briefly on certain general Neo-Confucian doctrines presupposed in Wang's discussion and what they might mean in contemporary terms. Chou Tun-i (1017–73) was the first great Neo-Confucian philosopher to set out the major themes that Chu Hsi and Wang Yang-ming took for granted.[10] His classic *An Explanation of the Diagram of the Great Ultimate* begins:

> The ultimate of Non-being and also the Great Ultimate (T'ai-chi)! The Great Ultimate through movement generates yang. When its activity reaches its limit, it becomes tranquil. Through tranquility the Great Ultimate generates yin. When tranquility reaches its limit, activity begins again. So movement and tranquility alternate and become the root of each other, giving rise to the distinction of yin and yang, and the two modes are thus established.[11]

From our standpoint, the crucial point of this passage is its assertion that the "Great Ultimate" is a vibratory movement wherein movement itself has a limit in which it is transformed and becomes tranquility which returns to the origin of assertive movement again. The ancient concepts of yang (the active part of movement) and yin (the tranquil part) are interpreted as derivative or partial functions of the Great Ultimate's movement. This accords with the interpretation of yin and yang in taoism given in Chapter 7. I take it to assert that the most primordial sense of what it is to be, feels "being" to be vibration. To be is to be one or several vibrations.

This interpretation clearly depends on Whitehead's language describing the cosmos as a set of vibratory patterns. Its utility for making connections with modern physics is equally clear.[12] Therefore, it is important to determine the degree to which this interpretation was in the minds of the Neo-Confucians and the extent to which it is a mere implication or possible reading of what they said. It must be admitted at once that they did not develop the notion toward a theoretical physics; nor did they elaborate a prescientific cosmology explicitly drawing out the implications of vibratory motion. Rather, they usually moved quickly from naturalistic statements to concerns about human nature, ethics, and politics. On the other hand, the sense that to be is to be a "change" illustrating the principles of yang and yin is ancient and permeated the Chinese culture that the Neo-Confucians took for granted. It was more basic than the splits between Confucian, taoist, and other schools. Furthermore, there was no school of thought in China that would have presented a substantialist alternative to the view of being as change. The closest candidate would be the common-sense view of things attacked by the Buddhists as illusion, and even here, it was the Indian, not the Chinese, sources of Buddhism that became most exercised about criticizing the theory of permanent substances. Those of us who have been frustrated by our Western colleagues in the attempt to present an alternative to the view that to be is to be a substantial "thing" can appreciate how the Chinese might never have seen the need to sharpen or even explicitly develop the concept of being as vibratory motion. Thus, I believe my interpretation, while not a paraphrase, would not be denied by the Neo-Confucians.

I state above that "the most primordial *sense* of what it is to be *feels* 'being' to be vibration." The language of "sensation" is deliberate. The "sense" that leads to ontology for the Chinese is not vision or touch, as it has been for the West. Nor is it the hearing of the "music" of things, as it has been for India.[13] Rather, it is the dance – particularly, the kind of exercise movement traditionally attributed to the Emperor Yü (2205 B.C.E.), for the purpose of bringing health through harmonizing with the universe and developed through the milennia into what we know as t'ai chi ch'uan and related movements.[14] The importance of this is that learning the rhythms of one's own movement is part of learning to perceive the being of others. Ontology requires cultivated experience, though all of us can feel something of what is intended in an ontology of vibratory movement.

Within the Chinese cosmology of vibratory motion, ascending and descending the waves is called yang and yin, respectively, Further concepts are needed to describe the amplitude of the waves. These are concepts that would relate a given vibration to its environment of vibrations with which it must harmonize. Each vibration has its intrinsic nature "given by Heaven," as the Neo-Confucians would say; but its nature is determined by the requirements of harmonizing with its background and the larger rhythms of which it is a part. The cosmology of vibratrory motion requires harmony as a central concept.

Although Wang did not develop the point, I believe he presupposed the cosmology of a harmony of vibratory motions as the background to his claim that the sage is one body with the universe. In one sense, every being is one body with the universe, in that its rhythms must at least be compatible with the vibrations around it. To be completely out of phase is to self-destruct. Some internal rhythms, however, can be so attuned that they register and reinforce the rhythms of distant vibrations. They are the ones that are "perceptive" of the distant or cosmologically con-

joined by virtue of mutually supportive or organically connected harmonies.

For Chou, the heart of normative human nature is sincerity, a concept
first developed in the ancient Confucian classic, *The Doctrine of the
Mean*.[15] For Chou, sincerity is the harmonizing trait that connects ideal
inner tranquility and all outer moral activities. He wrote:

> Sagehood is nothing but sincerity. It is the foundation of the Five Cons-
> tant Virtues (humanity, righteousness, propriety, wisdom, and faith-
> fulness) and the source of all activities. When tranquil, it is in the state of
> non-being, and when active it is in the state of being. It is perfectly correct
> and clearly penetrating. Without sincerity, the Five Constant Virtues and
> all activities will be wrong. They will be depraved and obstructed.
> Therefore with sincerity very little effort is needed (to achieve the mean).
> (In itself) it is perfectly easy but it is difficult to put into practice. But with
> determination and firmness, there will be no difficulty. Therefore it is said,
> "If a man can for one day master himself and return to propriety, all under
> heaven will return to humanity."[16]

What might this mean in terms of contemporary process philosophy?
Within an actual occasion, what Whitehead called "categoreal obligations" govern the passage of separately felt data, merely subjectively
unified, into a novel, concrete, subjectively harmonized occasion.
Because the obligations oblige a process if it is to issue in a thing, this inner process must satisfy them as a cosmological necessity.[17] I suggest
that the process of concrescence, of becoming concrete as directed according to categoreal obligations, is what Chou and the other Neo-
Confucians idealize as inner tranquility. But the inner process of concrescence is not isolated from other occasions. Each occasion has its own
value, the objective fact of its own subjective process of satisfaction of
the categoreal obligations. Properly, moral subjective concrescence
should respect the values of what it prehends and what will prehend it
later. That is, speaking very generally, an occasion should objectify its
data "truly," preserving their individually attained values, and superject
to its successors the best potentialities.[18]

These points about actual occasions are made as though actual occasions were people; they are not. At most, they are merely momentary
parts of people. Most occasions are not parts of anyone. The point of process philosophy is that the elements of subjectivity and value – indeed,
obligation – are found rudimentarily in every actual element. A continuing difficulty with process thought today is the facile slippage from personal language to cosmological language, and then the assumption that a

fully elaborated cosmology is a sufficient theory of the human person. Leaving the difficulties aside for the moment, the historical point should be stressed that the Neo-Confucianists did exactly the same thing, as I shall illustrate shortly.

For Chou Tun-I, sincerity, read in process terms, is the harmony of ideal subjective process with ideal objective perception and effect. Without that harmony there can be an elegant way of satisfying the categoreal demands for subjective harmony which, nevertheless, distorts the values of the world and merely contributes difficulty in the future. There can also be ways to respond objectively to the world and helpfully toward the future, which, without harmony, leave the self (or occasions) either in knots or in unwoven skeins. Sincerity is the peculiar harmony that maximizes both inner elegance and outer virtue.

It is apparent from these suggestions for interpretation that the model for sincerity is cosmological, not psychological. This was indeed the way Chou took the point. His small essay, *An Explanation of the Diagram of the Great Ultimate*, begins cosmologically with the generation of yang and yin from the Great Ultimate; from yang and yin come the Five Agents or material forces: water, fire, wood, metal, and earth, and from them all things are made. Then Chou argues:

> It is man alone who receives (the Five Agents) in their highest excellence, and therefore he is most intelligent. His physical form appears, and his spirit develops consciousness. The five moral principles of his nature (humanity or *jen*, righteousness, propriety, wisdom, and faithfulness) are aroused by, and react to, the external world and engage in activity; good and evil are distinguished; and human affairs take place.[19]

Because persons are the purest and best exemplars of the manifestation of the Great Ultimate, human virtues (at base, sincerity) provide the names for cosmological factors.

Consequently, in his book, *Penetrating the Book of Changes*, Chou said that sincerity is the foundation of the sage obtained from the originator of all things.[20] It is the original nature of persons and not of persons only but of all things, except not so clearly or excellently. Later, such Neo-Confucianists as Ch'eng Hao (1032–1085) and Cheng I (1033–1107) developed more straightforwardly cosmological concepts for interpreting the original nature of persons – namely, "principle of nature" and "material force." Roughly, "principle of nature" is the set of categoreal obligations, and "material force" is creativity organized in its basic ways (for example; as active and passive and as the physical elements). Chu

Hsi, the greatest Neo-Confucianist before Wang Yang-ming, argued that each thing in the universe has its own nature or principle and that this principle is antecedent to but never separate from the thing's material force.[21] For these later thinkers, the concept of *jen*, meaning love or humanity, took the place of sincerity in Chou's thought as describing the ideal harmony of inner process and outer connections.

Against this background, we can reinterpret Wang Yang-ming's claim that "the great man regards Heaven, Earth, and the myriad things as one body." "Great" because of their humanity (*jen*), sages harmonize their internal process with all things to which they are related. But what about the person who is less than a sage? Is humanity (*jen*) universal, or is it a special achievement of greatness? This is an ancient question for Confucianism.

Wang addressed this question from two sides. From the first, he argued by a series of steps that persons, great or inferior, identify with all things. If they see a child about to fall into a well, they feel immediate alarm and commiseration. The feeling of humanity, however, does not extend only to their "brothers." Wang wrote,

> Again, when he observes the pitiful cries and frightened appearance of birds and animals about to be slaughtered, he cannot help feeling an "inability to bear" their sufferings. This shows that his humanity forms one body with birds and animals. It may be objected that birds and animals are sentient beings as he is. But when he sees plants broken and destroyed, he cannot help a feeling of pity. This shows that his humanity forms one body with plants. It may be said that plants are living things as he is. Yet, even when he sees tiles and stones shattered and crushed, he cannot help a feeling of regret. This shows that his humanity forms one body with tiles and stones.[22]

Note that Wang explicitly rejected the view that love or identification, regarding as one body with oneself, is a matter of affinity with things *like* oneself. It is not a matter of appreciating by analogy with a sense of one's own feelings. Rather, it is a fundamental appreciation of the values of things' own natures and a pang at the loss of the values. This is similar to Whitehead's point that the primary objects of prehension are other occasions, or nexuses of occasions, replete with the subjective sense of their own satisfactions. In the process theory of actual occasions, the intrinsic, formal value of prehended things is quickly compromised by the need of the prehending occasion to value the things relative to the demands of its own satisfaction. The world is mostly transmuted to structures and lines of energy. Only in human beings – indeed, only in connoisseurs – is there a highly developed capacity to integrate prehended things into one's own subjective experience while acknowledging the objective natures and values of those things. For the most part, physical low-level occasions – and even people most of the time – forget the values things have in themselves and attend only on the values they have in their own coming satisfaction. Massive negative prehension, or rejection, is the price most things pay for subjective harmony. This is precisely Wang's point: the great man should learn how not to have to pay that price. The scope of prehensions unites all things in one body, but only sages can regard things that way because only they can minimize negative prehensions.

Wang does not infer from the above that sages are a higher grade of being than inferior persons. Rather, inferior people have the same nature sages do, but they obscure it by allowing themselves selfish desires. This is Wang's second approach to the question of the universality of humanity (*jen*). The effect of having selfish desires is not immediately immorality but rather the breakdown of the harmony between inner process and outer things. Having a selfish desire interposes between the categoreal obligations of subjective satisfaction and the objective values of things to be attended to a bad principle of valuation – namely, that things should be valued for their contribution to a personal *idea* of self. This is more than merely valuing things according to their potential for integration in satisfaction. It is also more than negatively prehending things to achieve integration; it is to value things according to how they serve an idea of self as distinct from the rest of the world. The idea of the self, so used, destroys sages' regard of the whole world as one body. As Wang put it, "The learning of the great man consists entirely in getting rid of the obscuration of selfish desires in order, by his own efforts, to make manifest his clear character, so as to restore the condition of forming one body with Heaven, Earth, and the myriad things, a condition that is originally so, that is all."[23]

Would Wang have said that the original human nature, manifested by sages as humanity or love, differs from the principle inherent in other things? In one sense it does; only people have the "clear character" according to which all things are regarded as one body, which it is the duty of the great person to manifest. In another sense, it does not necessarily. When a great person grasps another thing as part of his or her body, it is by appreciating its principle. As we shall see, Wang also argued that the principles of all things are identical to the principle to be found in one's own mind. What might that principle be? My suggestion is, the principle is categoreal obligations for grasping a world into a new valuable actuality. The character a person has, even if obscured by selfish desires, is the same that animals, plants, and tiles have; in nonhumans that character lacks clarity because of what process philosophy calls "negative prehension."

II. Loving the People

The second item of the learning of a great person is "loving the people." Wang explained the item this way:

> To manifest the clear character is to bring about the substance of the state of forming one body with Heaven, Earth, and the myriad things, whereas loving the people is to put into universal operation the function of the state of forming one body.[24]

This involved Wang in interpretation of the ancient Chinese distinction of substance from function. Roughly, the substance of a thing is what it is in itself; its function is what it is in interacting with others. A thing functions according to its own inner principle (as well as according to the possibilities offered by the things with which it interacts). When the thing is considered in its substance, the principle is there but inactive, undifferentiated and unmanifest. When the thing is considered in its functioning, the principle is the guiding force of its activity, diversely relating to the myriad things. In Confucian tradition, one touches one's substance in the meditation that attains tranquility; one's function is seen in one's relations as rightly ordered.

Here, Wang's contribution was to point out that the humanity by virtue of which the great person is one body with the world can be regarded both as substance and as function.[25] As substance, one's own personal being apart from overt expressions, humanity is the manifestation of the clear character by which the world is regarded as one body. As function, however, the person must live daily life in such a way as actually to weld the world into one body. This is a complicated theory. How can people regard the world as one body when they have the continuing task of making it one body? Is that not a simple confusion of the ideal with the real?

Wang's usual way of responding to this difficulty was to point out the identity of knowledge and action, his most famous doctrine. People do not really know themselves to be one body with others unless they interact with them in "bodily harmony." This is not merely a matter of their own intentions but also of the other's intentions. For a sage to love the people, the sage must also "renovate" them, that is, make them great too.[26] This picks up the traditional Confucian theme – the main theme of the *Great Learning* – that by perfecting one's own life one has a causal influence on perfecting the lives of others (a topic we return to shortly).

At the moment, let me stress a point that will pose some difficulty. It seems as though the world is not one body, regardless of how the sages would like to see it. If it were, there would be no need for effort. In this interpretation, reality has not measured up to the ideal. Wang and some other Confucianists see the matter differently. For them, the world at base is indeed ideal – one body, as it were. Evil is the superimposition by selfish desires of feelings and actions that pervert ideal harmony.[27] The bulk of the moral program, then, is elimination of selfish desires so the original clear character will shine through or so love of people will be fulfilled, with all that means for ordering the family, economy, and state. Put in theological terms, Wang believed that "after the Fall" human nature remains intact underneath and, moreover, that mankind remains in the Garden of Eden. Put another way, the disharmonies that rend the otherwise organic fabric of the world are all functions of individuals' selfishness. But is this so?

III. Abiding in the Highest Good

Before pursuing this point it is necessary to examine Wang's interpretation of the third item of the "Great Learning," namely, "abiding in the highest good." He wrote:

> The highest good is the ultimate principle of manifesting character and loving people. The nature endowed in us by Heaven is pure and perfect. The fact that it is intelligent, clear, and not beclouded is evidence of the emanation and revelation of the highest good. It is the original substance of the clear character which is called innate knowledge of the good.[28]

I take this to mean that the highest good is the heaven that endows us with our original nature or substance, and that in its substantiality – or, apart from expressive functioning – this original nature is innate knowledge of its own source. In its functioning, the clear character is an innate knowledge of the good as expressed in things: one's own mind and other things. This valuational quality of inner subjectivity carrying throughout experience is characteristic of Neo-Confucianism in general. Wang's special emphasis, and the chief point of his dispute with Chu Hsi, is that if the good can be found functioning within one's own mind, there is no need to investigate things outside the mind for the purpose of abiding in the highest good.[29]

The general theme of abiding in the highest good is the greatest contribution Neo-Confucianism makes to contemporary philosophy. It is the point at which an axiological theory of experience is put forward. Without the necessity of working through the fact-value dichotomy, Neo-Confucianism presents an understanding of the knowledge of things' inner principles in which those principles are values.[30]

Process philosophy can help explicate "abiding in the highest good" in modern terms; it can, in turn, learn from that doctrine some ramifications of its own view.

First, from an objective or coordinate point of view, everything has a pattern of structure; one interpretation of *li*, the Chinese term for principle, is "pattern." Process philosophy points out that patterns are not only facts or forms of facts, but also values, because each pattern or structured thing is a satisfaction or nexus of satisfactions. In other terms, a structure has the value of being a means to an end. The end is the satisfying of the categoreal obligations of harmony within the limits imposed by the initial data; concrete satisfaction is the means by which this end is achieved. Without the factual character of the structure, there would be no actual means by which the end is attained. Without the value of being a means to some end, however, a structure is radically unintelligible; it must always be somehow "mysterious," as Wittgenstein suggested, that there is such a thing as formal coherence.[31]

Most, if not all, structures of which we are aware in experience are not the result of single occasions but of nexuses of occasions. They exhibit many satisfactions. Most, however, are socially organized so the satisfaction of each member occasion is coordinated with the satisfactions of many others and so the value of the whole has extra coherence. With Neo-Confucianism, process philosophy offers as an empirical generalization the proposition that experience is shot through with valuing. To take in a structure is to take it in as the achievement of satisfaction. The factual character of the structure may be isolated from the value elements, and for many practical purposes it is; but this should be recognized as abstraction from the basic "principle" of the structure.

Second, from an internal, genetic or subjective point of view, the principle of a thing is the set of categoreal obligations that define the process of attaining satisfaction for its initial data. The initial data are the "material forces," as it were, needing regulation by "principle" – the categoreal obligations of creativity – in order to be existent or present.

When the situation is stated this way, we see that Wang Yang-ming must have been right, that there is only one "principle" in all things; things differ because of their diverse initial data. As I argue below, there is another source of difference which Wang does not explicitly take into account. Meanwhile, the common process theme should be mentioned here, that, from a genetic analysis of an occasion, *principle* would be "innately" present insofar as the categoreal obligations of creativity govern the genetic process. Moreover, the initial data incorporated in the emerging occasion are themselves innate exemplars of the categoreal obligations. The categoreal obligations, to use Wang's language, are the clear character of persons' (or anything's) original nature that the sage might manifest. They are also principles of other things to which the sage might be related. Because the obligations are present in process, Wang believed that they not only are innate but can be known innately. Although it might require sagacity to express this objectively, what he meant was that insofar as a person apprehends the value of something, the person apprehends it as satisfying "principle," that is, as being a means to the end of incorporating the categoreal obligations in the process of making an actual thing out of initial data.

Third, for both Neo-Confucianism and process philosophy, exhibiting "principle" allows of degrees. That is, although all processes and resulting structures must be harmonious out of conformity to categoreal obligations, some ways of meeting those obligations with certain data are more harmonious than other ways with the same data. In particular, as Whitehead expressed the theme, human beings can live with truth, beauty, and adventure, which are superlative ways of meeting the categoreal obligations as relevant to human life. The obligations *can* be met *without* truth, beauty, or adventure, or with only minimal attainments. In Neo-Confucian terms, abiding in the highest good is not merely to exhibit "principle," which all things do willy-nilly, but also to adjust those aspects of life under possible control to resonate with exhibiting principle. Wang and most other Neo-Confucians would have argued that the failure to exhibit principle in the highest degree is a result of corrupting selfishness, not one of lack of original attainment. The result is similar to that expressed in process philosophy, that harmony is minimally and not necessarily maximally embodied.

Fourth, the point of contact between Neo-Confucianism and process philosophy regarding value is that for both it is an ontological matter. For Wang and other Neo-Confucianists, principle is that by which things exist. For process philosophy, the ontological condition for existence is the satisfaction of the categoreal obligations; past occasions provide the cosmological data and causal constraints, but emergent existence is a matter of meeting obligations.

The ontological character of the innate quality of value raises another question: Why is *this* what it means "to be" rather than something else? Why are these categoreal obligations the way to harmony? That they do or do not fit our intuitive sense is an empirical matter. But *why* is harmony "that way?" No description of the conditions for harmony can give the normative reasons for being obligatory. The Chinese respond to this question by citing heaven as the source of principle.[32] Principle is the original gift that is native to every determinate thing and process. In itself indeterminate, heaven, or the "Great Ultimate," gives rise to a principled world.[33] This is a precise specification of our theory of creation. On one hand we have a sense of arbitrariness in the creative process; on the other, heaven is heaven precisely because its creation is principled. The theology concerned with most process thought asserts that God is finite and does not create in a radical sense. Because God is said by process theologians to be bound by the categoreal obligations, God cannot account for their being normative.[34] The more radical doctrine of creation defended in this book is not incompatible with a process cosmology, however, even if incompatible with process theology. As Chapter 7 indicates, God can be represented as a creator *ex nihilo* that, from the standpoint of the harmonies of the world, is similar to Plato's "form of the good."

Wang's interest in "abiding" in the highest good was more immediately moral than ontological. He point out that if superior persons do not abide in the highest good, their attempts to manifest the clear character or love the people are likely to go awry. The Buddhists and the taoists sought to manifest the clear character without abiding in the highest good and lost their minds "in illusions, emptiness, and quietness, having nothing to do with the work of the family, the state, and the world."[35] Those who want to love people without abiding in the highest good sink "their own minds in base and trifling things," losing them in scheming strategy and cunning techniques having neither the sincerity of humanity nor that of commiseration.[36] The point is, both the normative character of harmony within and the objective satisfaction without can be lost, with only factual consideration remaining, unless the value dimension of being is explicitly cultivated.

IV. Investigation of Things

From this point on in his essay, Wang deals with practical implications of his exposition of manifesting the clear character, loving people, and abiding in the highest good. They fall under three main heads.

Wang's First Theme

First is Wang's argument that the "principle" should not be sought in external things. Chu Hsi and others had argued that the foundations of Confucian learning, that is the "three items," are to be found by investigation of external things. Wang argues that this merely leads to the mind becoming confused.[37] Of course, Wang would admit that one must investigate things in order to know what they are; but one cannot discern the "principle" in them if one does not already have the principle both in oneself and identified there. Cultivation of "principle" in tranquility and peaceful respose, therefore, allows norms to be brought to deliberation instead of sought in deliberation itself. This makes sense in terms of process philosophy insofar as it means that (1) categoreal obligations are universal, and (2) it is by discerning them in oneself that one appreciates the satisfactions of others as normative. Insofar as there is a parallel with process philosophy at this point, two additional statements must be made about the problem. First, despite the universality of the categoreal obligations, each event in the universe is unique in having its own place, its own data to integrate, and its own subjectivity. As a result, the mean (the "satisfying" structure) by which any other occasion meets its obligations is unique to itself. Therefore, people cannot know anything about a particular thing other than themselves by knowing only the categoreal obligations in themselves or in abstraction. Second, even if a person knows the categoreal obligations and the initial data for another event, that event has its own subjectivity, by which it spontaneously weights the importance its antecedents have for it. Thus, in order to know how and to what degree "principle" is realized in another thing, it is necessary to investigate it directly.

Wang wrote: "People fail to realize that the highest good is in their minds, and seek it outside. As they believe that everything or every event has its own definite principle, they search for the highest good in individual things."[38] But everything *does* have its own definite "principle." Although *principle* or categoreal obligations are ingredients of everything, each instance is unique. Apart from structuring specific processes, *principle* is vacuous or indeterminate. The statement of principle in abstraction from specific processes, like Whitehead's exposition of the categoreal obligations, is merely an empirical generalization of nodal points in the way of becoming harmonious, not an exhibition of the normativeness of principle or of obligations.[39]

At this point it is relevant to recall the general Neo-Confucian conception of nature as a complex, harmonious configuration of vibratory changes. Suppose we said that a person appreciates a distant thing by grasping its vibratory character, its rhythms and the connections of its rhythms with the surrounding environment and across intervening space. This would be done by virtue of the extraordinarily complex rhythms within human experience wherein the core of the person's own experience is made compatible with the rhythms of external things, with minimal distortion, and whereby semantic rhythms within the person's experience point out the external reference. Whitehead's discussion of symbolic reference is a case in point. At that level of interpretation, experiencing a distant thing would be a kind of concrete feel for the harmonious nature in which both the thing felt and the feeler exist, a feeling of participating in the tao which includes the thing perceived. Put another way, one can feel oneself to be in natural connection with the distant thing. The thing can be isolated for strict observation only by a process of abstraction which somehow attempts to neutralize the intervening medium.

This feeling of harmonious connection with other things is perfectly concrete and, if it serves as a categoreally basic feeling, puts a new perspective on both the knowledge of principle (categoreal obligations) and the knowledge of particular other things arising out of their specific initial data. Knowledge of principle is abstract. As noted above, categoreal obligations are universal to all occasions and are actually indefinite without some specific initial data. According to process philosophy, the particular actual entities prehended are absolutely unique, both because of the uniqueness of their initial data and because of the individuality of their subjective processes of unifying those data. Within the ambience of process philosophy, experience of another thing is usually presented as a matter of receiving the other as data and then transmuting it to make it compatible with other demands within the experiencing occasion. The other-self dichotomy is strictly preserved, and doubtless there are important contexts where it is valid. But suppose there are, indeed, "feelings of harmonious connection" within which both the appreciation of categoreal obligation (principle) and the givenness of data about others are abstractions. One's self-constitution would be a vibratory response to the rhythms felt in the environing universe; but the character of that response would be a harmonic constituent of the larger "body" of the universe. The "morality" of self-constitution would include both acknowledgment of distant rhythms and setting up one's own rhythm to enhance the others. Bringing such feelings of harmonious connection to consciousness is unlikely to be a frequent occurrence. It is not incompatible, however, with Whitehead's views; indeed, it is closely allied to the sense of peace articulated in his later writing. What I call "feelings of harmonious connection" is not explicitly discussed and defended by Wang Yang-ming. Is there any ground for thinking he asserted something like these feelings in other terms? First, I believe they are natural extensions of the doctrine of vibratory motion that underlie yang and yin, a doctrine common to the heritage of Neo-Confucianism. Indeed, those feelings must be close to what the Chinese tradition meant by being aware of one's participation in the tao. Second, I believe this notion was what Wang was reaching for in his attempt to extend the concept of *principle* to cover what other Neo-Confucianists called "material force." Wang's insistence on monism is not intended to reduce the particularity and materiality of the world to an ideal principle in some subjective sense, although he did misstate his case when he called for seeking the principle within oneself instead of in external things. Wang's monism, rather was, the doctrine that genuinely human functioning is a concrete grasp of the rhythms of a universe in harmony. From the perspective of the actual rhythms of the universe, both particular initial data and universal categoreal obligations are partial and abstract. Third, Wang had other doctrines that make good sense on this interpretation (discussed below).

Wang's Second Theme

Wang's second main practical theme had to do with the continuity of process. "Things have their roots and their branches," said the *Great Learning*. Chu Hsi had likened manifesting the clear character to the roots and loving the people to the branches.[40] Wang objected that this inevitably leads to bifurcating these into two things. He argued, instead, that manifesting the clear character *consists* in loving people, and vice versa (so long as this continuous process abides in the highest good). To distinguish strongly between roots and branches is to encourage self-preoccupation on one hand and unintegrated moral activity on the other. So far so good; pragmatism makes a similar point.

If we remember the problem above concerning "principle" in things outside one's mind, however, we must cope with the problem of contingency. An act of love issuing from one's own clearly manifested character cannot flow smoothly through the world to its objectives as guided by principle. The specific expression of principles of other things might be different. Further, other things have their own subjective responses to make, which might thwart love (or renovation). The superior person simply does not have the control over others or over the inanimate part of the world that Wang and other Confucianists thought.[41] The metaphor of roots and branches might be too limited.

From the perspective of process thought, the problem is one of spontaneity. Although each occasion must constitute itself within the limits of its initial data and the tolerance of the environment, it exercises spontaneity in doing so; when the occasions are parts of complex human experience, that spontaneity may be significant. One person's self-constitution cannot affect the spontaneity of another's except through persuasion. Further, limiting one's attempts to influence others to mere persuasion is one way to show basic human respect. Where the self-other dichotomy is strictly observed, influence or control can be nothing more than presenting oneself as initial data to be done with as the other occasion sees fit. From the perspective of the world as an interlocking harmony of rhythm, though, one's action is the setting up of a chain of vibratory processes within which other people move. They, of course, behave with some spontaneity and many act so as to change the rhythms one intends for them. But the overarching concrete harmonic pattern is a larger matrix of value than either their own personal ideals or one's own initial intentions. My suggestion is that the metaphor of roots and branches should not be interpreted by identifying one's initiating actions as the roots and consequences of those actions in others as the branches; rather, the roots and branches are the proximate and remote elements respectively of the overall harmonic process of the universe. Wang was correct precisely in his insistence on not separating them. Here, the limitation is that people *do* have the spontaneous ability to fit within the overall harmonies in ways that minimally harmonize, that barely meet categoreal obligations. The price to be paid for this diminution of one's rhythmic answer to nature's pulses is the necessity of erecting a narcissistic image of self and world as a barrier to which one answers instead.

Wang's Third Theme

Wang's third theme brings out even more the critical elements in the others. Asked to explicate the passage from the *Great Learning* that says sages ordered the state by cultivating their personal lives in knowledge and will, Wang developed his view that the rectified will or innate knowledge of good is the foundation for action and for knowledge of external things. All things, from the inner mind to ordering the state, are "really one thing," according to Wang:

Now the original substance of the mind is man's nature. Human nature being universally good, the original substance of the mind is correct. How is it that any effort is required to rectify the mind? The reason is that, while the original substance of the mind is originally correct, incorrectness enters when one's thoughts and will are in operation. Therefore he who wishes to rectify his mind must rectify it in connection with the operation of his thoughts and will.[42]

Wang exegeted his statement with the comment that only when one is actually willing things or thinking thoughts does the question arise as to their goodness or evil. Before the "functioning" of will and thinking there is only the original nature or principle. A well-cultivated person responds to good thoughts and actions as good and to bad ones as bad. What does *cultivation* consist of? It consists of extending the innate knowledge of principle, the highest good, into all objects of thought and action so their real value character is manifested. But to *extend* that knowledge is to *investigate* those objects. The external world cannot be ignored; it must be investigated so as to manifest its structured value. Chu Hsi said that "investigating" means finding out what things are, whereas Wang said, "to investigate is to rectify,"[43] by which he meant that a person knows an external thing by rectifying it so that it is lovingly conformed to principle. Rejecting all strong distinctions between internal and external things, Wang defined a thing as an object of will. Possibly anticipating Josiah Royce, Wang argued that willing a thing's good is the way to know it. Concerning this view, it would not make sense to say one *knows* a bad thing; in the complete sense of *know* the sense appropriate to the sage, "to know" is "to will." Therefore, rectification of the mind so as to bring its functioning into consonance with the highest good is the foundation for all particular willed actions and acts of knowing, including matters of government. "If one sincerely loves the good known by the innate faculty but does not in reality do the good as he comes into contact with the thing to which the will is directed, it means that the thing has not been investigated and that the will to love the good is not yet sincere."[44]

This is a remarkable – and dangerous – strategy as it stands, for it amounts to saying that moral and political action flow naturally from a cultivated personal life. Let me briefly develop this line of criticism.

From the perspective of process philosophy, the events of the world are unique and perhaps interestingly contingent. This is particularly true of the events comprising one's personal and social life. Thus there are cosmologically built-in limits to the moral force of a person, indeed, to that individual's moral ideals. Whereas it may be true that there is an ideal state of affairs for all the things affected by a person's actions, it is *not* true that it is ideal that they should be made to realize their ideals by that individual's actions alone. In most human affairs, freedom to be self-governing is a somewhat higher ideal than most ideals about which governance decisions are made.[45] If Confucian sages could, indeed, strictly order the state by their investigative will, they would end up with a situation of totalitarianism. Confucians before Wang noted that a sage-king can order the state by encouraging people to imitate *his* virtue, but this is not the same thing as causing the people to be virtuous by the will that knows them.

I believe that if the concept of vibratory change is noted against the background of Wang's thought, a different perspective emerges. To know and to will a thing means both to reverberate to its rhythms in ways that reinforce what is good and to set up improved rhythms where possible. One can no more control another person than a dancer can force the movements of another dancer. But one dancer neither knows nor cares for the other without dancing in such a way as to acknowledge tenderly, and provide rhythms for, the other's initiative. A caring dancer evokes spontaneity in others with the very rhythms he or she establishes. Herbert Fingarette has developed an elaborate interpretation of Confucius in which the dominant thesis is that the ruler governs the empire, establishing harmony and peace by a kind of ritual dance or observance of propriety.[46] Wang did not mean to be a totalitarian!

V. Harmony and Creation

At this point it is necessary for me to admit that the interpretation I have been pressing, based on the notion of vibratory change and harmony, has raised an extreme taoist tendency in Wang, one that emphasizes communication with nature and people whose rhythms do not always respect the idiosyncracies of individuals. Particularly, it tends to dismiss as irrelevant those elements of spontaneity that are not significant for the grander harmonies of natural and social life, as well as those elements of degrading brute force whose existential harmony with nature thwarts humanity. The interpretation suggests that social and political strategy would not respect the rules of propriety or the integrity of private experience if propriety and private integrity stand in opposition to the larger rhythms of harmony and justice. Indeed, the Confucians traditionally criticized the taoists for taking propriety and private integrity too lightly, for being willing to use deceit in strategy and public affairs. I believe this to be a fair interpretation of Wang Yang-ming. His great achievements were as a military leader—a taoist occupation—rather than as a Confucian court scholar. His famous victory over royal rebels was based on deceiving envoys.

But where does this leave us with regard to ethics and political theory? Is it not the case that the problems we so often must deal with are the brute, disharmonic forces of poverty, malice, stupidity, and entrenched personal and group interest? To focus on the high-level harmonic connections of things is to mystify practical politics and permit what should be changed. Does not justice sometimes demand paying strict attention to the self-other dichotomy? Is it not the case, in fact, that the revolutionary Maoists were right in insisting on change of the basic material conditions of life before attempting subtler cultivations of character through interpersonal rhythms, and that the traditional approaches of both Confucianism and taoism were counterrevolutionary?

I suspect the answer to those rhetorical questions is yes, that resolution of the problems they pose involves distinguishing various kinds of experience and assigning to each a domain of appropriate roles. The taoist awareness of the harmonic connections of the universe has its place, particularly in contexts of cultivation of the spirit. The moral experience of dealing with resolutely opposed others also has its place. The norms for that kind of experience are not easily derived from considerations of manifesting the clear character, loving the people, and abiding in the highest good. A cosmology of social thinking is needed to sort and order these and other kinds of experience. The hallmark of such a cosmology would be an emphasis on free participation by all parties rather than an emphasis on the harmonic pattern in which they participate, for the pattern is moral to the extent that it is an extension of the individual, responsible exercise of spontaneity. So far, neither Neo-Confucianism nor process philosophy has contributed a cosmology of social thinking. The remarkable ethical point about Wang Yang-ming's thought was that in his vigorous, active life he continually kept his immediate practical concerns in contact with a metaphysical tradition concerning value.

A more general, important point underlies these considerations. Wang was the epitome and culmination of a long tradition that began in the dark mists of yin-yang theory in the third millenium B.C.E., which attempted, by reflection, to understand the interrelation of things in terms of continuities of change. This tradition was decisively different from the Greek tradition which attempted to reflect on the same problem in terms of substances in relation. The Western tradition foundered on the paradox that if substances are free enough to be independent, they are too separate to be genuinely related, and if they are sufficiently connected to be related, they are one substance and not an independent plurality. The Chinese tradition appears to surmount this paradox by treating things as changes related through external tolerance and internal resonance. But this is only an apparent success. Having acknowledged that the Chinese emphasis is on ethics rather than metaphysics, we see that a similar paradox arises. If individuals are patterns of changes that can dominate other changes sufficiently to control or, willy-nilly, rectify them, then those others cannot be sufficiently independent "changes" as to be accorded the dignity that Chinese tradition insists on. Or, if individuals have such depth of inner tranquility and privacy that they cannot be controlled by others, every individual is prevented from becoming great because no one can become one body with the world. The first alternative is bureaucratic totalitariansm, the second Buddhist "illusion, emptiness and quietness."

This chapter has uncovered the Chinese paradox in Wang Yang-ming, in several ways. Like most thinkers in the Confucian tradition, Wang believed in the power of individuals to influence others by their self-constitution; emperors, at least, are supposed to do this, and for Wang, so are sages. Note, however, that Wang, in denying the means for separating one person from another, must say that a great person cannot be great without rectifying others or achieving the results of love in them. Yet, to have such ideal control would be to brutalize Wang's other ideal of the dignified, centered person who need not look outside himself or herself to find principle. In light of this expression of the paradox, would Wang fall back on Plato's tragic vision that, since one cannot be just in an unjust world such as we live in, the wise man hides behind the wall as though a storm were blowing? Wang's attack on the separation of roots and branches encounters the same paradox: If the branches are of one piece with the tree wholly formed by the roots, there is no moral integrity in the branches. Ethically, the great person's purpose is to transform the branches of his or her actions into morally integral persons. Yet another expression of the paradox arises from the fact that Wang's insistence on the completeness of internal principle must be supplemented by what I have called "feelings of harmonious connection." The reason for this supplementation is that principle in another thing is vacuous and indeterminate without the specifics of the other thing's starting point. To know another thing's specific starting point from within oneself alone requires having among one's own starting point, feelings of concrete connection with the other. The paradox is that, even with feelings of harmonious connection, the starting points of the others are either contained within oneself – in which case, there is no genuine diversity – or merely replicated within oneself, which results in a mystery.

All of these expressions of the paradox are related to the fundamental concept of substance and function in Chinese thought. Although this concept prevents the notion of vibratory change from being merely objective, with no interiority in a rhythmic pattern, it remains incoherent. Whereas the substance side can be understood by reference to the subject of change, the function side requires a dual reference. On one hand, it refers to the subject of whose substance it is the function while, on the other, referring to those other things by virtue of which it makes the substance relative. The analogy of water and waves is sometimes used to illustrate the substance-function notion: water is substance and its turbulence is its function. But the turbulence must be understood by reference to both wind and water. Whence the wind if all is water in waves? Now, what relation holds between two substance-function entities or changes? Surely it cannot be a substance-function relation itself. Wang and his tradition seem to have no answer. For Wang, a great person needs other persons to rectify, but they must be other than the person's own substance for rectification to be a function. For him, one's rooting actions need functional expression in branches, yet they cannot contain those branches within the roots without denying contingency in social consequences. One must be harmoniously connected to others who are not reducible to one's own substance or function in order to have within oneself the determinate principle of others. But how can the specifics of the others be in oneself without being one's substance or function?

Let me suggest that a way around the paradox is to acknowledge that all functional, vibratory yin-yang relations are cosmological relations; they are matters of the conditioning of one thing by another. Further, such conditioning presupposes that the conditioned and conditioning thing are in a context of mutual relevance more fundamental than the particular condition. The reason for this is that to be a thing is to be a harmony of essential features and conditional features, as described in Chapter 3. In the Chinese view, the essential features are substance, the conditional features function. Each thing is a harmony of essential and conditional features. There are no substances without function or relation. There are no functions without substances functioning. Yet the relations between things affect only functions. Therefore, the things must be together in a more primordial context in which their essential features, their substances, are related ontologically. Things could not functionally condition each other unless the primordial togetherness of their essential substances allowed for it; for the very being of a thing is a harmony of substance and function.

The context of mutual relevance is ontological creation, as the notion is developed in this book. Although there is little warrant in Wang or in Chinese thought for attributing agency to creative ground by calling it God, there is a metaphysical necessity to acknowledge a ground that creates diverse substance-functions together so they can mutually influence one another. The kind of causation that functionally happens between things when interpreted on either Western or Eastern models is not the kind that makes things be in the first place so that there can be causation. Cosmological, functional causation presupposes ontological causation.

Just as inability to solve this ontological problem of the one and the many has led many Western moral thinkers to vacillate between Marxian totalitarianism and Millian individualism, it has also led the Chinese tradition to vacillate between bureaucratic totalitarianism and meditative quietism. I suggest that something resembling the ontological conception of creation is that toward which both traditions have been groping. That this is true even of the allegedly privatistic Buddhist tradition is the topic of the next chapter.

Chapter Nine
Buddhism and Process Philosophy

P ROCESS PHILOSOPHY in the tradition of Alfred North Whitehead considers itself the heir of a conceptual undercurrent in Western intellectual history. Whereas the mainstream of Western thought has supposed that substances are the basic elements of reality, Heraclitus' belief that "all things flow" has finally emerged as a commanding metaphysical position only in the last one hundred years. One easily understands, therefore, the enthusiasm with which process philosophers applaud the Western discovery of Buddhist philosophy as a commanding metaphysical vision of process whose profoundest technical expressions are themselves ancient.

The encounter of Buddhism with process philosophy is also of vital interest to the expanding culture of Buddhism. There are numerous indications that Buddhism's vitality in the West may rescue it from overcommitment to premodern cultures in Asia, just as in ancient times its flowering in East Asia offset its eventual subordination in India. Han China's civilization must have seemed as alien to the early Indian Buddhist missionaries as Western society seems to contemporary East Asians. Missionaries to the Han found a congenial resonance in indigenous Chinese taoism, however, and Buddhism transformed itself in China, taking on the naturalistic cosmic orientation of Chinese thought.[1] It is natural, therefore, for Buddhism to take an interest in indigenous Western philosophies which might provide a similar resonance.

At the moment, two Western philosophies seem to be of the greatest interest from the Buddhist perspective. One is the fundamental ontology of Heidegger, which is influential in the Kyoto school and currently provides a language for Tibetan tantric Buddhism in the work of Herbert V. Guenther. The chief point of Buddhist interest in Heidegger's approach is its epistemological, transcendental orientation. Although Buddhism as a whole has given some place to what in the West has been called the "transcendental turn," a stepping back to consider not what is experienced but the character of experiencing, some forms of Buddhism give this consideration a premier place. David A. Dilworth and Hugh J. Silverman call this intellectual strategy "de-ontologizing," analyzing it as a relativizing of cognitive commitments so as to avoid ontological commitments.[2]

The other Western philosophy of interest to Buddhism is American process philosophy and its naturalistic culture in pragmatism. In contrast to the transcendental orientation of Heidegger, process philosophy is responsive to those strains in Buddhism that interpret the epistemological critique naturalistically. That is, instead of experience being a second-order affair relativizing reality, it is a medium uniting subject and object in myriad complex ways. The taoist side of Chinese Buddhism is precisely that interest which focuses not so much on the transcendental form of experience as on its content as empty, impermanent, and interpenetrating. This is the interest that finds in process philosophy a congenial sounding board.[3]

The topic of the encounter of Buddhism with process philosophy, therefore, ignores several aspects of the encounter of Buddhism with Western thought in a larger perspective.[4]

The thesis of this chapter goes beyond the recognition that different Western philosophies are selectively responsive to different elements in Buddhism, and vice versa. The thesis is that the current encounter of Buddhism with process philosophy enables each to develop beyond its previous achievements as understood from the perspective of creation theory. Eventually, perhaps, the developing "subject" will be neither Buddhism nor process philosophy but their encounter itself with some as yet undetermined name. The following sections, though interpretive, attempt to advance the dialogue.

I. Process

The obvious point of similarity between Buddhism and process philosophy is in the rough analogy between the conception of *pratītya samutpāda* and Whitehead's conception of *process*. Stated in a general enough way to include most schools of Buddhism, from the early Abhidharma to the late Mahayana, the *pratītya samutpāda* doctrine expresses the Buddhist view of process to the effect that (1) nothing endures and (2) anything within a process can be analyzed reductively into other conditions. Buddhist schools disagree about whether there are any irreducibly basic elements and whether things have a moment of true existence even if they do not endure. They agree, however, that the world as we experience it ordinarily does not present basic realities and that its character is one of constant flow and passage.[5]

Resonant with this, Whitehead's theory claims that *process* consists of momentary occasions of experience, each perishing as soon as it has come to be.[6] Furthermore, each occasion can be analyzed into its prehensions or feelings of prior occasions, which of course themselves can be analyzed into still other prior occasions. There is no form in any occasion that cannot be traced to some prior condition. To this extent Whitehead's cosmology expresses the general Buddhist view. Further, in these two points Whitehead stands in opposition to almost the entirety of the earlier Western tradition, certainly among abstractly articulated metaphysical views.[7] The main current in the West believes that enduring substances must be postulated precisely in order to account for change, that although substances have causes, in an important sense they themselves can be conceived of without reference to external conditions. Thus Whitehead's is the first fully elaborated Western metaphysical theory to which Buddhism can look for sympathy.[8]

From a Western perspective, the price Whitehead paid for being able to say that things have only momentary existence was a concommitant emphasis on creativity within each occasion. Each occasion is self-creative in that the change it occasions from an antecedent state of affairs is not made by the activity of the antecedent conditions but rather by the self-constitution of the emerging occasion. Once having happened, the antecedent states of affairs are passive and are turned into determining conditions by the subsequent occasion or entity that forms itself from them. Although some forms of Mahayana Buddhism articulate the immediate "thisness" of experience in language evocative of what Whitehead might have described as the "subjective immediacy of becoming," Buddhism in general has no metaphysical category corresponding to creativity that could be internal to occasions. This, as I suggest, is an area in which Buddhism can learn from process philosophy.

Thomas J. J. Altizer, followed by David Dilworth, argues that a more precise interpretation of Whitehead's conception of process is that it bears a close similarity to the early dharma theory of the Hinayana schools.[9] Whitehead's actual occasions, their constituent prehensions and nexuses of occasions, are the "ultimate facts of immediate actual experience."[10] Further, with regard to concreteness, prehensions are incomplete in and of themselves, as Dilworth points out; they are abstractions from actual entities, and nexuses are groups of actual entities that are nothing more than the sum of the actual entities. Dilworth quotes

Whitehead: "actual entities . . . are the final real things of which the world is made up. There is no going behind actual entities to find anything more real."[11] Like dharmas, actual entities or occasions become instantaneously; they do not change themselves but cumulatively make up strands of occasions that change, and lie behind the appearances of the world of common sense.

Dilworth goes on to associate what he calls Whitehead's "process realism" with that aspect of the Abhidharma that came under criticism from later Mahayana thinkers. Although his argument is comprehensive and detailed, its central point comes down to this: Whereas the early Abhidharmists said that the common-sense things of experience are empty and that the basic dharmas, the unconditioned dharmas, alone are real, the Mahayanists argued that even the unconditioned dharmas are empty. Whitehead is like the Abhidharmists in claiming that the actual occasions alone are finally real. According to Dilworth, he is subject in part to the Mahayana critique in his failure to regard actual occasions as empty.

Let us consider the matter more closely. In what sense are Whitehead's actual occasions "more real" than prehensions, nexuses, or common-sense appearances? They are the "final real things of which the world is made up" with regard to two points:

1. Their analytical components, the prehensions, cannot exist except in actual occasions. In this sense, Whitehead critically developed the Western problematic of the *res verae*, the true atomic elements. But this is only to say that, whereas actual occasions are concrete, prehensions are not concrete by themselves. It is not to suggest that prehensions are any less real than the actual occasions, only that they are real as necessarily contained in actual occasions. In their turn, actual occasions have no reality except as they are integrated prehensions of antecedent conditions. From a causal point of view, a completed actual occasion is dependent on the creative drive of its component prehensions to find satisfactory integration.

2. Actual occasions are the only loci of decisive change, and therefore are the sole basis of the limited contingent character of things. This merely distinguishes their function from that of eternal objects; it does not make actual occasions more real. Eternal objects, in their turn, contribute the definiteness to things that might be chosen by actual occasions. Therefore, though it may be that actual occasions are more comprehensively *interesting* than other elements in Whitehead's cosmology, it cannot be said that they are more *real*. For Whitehead, to be is to

make a difference to something, to function (at least potentially) as a condition within process.[12]

The situation is more complex with regard to whether Whitehead sides with the early dharma schools or with the Mahayana regarding the emptiness of things. Whereas Dilworth puts Whitehead with the early schools because of the common belief that dharmas (at least unconditioned ones, such as Nirvana) and actual entities are "ultimate facts," I would stress the similarity of his views to those of the Mahayanists because of the common belief that nothing, not even actual occasions, has "own being." The heart of the Mahayana claim is that even unconditioned dharmas are empty and that emptiness means things lack any being in their own right. "Own being" does not mean the capacity to function as a condition but, rather, to be a reality somewhat independent of conditions.

The heart of Whitehead's conception of process, I believe, is his recognition that the achievement of objective reality entails the perishing of subjective immediacy, with the occasion dropping into the past. Processive emergent reality is not *being* in the sense of having an identity of one's own, but rather *becoming*. Within an actual occasion as it is happening lies the creative drive to achieve unification of prehended past occasions so as to be an object for prehension by later occasions. The immediacy of the creative process involves an indefiniteness regarding how the occasion can reach a determinate state. Resolution of that indefiniteness into a completely determinate form is what brings the occasion into existence. Until resolution, the occasion has no being, only becoming. It does not exist; it merely lusts for existence. That is why the instant time of an occasion is not an infinitesimally thin slice but an extended duration; whole lapses of time and change come into existence instantly. Having come into existence, they are objective, finished, past facts available for prehension by subsequent occasions.

At no time does an occasion possess "own being." When it is coming into existence, it is "not yet." When it has achieved existence, its own subjective immediacy – the only "subject" that could possess "own being" – has perished. The only "being" an occasion has is its availability to be a condition for a subsequent occasion. Is this not the heart of the Mahayana claim that nothing in experience has "own being"? If anything has "own being" in Whitehead's system, it cannot be actual occasions or the things they compose; for actual occasions are *subjects* of properties only when they are not yet. When they have achieved properties, only other occasions can be subjects entertaining them.[13]

At least with respect to the universal denial of "own being," Whitehead seems to agree with the Mahayana claim that everything is empty. There is more to the Mahayana claim than this, however, and it has to do with relationships and causation.

II. Relationships and Causation

Some people experience affairs in such a way that the enduring substantiality of things seems important. Others experience that substantiality as empty, as a puffed-up exaggeration.[14] Most of us have both kinds of experience. Which is the truer interpretation?

One cannot argue, as Madhyamika Buddhists might for emptiness or Thomist Christians might for inhering acts of *esse*, that the true view is that which results from successively cultivated meditative experience. The cultivation might be in the wrong direction; presumably a corrupt interpretation of experience might be "confirmed" by selectively cultivated intentionality.

Nor can one argue that there are two truths ordered as appearance to reality or, to quote Nagarjuna, as "the truth which is the highest sense" is ordered to "the world ensconsed truth."[15] Once the priority is established, whichever it is, it needs justification.

Nor can one make a simple pragmatic argument that one view is true because it leads to salvation. Both views have been held by sincere, sensitive, and intelligent people to be elements in salvific experience. Futher, not only is the character ascribed to salvific experience partly relative to the assertions about which are the true views, but salvation is also relative to the character of the problematic situation from which one is to be saved. Thus, whereas a Madhyamika Buddhist might say that salvation is from the sorrow stemming from (misplaced) attachment to (illusory) enduring realities, a medieval Thomist might say that salvation is from a self-centeredness that causes one to be detached from the enduring realities in which God is incarnate and whom one should love. The religious question, of course, is much more complex than this; it is a matter of the competition between taos of faith and practice. Religious success, however, cannot be used as a simple pragmatic criterion for choosing between an interpretation of things as empty versus an interpretation of experience as filled with enduring loci of the divine.[16]

Claims with regard to truth, therefore, need to be mediated by the broad apparatus of philosophy and complex cultural experience. This was recognized early in both the West and India; Nagarjuna's

Mūlamadhyamakakārikās is as near a classic experience of this task as the work of Parmenides or Plato. There are at least two ways of responding to Nagarjuna's chief arguments. One, expressive of the transcendental turn, interprets Nagarjuna's intent to be the soteriological goal of causing people to abandon attachment to views of reality altogether. According to Frederick J. Streng, for instance, Nagarjuna's inspiration was rather like Wittgenstein's, to show people that language does not refer to extralinguistic realities.[17] Rather, words are interdefined and interreferring, and the attempt to see them as referring to ontological realities outside themselves is one of the main sources of self-deception. By use of negative logical arguments, Nagarjuna demonstrated the futility of speculative thinking. Dilworth notes that this is partly true and that the deontologizing motive is strong in Nagarjuna. But there also is a pro-ontologizing motive. Dilworth writes:

> Despite its rejection of ontological pluralism, monism, and nihilism, however, the Mahayana position is not free from its own kind of ambivalence. A pro-ontological conception of "true reality" has crept back into the discussion. . . . A difficulty for the interpretation arises here in that this vivid pro-ontological claim is commingled by Mahayana philosophers with their de-ontological critique of dharmas. They say that the Absolute is the *Nirvana-dharma-dhātu*, the inmost essence of all things, the unconditioned, limitless, undivided, unutterable Reality. This Mahayana Absolute is experienced through *prajñā*, the "non-discriminatory wisdom" or "enlightenment." Needless to say, however, the experiential claim to enlightenment does not carry its own intellectual justification. The Mahayana tradition is clear on the point that such an appeal to "non-discriminatory wisdom" is itself a discriminatory claim – and thus as meaningless as other predications about the Absolute within the relative order of discourse. . . . Nagarjuna's dialectical logic of negations is designed to free the mind up from intellectual discriminations, and thus to reinforce the religious wayfarer's appreciation of the possibility of attaining the fruition of the yogic experience in his/her own awakening.[18]

Acknowledging the inconsistency of Nagarjuna's position, Dilworth, however, wants to reassert it again on a higher level by claiming that all speculative thought takes place within paradigms, that Nagarjuna's paradigm is one among several, and that none can be asserted as preferable except from the standpoint of yet another arbitrary paradigm.[19]

But is it the case that all speculative paradigms are arbitrary and relative? At the very least we can consciously move from one to the other, with a continuity in cross-paradigmatic thinking that is not itself immediately reducible to any of the paradigms crossed. In various practical senses we approve certain paradigms over others because of the fruitfulness of their interpretation of experience. This would seem logically impossible if the only factors were brute experiential data preformed by a given paradigm's categories and by the paradigm itself. In this case all thinking and experience would be dictated in form by a given paradigm. But many diverse factors contribute to the forms of experience at many levels, including the theoretical. One of the most forceful contributors of form is the need to make prima facie sense of ordinary experience, in particular, of the causal factors in nature and human effort and of change in general. Now, it may be the case that causation and change are inherently irrational. If a theory can be proposed that renders them rational, is not that paradigm to be preferred to those according to which they are irrational? What would be the justification for rejecting a theory if not that it is irrational to accept it?[20]

The answer sometimes offered to this rhetorical question is that the whole business of theories or paradigms is a mistaken enterprise, that speculative theories about the nature of the world are inherently misguided. But then, if someone were to propose a theory that does not lead to egregious logical or practical difficulty, and if that someone could couple the theory with a theory about how theories interpret the nature of reality, would not the speculative enterprise have made a straightforward advance?

That is precisely what process philosophy claims to have done.[21] According to process philosophy, the reason for both the ancient Buddhist and the contemporary transcendental interest in denying the validity of speculative metaphysics is that they suffered from impoverished metaphysical ideas. With improved ideas there should be no such antispeculative or deontological motive. (That soteriological interests require deontologizing is criticized below.)

Let us, then, review the problem with respect to Nagarjuna and Whitehead, arranging a dialogue between them (and apologizing for the terse technicalities) that centers on ten points of debate. In the first two chapters of the *Mūlamadhyamakakārikās*, Nagarjuna attacked the conceptions of conditioning causes and change, showing that on certain assumptions of what they must be, they are impossible. Does his negative argument apply to process philosophy's conception of causation and change?

To be more specific about Whiteheadian process philosophy, an occasion of experience (or an actual entity) comes to be with both passive and active factors. The previous actual occasions are objects to be prehended or felt by the emerging occasion; although they do not act, they constitute the given initial data from which the new occasion emerges through transforming, eliminating, and/or integrating them. Each set of data has various possibilities of integration to which the emerging occasion must conform. But the activity of the actual integration, by which the initial data are transformed into a pattern that satisfies the requirements of integrity, is the creative self-constitution of the emerging occasion; this is the active factor. The previous occasions are conditions for the emerging occasion, but the emerging occasion itself transforms the previous occasions into conditions by incorporating them in its integral nature, objectified for subsequent prehension. In some cases the emerging occasion has considerable leeway as to what role the antecedent conditions will play in its constitution. (The crucial factor in Whitehead's analysis, one lacking in the Buddhist analysis, is the creativity exercised within each occasion's coming to be.)

1. Turning to Nagarjuna, he argued, first, that a cause can neither possess its own cause nor can it *not* possess its own cause.[22] For process philosophy, however, a cause in one sense possesses its own causes, in that it incorporates them in its own integral reality, enjoying them as their subject. In another sense it does not possess them because they are objective for it, their own subjective reality having passed away when they achieved their own satisfactory integrity.

2. Next, Nagarjuna argued that a conditioning cause is such only when that which it conditions comes upon them, but that it would not have existed before conditioning anything. Further, when the conditioning cause exists, its effect is not yet, and when its effect exists, the cause has passed.[23] But this is no paradox for process philosophy. The subjective reality (the reality as subject of experience) of a condition passes when it achieves objectivity, and it has objectivity in the sense of being available for prehension ever after. It does not actually condition anything until prehended into a new occasion, however. Whereas the subjective reality of the condition passes away, its objective reality is everlasting, and its efficacy as a condition depends on the subjective creativity of subsequent prehending occasions, not on any impoverished life of its own.

3. Nagarjuna said: "If an element occurs which is neither real nor nonreal nor both real-and-non real, how can there be a cause which is effective in this situation?"[24] If the element is a Whiteheadian occasion, it is subjectively real and objectively nonreal in its occurrence and subjectively

nonreal and objectively real when it has achieved satisfaction. An antecedent cause for that occasion cannot be effective creatively in the coming to be of the occasion, because all efficacy of that sort belongs to the subjective life of the emergent. But it can be effective in the sense of a resource and determining limit. If the condition is objectified by the emerging occasion, then it is effective yet beyond the first occasion it conditions.

4. Nagarjuna said: "Just that which is without an object of sensation is accepted as a real element; then if there is an element having no object of sensation, how is it possible to have an object of sensation?"[25] Whitehead would answer that a conditioning cause, in itself, is an objective datum, possibly possessing no intentional character. But when it is prehended, the form by which it is integrated with other things prehended may be such that it functions propositionally as an object of intention. Being an object of intention does not entail being intentional (or mental), because intentionality is a function of the subjective form of its being prehended.

5. If an element has appeared and disappeared, said Nagarjuna, there could be no immediately preceding cause of it; for if there were the cause, it would not have ceased.[26] Because, for process philosophy, what "arises and falls" with respect to dharmas is the subjective immediacy of their self-creative coming to be, and since this self-creativity is unique to each thing, an immediately preceding cause must have disappeared subjectively in order to be an objective condition. The effectiveness of the condition is temporary with respect to its being grasped by the self-creativity in the coming to be of the effect, and once the effect has reached its own integration, both the immediately preceding cause and the newly finished effect are objectively immortal as potential conditions for further occasions.

6. If a thing derives its existence from another, said Nagarjuna, it has no existence of its own and hence cannot exist.[27] For Whitehead, the subjective existential activity producing an integrated new datum is an occasion's own self-creativity, which is not derived from anything else. But the conditions integrated are derived from past acts of creativity and are the objective data. The objective data of the past are carried forward insofar as the new occasion does not eliminate or transform them, but rather objectifies them in its own satisfied integration.

7. If the product does not reside in its causes, asked Nagarjuna, how can it result from them?[28] Process philosophy answers that the antecedent occasions are the conditions making up the product, but the subjec-

tive reality of making up the product derives from the product's own self-creative act of integrating the antecedents.

8. Since a product consists of its conditioning causes, said Nagarjuna, and since those causes in turn consist of their own causes, indefinitum, how can anything come to be a product?[29] By the fact, answers process philosophy, that each occasion in the causal chain constitutes its own novel subjective reality out of whatever antecedents it has by its own creative act. Nothing could come to be without antecedents, since it would have nothing to integrate. But the antecedents alone do not cause the sui generis occasion.

9. If a condition does not produce its effect, how can it cause (or not cause) when no product is produced, asked Nagarjuna?[30] Products are produced out of the conditions by their own creativity, says Whitehead. The conditions cause by being incorporated in the new occasion. If no occasion incorporates them, they are no less objective and available for prehension than otherwise.

10. Nagarjuna's analysis of motion or "going to" in Chapter 2 can be dealt with more briefly. There is no motion without that which moves, he said; yet that which moves is not a mover without moving. Further, no motion takes place except insofar as movement is achieved; yet once the motion is achieved there is no more anything. This is a familiar Western theme for which process philosophy has a clear alternative treatment. The subject of an occasion itself emerges as the integration within which its coming to be takes place. There is no agent in an occasion doing the integration; rather, the occasion is the arising of a new integration which is the emergent entity. The sense of motion involved in coming to be is not existent motion, for only the achieved change from the antecedent conditions "exists." Rather, it is simply a subjective coming to be of an objective new datum. Existent motion, on the other hand, is the measurable change from the antecedent conditions to the situation with the newly emerged occasion. Any talk of agents that move must refer not to individual occasions but to trains of objectified emerged occasions. The subjective immediacy of coming to be is not something done by agent movers but the emergence of subjects of the integration process.

Nagarjuna's other arguments concerning the reality of dharmas and other features of the world depend similarly upon criticizing positions unlike process cosmology. Since the process cosmology can give pima facie explanation of them (or at least of causation and motion), it is immune from his attack; therefore, one cannot conclude, on Nagarjuna's authority, that all speculative views are false.

Dilworth interprets the situation as follows. Nagarjuna, like F. H. Bradley, assumes that any real relation must be an internal one. For instance, the product must be *in* the cause, or it is not related to the cause. Whitehead, however, said that subsequent prehending occasions are external to the objective constitution of the conditions, though the conditions are internal to the prehending effects. Dilworth puts this down to a difference in paradigm; but that obscures the logical situation. Why would Nagarjuna or Bradley believe that all relations must be symmetrically internal? Either they could not think of a logical alternative, such as Whitehead's asymmetrical view, or they believed that the symmetrically internal relations view better interprets phenomena. Whitehead's theory is indeed a logical alternative (unless someone shows it to be contradictory); it does not require one to say paradoxical things about causation or motion.

Of course, there is no reason to suspect that Whitehead's theory is anything more certain than a hypothesis that is dialectically superior to a finite set of alternatives. Surely it will be improved on, and it has been subjected to criticisms. It does seem to be superior to the theory Nagarjuna showed to be paradoxical. Hence, Nagarjuna's claim to have proved all dharmas empty, in the sense of their being self-contradictory, is unjustified. We can, in fact, entertain a cosmological theory of process that interprets basic categories such as causation and motion with prima facie plausibility. As has been remarked, this process cosmology allows that things are empty in the sense of not having any "own being"; it does not allow that speculative thinking must be misguided, contradictory, or erroneous.

As a result, the transcendental interpretation of Nagarjuna is not as interesting as the ontological interpretation. If Nagarjuna objected to speculative thinking, it should not have been on intrinsic grounds, as his apparently logical arguments allege. The objection would have to be based on other, perhaps soteriological, grounds.

Streng interprets the positive side of Nagarjuna's visions as an articulation of the interconnectedness of all things. Sunyata, he suggests, can be translated, following Stcherbatsky, as "relativity."[31] Rather than allow metaphysical theories to stand between ourselves and the world, especially other people, he urges, we should see our language merely as the medium making the connection.

The conclusions of this part of the discussion are that, though process philosophy agrees that process is empty, it disputes that strain in Buddhism which says process is illusory or that theories asserting and interpreting the causal flow are logically inappropriate. Nagarjuna's refutation of causation and change fails with respect to the theories of causation and change in process philosophy.

III. Unity and Interpenetration

Thomas J. J. Altizer, while likening Whitehead's theory of process to early dharma theory, points out that his greatest parallel with Buddhism lies in his religious vision of the interconnection of all things. In the most imaginative treatment of the encounter of process philosophy and Buddhism prior to Odin's *Process Metaphysics and Hwa-Yen Buddhism*, Altizer notes that Whitehead and Mahayana Buddhism uniquely identify the factual and the religious and that both characterize religiously ultimate elements in terms of interrelation and the coincidence of opposites.

In Altizer's view, Whitehead was fundamentally a religious thinker. But the imaginative ground for Whitehead's religious vision is not to be found in the West. For Altizer, the West has been ineluctably wedded to concept of transcendence, dichotomizing God and nature, sacred and profane, real and apparent. Rather, the imaginative ground for Whitehead's vision is to be found in Buddhism, not Christianity. Not that Whitehead learned his vision from Buddhism, but that his vision is uniquely available and publicly penetrable through the language and imagery of Buddhism.[32]

Altizer's remarks suggest a different way of interpreting Nagarjuna. Whereas the particular, symmetrical, internal-relations theory attacked by Nagarjuna accentuates dichotomies and the transcendence of the genuinely religious from the flowing world, destruction of that theory and its way of thinking allows the spiritual dimension to appear in the immediacy of fact. This might have been Nagarjuna's intent. As Dilworth points out, that is what the yogic experience is supposed to reveal.

In light of the discussion above of process and *pratītya samutpāda*, however, two new complexities arise regarding the parallel between Buddhism and Whitehead on interrelation. The first arises from a point best made by Altizer:

Already in *Religion in the Making*, Whitehead says that the realization of the togetherness or the interdependence of the universe is the contribution of religion to metaphysics. . . Cosmic relatedness is the core of Whitehead's cosmology, which is concerned with the becoming, the being, and the relatedness of what he terms actual entities. . . . Whitehead believed that "everlastingness" (the "many" absorbed everlastingly in the final unity) is the actual content out of which the higher religions historically evolved. Now in this context it might be instructive to examine Whitehead's doctrine that the salvation of reality lies in its obstinate, irreducible, matter-of-fact entities. Is this doctrine grounded in a religious apprehension of the togetherness of the universe, leading to an understanding of actually as complete togetherness? . . . What else but a religious vision could not only make manifest the totality of the interrelatedness of the universe but also unveil the intrinsic and even total interrelatedness of matter-of-fact entities? Do we not find lying at the center of Whitehead's vision a non-dualistic apprehension of the union or coinherence of the macrocosmic and the microcosmic, of the outer and the inner, of the beyond and the near at hand which has no genuine precedent in the Western historical tradition?[33]

It is the religious vision of interrelatedness that Altizer believes has imaginative grounding in Buddhism but not in the Western imagination.

Unfortunately, Altizer's interpretation of Whitehead is incomplete. First, with regard to the existential coming to be of things, occasions are entirely separate from contemporaries. They prehend only the finished past and can be prehended only by future occasions when they themselves have perished in their subjective immediacy. The cosmic interrelatedness, therefore, pertains only to occasions that are finished insofar as they are objectively resident in other prehending subjects. Whitehead's conception of God provides a model by which all things that are finished can be prehended without loss and, once they have occurred, are everlasting in the experience of God. But this leaves out of the relation both the immediacy of occasions' existence and their projections toward the future which, if they are related, are only potentially so.[34] Second, because it requires a separate act of self-creation for one occasion to be a subject entertaining other occasions in an interrelated way, this aspect of Whitehead's theory is ineluctibly dualistic. With respect to the doctrine that God is the everlasting subject making it possible for each fleeting occasion of the world to be entertained immortally, the finitude and over-against-ness of God leads to a dualism even stronger than Western theories that represent God as a higher principle in which finite things participate. Altizer would interpret Whitehead as using God language to set forth a Buddhist perspective, not a doctrine of a transcendent God. Yet, if one eliminates those elements from Whitehead's philosophical theology that set God off as an other over against the world, one also eliminates those elements allowing for cosmic interrelatedness. Process philosophy must find a different conceptuality from its theism to articulate Whitehead's and Buddhism's aesthetics of inter-relatedness.

The second complexity for interrelation and process philosophy builds on the first. As mentioned, process philosophy's conception of causation is asymmetrical. That is, later moments are in part external to earlier ones, whereas earlier ones are internal to later ones that prehend them. Interrelation is thus a function of earlier moments being prehended into unity by later moments or by God in the divine consequent nature. Temporal flow is fully real, for process philosophy, not only in the subjective immediacy of coming to be but in the characters of relations between temporal moments. This stands in contrast to the scale of inter-relatedness in at least one school of Mahayana Buddhism – the Hwa Yen. Hwa Yen's distinctive contribution is its elaboration of the doctrine of mutual interpenetration.

In his *The Buddhist Teaching of Totality*, Garma C. C. Chang notes the similarity of Hwa Yen's doctrine of mutual interpenetration to Whitehead's organic philosophy.[35] But the parallel breaks down with regard to the symmetrical inclusion of past and future in each other. The first of the "ten mysteries" of Hwa Yen is "the mystery of simultaneous completion and mutual correspondence." Chang says of this principle:

> [it] implies not only the Non-Obstruction of space and time but more significantly, it implies the simultaneous existence of all causes and effects, regardless of kind or of realm, must be simultaneously established without hindrance or omission. Should we consider this to be a form of absolute determinism? From men's viewpoint, this certainly appears to be the case. How can effects in the future be brought into the past without first being determined? Here again we enounter the familiar Svabhāva way of thinking: determinativeness precedes all entities and events.[36]

Francis H. Cook, who also notes the parallel between Hwa Yen and Whitehead, stresses Fa-tsang's use of the part-whole construction to interpret interpenetration.[37] Just as a rafter is not a rafter except insofar as it is in place in a building, so the building is not what it is except insofar as it has that rafter. Now the part-whole model, being a spatial form, is not necessarily expressive of the temporal dimension. But Cook draws out its temporal implications in his discussion of the bodhisattva. If a bodhisattva at any stage already contains the later stages, what is the point of effort and vows? He quotes Fa-tsang:

> If one stage is acquired, all stages are acquired, because (each stage) possesses the six characteristics (of universality and particularity, etc.),

because of the infinite interrelationship of primary and secondary, because of mutual interpenetration, because of mutual identity, and because of mutual interfusion. The *Avatamsaka Sūtra* says, "One stage includes the qualities of all stages throughout." Therefore, what is meant here is the acquisition of all stages as well as the stage of Buddhahood as soon as one has reached that part (of the path) which is called "superior progress," which is the perfection of faith. Because all stages including the stage of Buddhahood are identical, then cause and effect are not different, and beginning and end interpenetrate. On each stage, one is both a Bodhisattva and a Buddha.[38]

Cook's answer to that question is a somewhat thin expression of the commitment to complete the path and to live *as if* one were already the Buddha.[39]

As Hartshorne and others argue, human action, even that of a bodhisattva, is morally significant and responsible only if the results of the action depend in part on a choice that could have been made another way. Further, as Hartshorne points out, Buddhism and Whitehead have been at one in their recognition that the base of moral motivation is the identity of any future outcomes with oneself, undercutting all egoistic theories which might claim that some special outcomes are in one's self-interest.[40] Compassion is a metaphysical truth, not merely a psychological achievement. Essential to this view of responsibility and compassion is the recognition of asymmetry in the causal, temporal process. As we noted in Section II, that Nagarjuna did not refute the claim that nature involves asymmetrical causal procession, we may now note that at least within the moral sphere one ought to adhere to such a view of asymmetry.

In a crucial sense, however, we should not say that past and future interpenetrate. We should deny that the future must be fully determinate in the past. Put another way, from the standpoint of our present activity, there are some relations that will come to be in the future that are not determined now. Thus responsibility for the future rests partly in our own activity and cannot be traced back to infinitely remote prior causes, as in an everlasting and reversible game of billiards. Process philosophy has helped articulate the importance of nondeterminism in causality.[41] This suggests that it is a mistake for Buddhism, a la Altizer or Hwa Yen, to interpret interpenetration or interrelation as entailing the symmetry of earlier and later times.

Perhaps Buddhism need not interpret causality that way. As Fa-tsang said (cited by Chang; italics are mine):

The mystery of simultaneous completeness means that all the above mentioned ten principles simultaneously establish themselves in correspondence, to form a (totalistic) dependent-arising, without the differentiation of past or future, beginning or end. In this dimension, all and all establish themselves in perfect consistency and freedom. This establishment of totalistic dependent-arising makes all things and principles mutually penetrate into one another, *yet does not upset their orders in any individual realm.*[42]

What Fa-tsang *should* mean by this (whatever he, in fact, meant), I believe, is that within the causal realm of process, particularly moral process, there exists whatever indeterminacy and asymmetry as would be found in an ordinary analysis, *and that the mutual penetration is to be understood on a different level.* The theory of creation *ex nihilo* expresses this distinction. Let me review.

Anything that has an identity – any occasion, eternal object, dharma – is determinate. For a thing to be determinate is for it to be itself in relation to as least one other thing, to be determinate with respect to something. To have an identity, therefore, is to be a complex of two kinds of features, conditional features and essential features. Conditional features are those a thing has by virtue of the things with respect to which it is determinate. Essential features are those it has intrinsic to itself by virtue of which it can stand in relation to what conditions it. Without essential features, a thing could not be different from other things and therefore could not relate to them as being conditioned. Without conditional features, a thing could not be determinate with respect to anything.

A thing is a de facto harmony of essential and conditional features. This statement has two aspects. First, the thing would not be determinate at all without both. Without essential features, the conditional features would not be different from the set of other things with respect to which the thing is supposed to be determinate. Without conditional features, the essential features would not be determinately different from anything else, hence not determinate in any way. Thus, determinateness itself, the very being of determinate being, requires the de facto harmony of both kinds of feature.

The second aspect is that the harmony is called "de facto" because it cannot be grounded in either the conditional features or the essential features. The harmony of both together is a condition for both. The conditional features, which are what we often refer to as "external causes" contribute to the harmony but do not sufficiently account for it because they do not cause the essential features. With the conditional features alone, there would be no new determinate thing, only the things with respect to which it *would* be determinate *if* it were determinate. The essential features do not account for the harmony because they are indeterminate except insofar as they are already harmonized with the conditional features. They presuppose their togetherness with conditional features and therefore cannot account for it. Lacking all "account," the de facto harmonies are "empty" in the profoundest ontological sense. Emptiness should not be thought to consist in the fact that each thing reduces completely to its conditional features and thus to the things that condition it. This is a common but erroneous interpretation of *pratītya samutpāda*. Neither does emptiness consist in the identification of a thing with its essential features which are indeterminate and thus mystically merged with the essential features of all things. The first leads to nihilism and the second to mystical eternalism. The "middle way" is to acknowledge that emptiness consists in what the philosophical theology of creation reveals as the de facto harmony of essential and conditional features.

These distinctions are illustrated in Chapter 3 along with the conceptions of process philosophy. An *occasion* is a de facto harmony of antecedent occasions prehended, plus those features that determine the subjective form by which the prehensions are integrated. The occasions prehended are the conditional features, though how they condition the occasion depends on how they are determined to fit together in and by the emerging subject. The essential features that can determine the fit may be of three kinds. Essential features stemming from the past are past occasions prehended objectively, which also function to determine the emerging subjective form; continuity of an individual through time, for instance, expresses some of these reiterating, essential features. Essential features stemming from the future are those determining obligation and what Whitehead called the "superjective character" of the process of integration. Most interesting, however, are the essential features stemming from the immediate moment of coming to be. They are spontaneous relative to what the past entails and creative of whatever new realities of integration come to be that allow the new occasion to emerge. The subjective immediacy of coming to be is the reality of, and sometimes the awareness of, the emerging de facto harmony of essential and conditional features.

A further distinction may now be drawn, which is crucial for rendering the Buddhist sense of interrelationship. The character a thing has, and all the relations involved in that character, may be called cosmological, as I have argued. This includes both essential and conditional features and all the causal and other determinate ways in which things are related to one another. However, *that* a thing is, with whatever cosmological nature it has, is ontological. A thing can be understood in both a cosmological and a ontological dimension. Understanding *what* it is, is cosmological; understanding *that* it is, is ontological.

From a cosmological perspective, as a de facto harmony, a thing is empty. The same characteristic viewed ontologically, however, reveals something different, namely that to be at all, things must be in an ontological context of mutual relevance deeper than their cosmological, relative conditioning. The proof is as follows. Consider two things, each of which has conditional features relative to the other. The cosmological relations between them are limited to those conditional features, for instance, how one limits the other. The cosmological relations make possible the determinate relations between the two de facto harmonies; but, for there to be cosmological relations, the conditional features must be determinate, which is possible only when the conditional features are in harmony with the essential features. Therefore, for cosmological relations to be positive, there must be an ontologically enabling context in which the two things, with their essential features, are mutually together. the ontological context of mutual relevance is a togetherness of determinate things more basic than their conditional relations, because it also involves a togetherness of their essential features. For a thing to be determinate as a harmony of essential features, it must be together with other things, not only conditionally but with regard to essential features.

The Buddhist aesthetic vision of the interrelationship of things in their immediate factual character is, I submit, an appreciation of the ontological context of mutual relevance, even if Buddhist metaphors and philosophical categories do not achieve this radical perspective. It is a basic ontological vision of what it is to be determinate, to be a dharma. It is also compatible with any cosmological relations we might find to exist, because all cosmological relations are matters of conditional features. Consider whether a future state of affairs is completely determined in an antecedent state. If it is (the doctrine of causal symmetry), then the later and earlier states have de facto harmonies determined entirely by their conditional features relative to each other; or, at least, the essential features of the later state make no objective difference. If the causal process is asymmetrical, however, there are some important essential features in later events that do not derive from earlier ones.

If there are independent cosmological reasons for preferring an asymmetrical, nondeterministic account of process, this is perfectly compatible with the deeper ontological interrelatedness or interpenetration that consists in the ontological context of mutual relevance. In the case of indeterminism, the later event would not be able to have those novelty-producing essential features that make it different from the antecedent event if the earlier and later events were not ontologically together in a context of mutual relevant. If they were not in that context, then the novelty-producing essential features would be indeterminate and hence incapable of producing novelty.

IV. Creation

The metaphors of whole versus part and of all-time-together versus a finite time are cosmological metaphors, taking their force from conditional features of spatial and temporal relation. The abstract categories defining "ontological context of mutual relevance" can indicate that the religious vision grasps a genuinely ontological interrelatedness, not cosmological connections.

There is an even greater religious depth to the ontological dimension. The phrase "ontological context of mutual relevance" connotes the passivity of being a presupposition. To grasp or envision the ontological dimension is to become aware of the immediacy of reality. Without the ontological context, there would be nothing, no de facto harmonies, no conditional features, no essential features, no dharmas. The immediate facticity of things – their dappled presence, their shining forth – suggests what has been construed in the West as divine creativity. It has been common to construe divine creativity cosmologically; that is, God is interpreted as one entity causing others, often in a temporal sense. But if God is a determinate causal entity, then God must be in an ontological context of mutual relevance with the world, and that ontological context would be more "creative" than God. Whitehead believed that God interpreted as a cosmological actual entity must be different from the creativity that underlies the prehensive relations between God and the world.[43]

Divine creativity need not be interpreted cosmologically, however. The mystical tradition, and in their most reflective moments many of the great Western theologians, have interpreted creativity ontologically. That is, the "presence" of God in the world is the world's own "acts of existence." But precisely because the ontological possibility of things requires that they be in an ontological context of mutual relevance, the creative act by which things are is "unified." The unity is not in the cosmological characters of the created things, for the creative spontaneity of some things is over here rather than over there and at this time rather than some other time; rather, the unity is at the level of the ontological context of mutual relevance. In Whitehead's view, the immediate creative spontaneity of an occasion must combine with the occasions it prehends, and each occasion is a combination of its own spontaneity with what it, in turn, previously prehended. Whereas the dates and places of creative manifestations are diverse, the connection in the ontological context of mutual relevance is unified. Otherwise, creativity would not ground the de facto harmonies of things whose essential features are cosmologically disjunctive.

The ontological function of divine creativity, as appreciated in yogic awareness, or enlightenment, stands in an advanced relation to both Buddhism and Western thought. Since there is no determinate divine creator who transcends the de facto, empty, created dharmas, it is true to say, on the theory proposed, that Nirvana is samsara. But the theory rejects any attempts to render the underlying unity of the world in a cosmological way, to deny differences, to say, as in the common water-wave metaphor, that absolute unity is real and that phenomenal diversity is extrinsically caused. Differences are precisely what is created, yet the unity of the creative act constituting the ontological context of mutual relevance is not to be reduced to the cosmological plurality of the thises and thats.

On the theory proposed, the appeal to creativity is not an attempt to explain things by a determinate principle of creativity; as determinate, any principle would have to be among the things explained. Rather, it is an appeal to what for lack of a better term can be called a creative or decisive "action." To know that is not to grasp a principle but to locate and respond in wonder to an act. Buddhistic enlightenment captures very well the empirical sense of *finding* the ontological ground, not grasping it rationally.

With respect to Western thought, it is plausible to interpret divine creativity as God. Insofar as "God" is supposed to be a determinate entity with a character apart from the product of creative exercise, it is incompatible with our theory which is then atheistic. But there are many precedents in Western thought for construing God as determinate only in the world and as indeterminate apart from the world. Since names are bestowed and not claimed, it is best to leave it to others to label our theory.

By way of conclusion, I simply note that the service process philosophy can perform for Buddhism is to force it to a recognition of the difference between cosmology and ontology and to abandon its sometimes too-cute attack on speculative thinking when it means to be attacking only a cosmological rendition of religion. Whitehead has provided, even with various modifications, a theory that adequately articulates the Buddhist insights regarding process and causation, its doctrine of *pratītya samutpāda*. What Buddhism can do for process philosophy is not merely to provide it with allies in its repunctuating of the history of the West, but to call it to abandon the inadequate conceptions of God as distinct from creativity and develop a more profound ontology. For thinkers unconcerned about "representing" positions, East or West, the encounter of Buddhism with process philosophy has already made a creative advance beyond what each philosophy originally brought to the encounter. This is a middle way between the eternalistic theory that "all is one", which mistakenly denies the truth of event pluralism in process, and the nihilism of the modern West which, noting the death of the cosmological God, concludes that nothing is holy.

Chapter Ten
The Daimon and the Tao of Faith

TO CREATE A DIALOGUE between the most metaphysical forms of Mahayana Buddhism, the Madhyamika and the Hwa Yen, and one of the most advanced twentieth-century Western speculative traditions – process philosophy – illustrates a certain mood of philosophical theology. An unrelieved metaphysical mood! Chapter 9, which did this, came round again in its metaphysical way to advertise the virtues of the abstract theory of ontological creation, of God the creator (to use Western terms). Buddhism is a concrete tao of faith and practice. Can philosophical theology make a contribution to understanding its concrete encounter with the daimon introducing the metaphysics of creation only in response to concrete problems of understanding the tao? In this chapter we explore the tao of faith in Mahayana; Chapter 11 explores the tao of practice.

The Treatise on Awakening Mahayana Faith is an ancient, central, and influential text in Mahayana Buddhism.[1] The West has no single treatise of equal importance on the subject, though certain discussions of faith, such as that in *Job* or in Paul's *Letter to the Romans*, have been important subjects for discussion. The importance of *The Treatise* justifies examination of its treatment of faith as a path to the topic of faith in Mahayana Buddhism. Since the following discussion involves close analysis of the text, readers who lack first-hand knowledge will have to decide whether to accept my interpretation for the sake of following the argument or inquire into other interpretations in order to decide about the text itself.

Three fundamental Buddhist theses about faith are particularly interesting because of their near parallels and significant contrasts with Western conceptions. The first is the thesis that faith is a preparation, a means of ascent through early stages of spiritual development, to be superseded by stages wherein faith is not needed as a hedge against backsliding. The second thesis is that faith is a kind of certainty and stands in contrast to doubt. Third is that faith is the vehicle for abandoning wrong attachments and thus is more a practical force than a cognitive state of certainty. Although these three theses are obviously connected, they may be examined in turn.

I. Faith as Preparation

The cosmology underlying Mahayana conceptions of spirituality involves a stepwise progression through many stages. Mythologically, if not literally, this is represented as requiring many lifetimes. With regard to faith, the great watershed is the step from being "undetermined" in the Buddhist faith (*aniyata rāśi*) to being "determined" (*niyata rāśi*).[2] The external mark of "undetermined people" is that they remain in danger of backsliding to no faith; their reincarnational destiny may take a turn for the worse. By contrast, "determined" people cannot backslide. As *The Treatise on Awakening Mahayana Faith* describes them:

> Those who are thus able to develop their aspiration through the perfection of faith will enter the group of the determined and will never retrogress. They are called the ones who are united with the correct cause [for enlightenment] and who abide among those who belong to the Tathagata family.[3]

Only after ten thousand aeons (or a very long time) of perfecting faith in the "undetermined" state can the transition be made to the kind of faith characteristic of the "determined."

Sung-bae Park advances a helpful interpretive thesis to explain the internal characteristics distinguishing the "undetermined" from the "determined." In its title and first three chapters, *The Treatise* characterizes the perfected faith of the "determined" Bodhisattvas. That faith consists in the realization of nonduality or the nondualistic consciousness as discussed in those chapters.[4] The fourth chapter, "On Faith and Practice," characterizes faith of the sort to be perfected by the "undetermined"; Park translates the relevant passage as follows:

> Briefly speaking, there are four faiths . . . . (1) To believe in the Ultimate Source, in other words, to be mindful, with the utmost willingness, of the principle of Suchness. (2) To believe that the Buddha has innumerable excellent virtues, in other words, to think always of being close to the Buddha, to make offerings to him, and to respect him. Furthermore, it means to awaken the capacity for goodness, which is wishing to have the omnis-

cience that the Buddha has. (3) To believe that the Dharma is the source of great benefits, in other words, to think always of practicing all the perfections. (4) To believe that the Sangha is able to correctly practice the Mahayana ideal of benefitting both oneself and others, in other words, to rejoice always at being close to the assembly of Bodhisattvas and to pursue genuine practice as it does.[5]

What is characteristic of these four faiths is that they primarily involve intellectual assent. Assent given in faith can also be taken away; hence, the ever-present danger of backsliding. That backsliding is possible *because* faith is intellectual assent is an important point, and we will return to it. The faith characterized in the first three chapters of *The Treatise*, by contrast, is not assent but realization, and experience cannot be "de-realized."

At this preliminary stage in the discussion an important contrast with Christian thinking can be introduced. Christians would tend to say that no stage can be reached in this life for which backsliding is not a danger. The reason for this is a central theme of Western culture, namely, that faith is a function of will as well as knowledge. Will is somewhat distinct from both cognition and desires, and however these are integrated within a person, the will with its faith always has the capacity to be abstracted from and set against the whole.[6] Therefore, as the faith becomes stronger and the will freer, the danger of backsliding and the real demonic spirit become all the greater. Satan was the spirit next in rank to God. In contexts where faith was associated with intellectual assent, the will was the faculty making the assent precisely because the cognitive faculties could not grasp it; when we come to see things face to face, faith will be unnecessary. In the context where for Christians faith means a reordering of the person so as to appropriate God's forgiveness and be born again, faith is the principle of psychic integrity. Because the will can assent to falsehoods, however, and because psychic integrity can be misprincipled and always stands in danger of coming unravelled, will is always fallible and faith is liable to error and backsliding.

Is there anything in the Mahayana conception of faith that avoids this consequence? For the "undetermined," faith can clearly be construed as a matter of will. According to the passage quoted above from Chapter 4 of *The Treatise on Awakening Mahayana Faith*, the first faith has to do with paying attention. The second recommends imitating the Buddha, the third counsels effort, and the fourth encourages confidence in certain personal associations. These are all nuances of will and involve binding the person to activities the fulfillment and worth of which are not immediately present. Thus, a person's faith can backslide.

According to Park's interpretation, the "awakening of Mahayana faith" has to do not with the faith of the "undetermined" as such but rather with the transition from that faith to the faith of the "determined."⁷ In Asvaghosha's text the transition is discussed explicitly in the final main section of Chapter 3, "On Interpretation." Here, the transition to enlightenment is analyzed in terms of three paths. One is faith, the second is understanding and deeds, the third is immediate insight. The first path takes one to the stage of being determined in the faith; the second and third paths are aspirations guiding the higher stages of determined life. Whereas the first, as we have seen, allows for backsliding, the second and third do not.

Or do they? Consider "the aspiration for enlightenment through understanding and deeds."⁸ People at this stage are characterized essentially (*t'i*) by a "profound understanding of the principle of suchness" and functionally (*yung*) by "no attachment to their attainments obtained by discipline." This is then explained by a series of *t'i-yung* relationships between items of knowledge and corresponding devotions of activities or functions:

1. "Knowing that the essential nature of Reality is free from covetousness, they, in conformity to it, devote themselves to the perfection of charity."
2. "Knowing that the essential nature of Reality is free from the defilements which originate from the desires of the five senses, they, in conformity to it, devote themselves to the perfection of precepts."
3. "Knowing that the essential nature of Reality is without suffering and free from anger and anxiety, they, in conformity to it, devote themselves to the perfection of forebearance."
4. "Knowing that the essential nature of Reality does not have any distinction of body and mind and is free from indolence, they, in conformity to it, devote themselves to the perfection of zeal."
5. "Knowing that the essential nature of Reality is always calm and free from confusion in its essence, they, in conformity to it, devote themselves to the perfection of meditation."
6. "Knowing that the essential nature of Reality is always characterized by gnosis and is free from ignorance, they, in conformity to it, devote themselves to the perfection of wisdom."⁹

Since people at this stage still need work on their charity, precepts, forbearance, zeal, meditation and wisdom, it is clear that they can backslide with respect to these virtues. But the sense in which they cannot backslide, the passage implies, is that, given their knowledge, they are unassailable in their devotion. Knowledge expresses itself without fail in devotion in the appropriate senses.

Yet, is this so? What can devotion mean except that in the face of imperfect charity, for instance, one wills to act charitably, hoping that the genuine charitable springs will develop? To be "devoted" in these cases means to will oneself to become perfect when one's natural or spontaneous behavior is still imperfect in the relevant respects. And cannot this devotion cease or become perverted? That one knows the essential nature of reality, knows what one ought to be, knows one can in fact attain that with proper effort, entails that it would be *irrational* to fail one's devotion. But that does not imply that one *cannot* fail one's devotions. We often do what is irrational. The very mark of the possibility of irrational behavior is the imperfection of those aspects of the person that are more than mere will – for instance, traits that should be charitable, moral, forbearing and the rest. So long as "deeds" are imperfect, regardless of perfect understanding of the principle of suchness, one can backslide in one's devotions. Prima facie, Asvaghosha's case is not persuasive, at least to a Westerner.

It might be argued, in rebuttal, that knowledge of the essential nature of reality is a special kind of knowledge which automatically guarantees fulfillment of the devotions. This is suggested by interpreting the parallels of knowledges and devotions according to the *t'i-yung* construction for which the essential and operational sides are merely different aspects of the same thing: to have the knowledge is *to be* devoted. This would be congenial to Wang Yang-ming's use of substance-function thinking. But that completely "spatializes" the relation between knowledge and devotion and eliminates the causal connotation according to which the devotion springs from the knowledge. The sense in which faith involves knowledge is complex, as is the presupposition of the *t'i-yung* model (examined in greater detail in the next section).

It might further be argued, again in rebuttal, that attaining this first stage of the "determined" life is such a transformation that the usual understanding of categories simply does not apply. Knowledge is not knowledge; devotion is not devotion. Unless this argument is merely ad hoc, backsliding would also not be backsliding, perfection would not be perfection; and so forth.

Consider the third group of aspirants, those whose path is insight. These people are at the highest stages of Bodhisattvahood; instead of "knowing" suchness, they are said to "realize" it. Part of the meaning of this distinction is that, whereas suchness may be an object for knowledge, in realization, the dichotomy of subject and object is overcome. Aspiration for enlightenment through insight

> can be identified in terms of the three subtle modes of mind. The first is the true mind, for it is free from [false intellectual] discrimination. The second is the mind [capable] of [applying] expedient means, for it pervades everywhere spontaneously and benefits sentient beings. The third is the mind [subject to the influence] of karma [operating] in subconsciousness, for it appears and disappears in the most subtle ways.[10]

It is tempting to consider these considerations the perfection of mind, enlightenment in its fullest sense. What is there that distinguishes these people from perfect Buddhahood?

Hakeda suggests that what differentiates the path of insight from the perfection of insight is the third characteristic. Being subject to the subconscious influence of karma, mind still arises and ceases. Furthermore, if Fa-tsang, who commented on *The Treatise on Awakening Mahayana Faith*, is correct as Hakeda cites him, then this operation of karma in the subconscious storehouse consciousness underlies the first two "subtle modes of mind" as well.[11] In the worst case for backsliding, then, even "true mind free from false intellectual discrimination" and the mind capable of spontaneously and beneficially applying expedient means are unsteady, subject to arising and ceasing. Precisely that unsteadiness constitutes the possibility of backsliding. In the best case, the true mind capable of expedient means might be independent of the mode of mind according to which things rise and cease due to karmic operations in the subconscious. Still, that third characteristic means the realization of suchness is unsteady in some measure or other. Because it is unsteady, one must will to perfect it. When the realization of suchness becomes clouded, however, temporarily, one can backslide. What more dangerous sinner might there be than one who is never fooled by false discriminations and whose power of expedient means is perfect?

Several conclusions follow from these considerations.

First, Mahayana Buddhism, at least in *The Treatise on Awakening Mahayana Faith*, has categories paralleling those in the West that articulate the peculiar character of will. The spiritual necessity to have faith as a characteristic of will precisely because will can ruin the profoundest knowledge and most charitable desires of the heart is characteristic of both traditions. *Devotion* for those seeking enlightenment through understanding and deeds is a resolution of will. For those seeking enlightenment through insight, will and, therefore, faithfulness are needed because of the unsteadiness of insight caused by the actions of karma on the subconscious storehouse of mind.

Second, the claim that backsliding is impossible once one has become "determined" (*niyata rāśi*) is misleading. As we have seen, both devotion and insight depend on will, which might go astray. Of course, the quality of faith may change when one is transformed from the "undetermined" to the "determined" state; but it does not change, contrary to the text, with regard to the absolute possibility of backsliding. Park characterizes the "determined" state as the realization of Buddha-mind. This may well be true, although the text of Asvaghosha stresses this only for those most advanced folk whose path is insight. A realization of Buddha-mind may well be an indelible experience; it may be that one cannot backslide in the sense of returning to a stage where it is as though that realization had never happened. Yet, because one needs faith even after "determination," in order to perfect understanding, devotion, and insight, it is possible that one's will can cloud that original realization of Buddha-mind. What is more common in us ordinary folk is that we forget, distort, and deliberately put aside our best spiritual knowledge, insights, and realizations. The more powerful and important our understanding, the more it challenges our perverse desires and the more effectively and surreptitiously we deceive ourselves about it. When it is convenient to do so, we deliberately forget. How do spiritually advanced people differ from us here? Their insights may be broader and deeper, but the insights may be all the more perverse when perverted. Their desires may be more refined, well ordered, and focused in genuine compassion, but all the more powerful when misguided. The likelihood of backsliding may be radically reduced for the spirtually advanced, but more dangerous for all that.

Third, the claim that faith is preparatory to the "determined" stages of Bodhisattvahood, to be replaced by aspirations through understanding and deeds and through insight, is also misleading. As we have seen, the will also needs faith in the higher stages. Park suggests that the faith of the undetermined people is *hsin-hsin* and the faith of the "determined" is *fa-hsin*. *Fa-hsin* is uniquely grounded in realization of the Buddha-mind, or nonduality. But it must be stressed that even when grounded in a realization of nonduality, understanding, deeds, and insight need to be guided by *fa-hsin*. The *ch'i-hsin* in the title of *Ta-ch'eng ch'i-hsin lun* refers, according to Park, to effecting the transition from *hsin-hsin* to *fa-shin*. He likens *hsin-hsin* to *assensus*, intellectual assent.[12] The problem with intellectual assent in this sense is that assent does not derive from intrinsic intellectual understanding. It is precisely because of the imperfect quality of understanding, both in terms of the beliefs described in Chapter 4 of *The Treatise* and the knowledge and realizations described in Chapter 3, that the will requires faith to assent to the truths. The imperfection of the knowledge of those who are determined is not that the truths are misunderstood but rather that understanding by itself is insufficient to perfect the whole of life. The Buddhist name for final perfection, *enlightenment*, may be a cognitive metaphor; but it denotes a perfection of the whole inner essence of a person, the outward behavior, and indeed the cosmic effectiveness of charity.

II. Faith as Certainty

This brings the discussion to the second main thesis to be considered, the claim that the faith to be awakened (*fa-hsin*) is a kind of certainty. In his commentary on the title of *The Treatise on Awakening Mahayana Faith*, the Korean monk Wonhyo wrote,

> This treatise causes people's faith to be awakened, hence the words "Awakening Faith." Faith is a term which indicates being certain. What is called [faith means] faith that the principle really exists, faith that practice can get results, [and] faith that when practice does get [results] there will be boundless merit.[13]

In all these points, and in the elucidatory ones that follow, Wonhyo emphasizes that faith is a matter of certain belief. Thus the cognitive, mentalistic, or intellectual metaphors for spiritual life characterize not only Chapter 4 of *The Treatise on Awakening Mahayana Faith*, where as Park urges, faith means assent, but also the initial and central portions. Mahayana generally employs mentalistic metaphors for its spirituality, the fulfillment of which indeed is called "enlightenment." Although these metaphors are stretched far beyond ordinary mentalistic usage and are carefully cut and polished to take on metaphysical and moral connotations, they stand in contrast to other root metaphors, for instance, Judaism's glorification of God in righteousness or Christianity's "salvation," which means being healed and becoming whole.

The choice of root metaphor distinctively affects the predominant contours of "faith" in a tradition. The importance of covenantal righteousness in Judaism reinforces the sense of faith as obedience to the law; to be faithful is modeled on such paradigms as being a faithful servant. The Christian double sense of salvation—being healed and becoming whole—suggests paradigms for faithfulness such as confidence in God (or Christ or the Spirit) as the Healer whom one can trust (not confidence that one's own practice will get results). It also suggests the imitation of Christ as a model for wholeness, restoring the lost image of God. Whereas the great religious traditions each extend and work their root metaphors to address a more or less common range of spiritual interests, the difference in metaphors contributes to the distinctiveness of the traditions.

Although faith as belief may be the dominant metaphor in Mahayana, it is not the only one. *The Treatise on Awakening Mahayana Faith* fixes it to the *t'i* side of a *t'i-yung* construction, the *yung* side of which is ridding oneself of attachments. In his "Invocation" Asvaghosha wrote:

> Because I wish to cause sentient beings to eliminate doubts and forsake wrong attachments, and in order to awaken [in them] right Mahayana faith so that the Buddha seed not perish.[14]

Commenting on this passage, Wonhyo said,

> Sentient beings fall into the sea of life and death for so long and do not hasten to the shore of Nirvana only because of doubts and wrong attachments. Therefore, the essence of [what is] here [meant by] saving sentient beings is causing [them] to eliminate [their] doubts and forsake [their] wrong attachments. . . . Two things [specifically] are doubted by those seeking Mahayana. The first is doubting the principle, which prevents the production of [wisdom] mind; the second is doubting the method, which prevents practice.[15]

Faith as the elimination of wrong attachments is the topic of Section III; therefore, the focus here is on the interpretation of faith as belief where that means elimination of doubt.

Although faith as belief without doubts has not been a predominant theme in the West, it has had its moment. The desperate father said to Jesus, "I believe—help my unbelief!" (Mark 9:23–24) During the Christian Middle Ages the form of disputation reflected a concern to overcome doubts about the "truths" of the faith; this concern arose in some part, perhaps, because of the pitiful miseries of the conditions of life – hardly the kingdom of the resurrected Christ. But the dominant intellectual stimulus to doubt was the encounter with Aristotle and Islam. The twentieth century has seen some discussion of doubt, for instance, in the work of Tillich. But the concern now is not that the truths of the faith may be false (in contrast to those of, say, Islam but that they may be meaningless. Doubt as a central theme in the West has had its heyday not in religion but in philosophical skepticism where it remains a serious interest now mainly to some academic analytic philosophers.

Wonhyo analyzed "doubting the principle" in the following way:

> The words "doubting the principle" mean creating this doubt: is the essence of the principle of Mahayana one or many? If it is one, then no other principle exists. Because no other principle exists, then no sentient being exists. [Then] for whose sake should the Bodhisattva make the great vow? If there are many principles, then there is not one essence. Because there is not one essence, the thing and I are separate [from] each [other]. [Then] how can [one] get the great compassion by which one regards others as his own body to arise? Due to these doubts, [people] are unable to produce [wisdom] mind. . . .
>
> Establishing the principle of One Mind causes that first doubt to be eliminated. [It] clarifies that the principle of Mahayana is only One Mind; apart from One Mind there is absolutely no other principle. Only because of ignorance are [people] deluded as to their own One Mind, which causes all [sorts] of illusion and transmigration through the six destinies to arise. Although the waves of the six destinies arise, they do not exist except in the sea of One Mind. Indeed, it is due to the movement of One Mind that the six destinies are created. Therefore, it is possible to make the vow of saving all [sentient beings]. [Also], the six destinies do not exist except in One Mind; therefore, [one] can make the great compassion by which one regards others as his own body arise. [By thinking] like this [one] eliminates doubts and can produce Great Mind.[16]

The first thing to notice about Wonhyo's view is its intellectualistic cast. One eliminates doubts by thinking according to a correct theory. The second thing to notice is that the problematic doubt concerns a standard problem of metaphysics, the problem of "the One and the Many." Wonhyo's solution, following *The Treatise on Awakening Mahayana Faith*, is the theory of One Mind with two aspects, the absolute aspect and the phenomenal. The intellectual success of this position is therefore significant not only in matters of theory but in matters of awakening faith, justifying the great vow to save sentient beings, and compassion. It is apparent that this approach to the one and the many is in the same family with Buddhist and process attempts to find a ground for inter-relations and with Wang Yang-ming's attempt to idealize being "one body" with many moral centers.

The relation between absolute and phenomenal aspects of One Mind is a central, pervasive theme of *The Treatise*, as is evident in its second and third chapters. With regard to the problem of the one and the many, Mahayana theory is that One Mind is one principle in the sense that it is absolute; since the whole of sentient beings (and everything else) is absolute, they can all be regarded as one body, the common object of universal compassion. But the phenomenal aspect of One Mind is the set of all things that arise and pass away, including the diverse separate sentient beings for whom common compassion is only a potentiality. Assuming for the moment the validity of the intuition of things as absolute, the question is: How are the absolute and phenomenal aspects related?

Perhaps the most natural solution to this problem is to say that the absolute aspect creates the phenomenal aspect. This has been a frequent solution to the problem of the one and the many in the West, though it is not the idea of creation advocated in this book. The absolute is "nonrelative" to anything else, according to the suggestion, in the sense that there is nothing else to be relative to except what the absolute creates. The phenomenal realm not only may contain risings and ceasings within itself, but literally arises from the absolute and may cease with the end of creation. As mentioned above, the *t'i-yung* construction used to render the absolute-phenomenal relation in *The Treatise* connotes in part that the *t'i* side gives rise to the *yung* side.[17] A similar construction is used in the *Doctrine of the Mean* to indicate that heaven-imparted human nature gives rise to feelings that are relative to separate objects.[18] In that book and in the *Great Learning*, the correction of the relative aspects of one's life is dependent on purifying the inner more absolute aspects which control or produce them.

The theory that the absolute aspect creates the phenomenal has difficulties both for interpreting Asvaghosha's text and for philosophic purposes. The difficult of interpretation is that then there are clearly two things, not just One Mind or one anything. The constant emphasis in *The Treatise* on permeation of the phenomenal world by the absolute realm, and vice versa, is incompatible with such a difference between the creator and the created realms.[19] The philosophic difficulty is that the concept of creation in this naive sense is equivocal. Either the absolute aspect gives the phenomenal aspect a being of its own (perhaps only a mental being), in which case there is a radical ontological dualism, or the being of the phenomenal realm is mere appearance and illusion, in which case the Bodhisattvas need not bother with their vows.

A more subtle creationist interpretation is to say that the absolute and phenomenal aspects emanate from the One Mind. The logic of "emanation" as a special kind of creation was developed by Plotinus.[20] This interpretation has three hermeneutical difficulties, however. First, within the logic of emanation, the difference between the One Source and that which is emanated is that the latter is a dyad, or dualistic. That which is emanated is determinate by virtue of being at least two things that are contrasted with each other. The absolute and phenomenal aspects would thus have to be interpreted as two determinately different things. But this stands against the constant theme of Asvaghosa's text, that absolute and phenomenal aspects are one.

The second hermeneutical difficulty is that the One Source and the emanated absolute-phenomenal realms are different and therefore two. The very act or process of emanation makes the difference. Therefore, the same objections to be lodged against the thesis that the absolute creates the phenomenal realm are to be lodged against the thesis that the One Mind emanates the absolute and phenomenal realms together: the text is against radical ontological pluralism.

A third hermeneutical difficulty is that, although the text does indeed express tiers of relations in a form typical of emanationist philosophies – One Mind, two aspects, three attributes, four faiths, etc. – this is a rhetorical structure (possibly with mnemonic intentions) which the text does not support by parallel claims for ontological creation. On the contrary, the text frequently rejects relations of ontological priority such as would be required for a serial emanation.[21] Besides, from a logical standpoint, Plotinus showed that what comes after the One and its emanated Dyad is interpretive Mind or consciousness, not the three attributes!

Quite apart from the text, to suggest that One Mind emanates its two aspects suffers the philosophical inadequacy of emanationism. Emanationism is a soft form of creationism, distinguished from stricter creation theories by the claim that the One produces the Dyad by introducing only negations into its own reality. (Strict creation theory says that the creator makes positive determinations.) The advantage of emanationism is that, lacking anything positive, the Dyad (or contrast of the absolute-phenomenal aspects) has no reality of its own separating it from the One Source. Therefore, the One and the Dyad are not "really" different. But where does the One Source derive the power to make such effective

negations as to produce determinateness within the Dyad? Put differently, how can arising and ceasing be produced by that which can only
negate something in its own being? Most emanationist theories cheat by
having the One Source create something positive by way of determinateness in the Dyad. Indeed, *The Treatise on Awakening Mahayana
Faith* not only denies but affirms the positive reality of the phenomenal
realm, as well as the positive reality of the absolute; otherwise One Mind
would have only one aspect.

We may ask now whether a philosophical theology structured by the
ontology of creation and cosmology of process developed above can be
specified by Asvaghosha's and Wonhyo's interpretation of the problem
of the One and the Many, for their conception of faith is indeed embroiled
in that metaphysical issue.

To recapitulate, let us say that in the theory there is a process of hap-
penings or occasions as described in contemporary process philosophy.
Each occasion comes into existence as a novel synthesis of prior occasions and presents itself as an objective fact to be synthesized in subsequent occasions. For each occasion, past occasions are conditions; it has
no being of its own except for its way of putting together its antecedent
conditions. Since an occasion is a coming into existence, when it has
come into existence it ceases to have subjective reality and exists only as
a conditioning element in subsequent occasions. Therefore, there is no
svabhāva in existence; all that exist are things conditioning other things.
All this is argued in Chapter 9. The coming into existence of occasions,
however, is a creative process of synthesis with subjective immediacy.
Within human experience there can be an immediate awareness of this
creative process, with the conditioning elements present insofar as they
are involved in the synthesis. Also within human experience, it is possible to focus on the conditioning elements as objects in their own right;
this is a kind of dual interpretive consciousness. Attending to conditioning elements as objects introduces not only the conditioning elements
but the *relations* of those elements as objects to the emerging occasion
as further elements within the creative synthesis.

It is apparent that this process cosmology can be read as an interpretation of the Buddhist theory of *pratītya samutpāda*. The interpretation
could be extended to give precise accounts of particular analyses of ris-
ing and falling—for instance, the theory of the "marks" of a thought—
jāti, sthiti, anyathātva, and *nirodha.*

The distinction in Mahayana between absolute and phenomenal realms can be rendered with a distinction already developed. The occasions and their relations of conditioning and being conditioned constitute the cosmological, or phenomenal, aspect of reality. This includes not only the causal elements of conditioning but the value elements as well. One's moral obligations, for example, include both the norms that apply to the occasions making up one's own person and to those constituting other people. All human matters having to do with effort, interpretation, and enjoyment are cosmological-phenomenal matters precisely because they involve the relations of other occasions to oneself. Consider, however, that any delineated portion of the cosmological process is what it is and is not nothing. *What* it is results from its conditions and synthesizing activity; *that* it is constitutes its ontological reality. Here, the scope of delineation of the subject is arbitrary. One may consider only a single occasion whose conditions are all external or many occasions, some of whose conditions are external but some of which are conditioned by others within the group. Having made the arbitrary delineation, the circumscribed portion of the process is absolute – irrelative as regards ontological reality.

That something is real is not another feature over and above *what* it is. Therefore, everything absolute is permeated, as *The Treatise* puts it, by the cosmological-phenomenal. Whenever we ask *what* something is, we seek a cosmological-phenomenal answer; it is never a relevant answer to cite some extraphenomenal ontological-absolute cause.

Anything phenomenal – anything that is a condition or that is conditioned, any occasion or relation between occasions – *is* what it is. Therefore, everything cosmological-phenomenal is permeated by the ontological absolute. No matter what phenomenal characters a thing has or how it relates to our own experience, it is possible, in principle, to appreciate *that* it is.

One Mind is simply the process. It cannot be spoken of except in terms of the occasions and their conditions. The aspect under consideration might be either the cosmological-phenomenological or the ontological-absolute aspect. If one can be spoken of, it must be possible to speak of the other. For the most part, our interest in experiencing the world is our own cosmological-phenomenal interests, reacting to our conditions or anticipating future ones. It is always possible – at least, in principle – to abandon interests deriving from our own position and merely intuit the absolute thatness or suchness of something or some stretch of process.

The intuition of the absolute reality of things can be characterized in two ways. One is to see that the "that" or "suchness" of the things is the product of conditions, such as they are; in this sense, things as suchness are "truly empty."[22] The other is to notice that everything in the world, or in all the worlds, can be appreciated as absolute; so suchness is "truly non-empty."[23]

If the phenomenal world is simply the occasions in their cosmological relations, what is the spiritual problem? According to *The Treatise*, it is that one not only thinks things but becomes attached to thoughts of them.[24] This establishes a duality within conscioiusness between the perspective of the thinker and the objects of thought that define the perspective. Instead of *simply* thinking, through "ignorance," thinking takes on a concern to determine *that* the thinker is real by zeroing in on the thinker's position through the subject-object distinction. The cosmological and ontological aspects are thus confused. Rather than merely allowing oneself to think (which can be as complex as interpreting, reasoning, evaluating, and attempting to think well rather than poorly), one attempts to establish oneself as real by making one's absolute nature a function of cosmological perspectives within experience. That is, instead of resting in the straight ontological reality of thinking, one attempts to construct an ego out of cosmological relations that might serve a special ontological purpose. But an ego is no more ontological than an unattached thought, it is merely a more complicated cosmological structure. If one believes the ego is ontologically special, the belief only makes one ignorant of the real relation of thinking to objects. Because even this confused, ignorant thinking, considered absolute, is still *simply* thinking, the text says that enlightenment is original and inexpungable. But because the cosmological-phenomenal character of ignorant thinking serves to provide a needless and painful concern to define one's ontological existence, ignorance might pervade one's thinking.[25] Attaining enlightenment therefore involves giving up the concern about defining one's ontological reality, and giving up consists in taking apart the relation between thoughts, on one hand, and the egoistic perspective for thinking them step by step, on the other. *The Treatise* analyzes these steps in terms of the four marks.[26] The result is a return to the original mind.

The philosophical categories employed to distinguish the ontological-absolute aspect of process from its cosmological-phenomenal aspect, showing both to be aspects of the same process, or One Mind, constitute a hypothesis for interpreting Asvaghosha's and Wonhyo's point about doubting the "principle."

Before we explore the fruitfulness of that hypothesis, however, it is important to raise a question not raised in the text or even stressed in Mahayana. Granted, there is One Mind – process – one in its absolute ontological character and plural in its phenomenal cosmological structure, *why* is there this One Mind, or process? This leading question reintroduces the theory of ontological creation.

Why there is One Mind is not a cosmological-phenomenal question to be answered by finding conditions for its dependent origination; rather, it concerns One Mind in its entire cosmological aspect (as well as its entire ontological aspect). Some thinkers would say that the "why" question therefore makes no sense, because all "why" questions, by nature, seek cosmological, phenomenal conditions. What, then, is the occasion for asking why something exists or is real? The occasion is that the thing about which the question is asked unifies some complexity not accounted for by the unified complexity itself. Within the realm of the phenomenal, a thing is questioned regarding the conditions from which it arose. The One Mind itself is a complex unity in its own way, allowing analysis cosmologically as well as allowing intuition ontologically. Although these permeate each other in the senses mentioned above, they are not in all respects identical. If One Mind is complex, one can ask, why is there One Mind? Why not no mind at all? No process? No nothing? Since the absolute, ontological character of reality is that things are such as they are, that reality is positive, partly determinate, and partly harmonious, why is there such a thing?

The answer given in several chapters above is that the positive reality is created *ex nihilo*. The West has often said that the creator is a God with determinate characteristics of its own apart from what is created; but that merely reintroduces the difficulties of relating the creator to the created product noted above in our discussion of the absolute as creator. Rather, a satisfactory answer to the "why" question requires us to say that the creator is indeterminate except insofar as the creator is characterized by creation itself. Even the Christian notion of the trinity can be interpreted according to this model. From the Western perspective, it might come as a surprise that Buddhism, too makes sense in the creation model.

But let us set aside this high ontology and return to Wonhyo's issue. How does understanding "principle" to be One Mind with two aspects eliminate doubts and lead to faith?" And what kind of faith is that?

In the passage quoted above, what Wonhyo claimed for understanding the One Mind-two aspects doctrine is the realization that there is no principle apart from One Mind and that illusions and all "transmigrations through the six destinies" take place within the One Mind. That is, everything is one process. Within Wonhyo's problem, there are two features that seem to require pluralism; first is the justification or meaningfulness of the Bodhisattva's vow to save other sentient beings, and the other is the moral requirement of compassion regarding everything as one body. Within Wonhyo's own text there is an unsteady bias toward making the One Mind more important and real than the needed diversity within it. But our own hypothesis need suffer no such bias. The occasions within process have their own individuality, arising out of past conditions and becoming conditions for future occasions. They have no self-nature over against the process; within the process, they have their own absolute suchness. The occasions making up a Bodhisattva (or any of us) are related to the occasions of other sentient beings, both as being conditioned and conditioning; therefore, the vow to save others is meaningful. Compassion is a meaningful problem because it is not automatic that one feel true continuity with what one conditions and what one is conditioned by. Insight into the common "principle" must be attained in the face of clear diversity.

Suppose, now, that the One Mind-two aspects doctrine can be interpreted and approved in contemporary terms. How does it bear on faith?

In one sense, it need not bear on faith at all. It is an intellectual hypothesis whose plausibility derives from a host of sources. Hermeneutically, it makes sense of many ancient texts which themselves have been approved and developed for ages, rendering those texts in contemporary terms and making them current, live options. Dialectically, the hypothesis has advantages over alternative hypotheses. Culturally, the hypothesis may receive support and help enliven current movements in the sciences, arts, and humanities. But it is only a hypothesis; after being developed and exploited for an age or two, it will be modified beyond recognition or will be replaced by alternate hypotheses.

Not to recognize the hypothetical character of the philosophical categories is to fail to appreciate the finite logical character of thinking. The point also holds for the One Mind-two aspect concept of Wonhyo and Asvaghosha, though they would not have recognized it perhaps. The typical response of classic Buddhist (and many Hindu) thinkers to the finiteness of thinking was to say that it is an inadequate metaphorical vehicle for experience. But that was often a facile way of neglecting the sense in which hypothetical thinking is indeed the way thinking grasps reality, with the moral consequence that it should be done well with artful development and criticism of hypotheses. For the integrity of thinking, for preserving and enhancing the dialectical community that provides the hypotheses by which we may experience the world, it is necessary to insist that hypotheses be treated as properly intellectual. They must be considered and criticized against a background of alternatives. Critical thinkers must be open-minded regarding the possible outcomes of critical deliberation. If the hypothesis of one's neighbor turns out to be better, on public grounds for adjudicating hypotheses, one should admit that and give up one's own. Before anyone can adopt a hypothesis as a basis for faith, the hypothesis should be subjected to the objective scrutiny of the intellectual community, as much as possible apart from the biases of commitments to faith.

Yet it is by hypotheses that our thinking experiences the world. Thinking is a form of intellectual engagement, but what is intellectual engagement? It is not merely having a belief about which one is certain and which one demonstrates in argument. Rather, it is the (possibly nondual) way one *takes in the world and comports oneself toward it* insofar as that way involves mind.[27] The importance of the Buddhist mentalistic metaphors for life is shown precisely here: life reaches its apogee in intellectual engagement.

The *content* of the One Mind-two aspects is not enough, however, to make clear its bearing on faith. It is necessary to understand the *use* of the hypothesis in engagement. The use of the hypothesis, in turn, is best understood in terms of the parallel doubt discussed by Wonhyo, about *method* that prevents practice. Faith is more than intellectual opinion when it is the heart of practice; without being the guide of practice there is no engagement, only undisciplined engagement. Correcting the doubt of principle is *t'i* and correcting the doubt of method is *yung*. Wonhyo wrote:

> As to [what is meant by] saying "doubting the method," if the teaching method established by the Tathagata is manifold, then according to which method should one first start practicing? If all may be depended on, then [one] cannot immediately enter [the way]. If [one way] depend on one or two, which is to be ignored and which is to be followed? Because of such doubts [people] are unable to start practicing. Therefore, for the sake of

eliminating these two doubts [the author] here establishes the principle of One Mind and reveals [its] two aspects. . . .
The revelation of two aspects [in One Mind] removes the second doubt. It clarifies that although teaching methods are many, there are not more than two methods in first beginning to practice. Based on the aspect of Suchness the practice of Tranquilization is cultivated, and based on the aspect of arising and ceasing the practice of Clear Observation is begun. If both Tranquilization and Clear Observation are practiced, myriad practices are thereby performed. If [one] embarks on these two methods, [one] is practicing all other methods. [By thinking] life this [one] eliminates doubts and can begin to practice.[28]

According to Wonhyo, the first thing to notice in these passages is that the hypothesis that removes the doubt about principle also removes the doubt about method. He said that practice needs to attend to the ontological-absolute "suchness" aspect of things and also to the cosmological-phenomenal, "arising and ceasing" aspect. Between them, these aspects exhaust the stances one might take toward One Mind which is the ground and goal of practice.

The second thing to notice is that by saying these two methods – tranquilization (*śamatha*) for suchness and clear observation (*vipaśyana*) for phenomenal matters – include or encompass all others, Wonhyo implies that all the disciplines of life, insofar as they are needed, are both legitimated and commanded. For instance, if it is true that the mindful grasp of things requires a dialectical development and criticism of hypotheses, then that is a requirement for clear observation. If it requires an effort to participate in culture so that one gains access to what does arise and cease, that too is a necessary discipline. The demands for practice in ancient times when it might be assumed that everyone had the skills and access to things were perhaps less awesome than what we see now to be relevant (though the Confucians were not naive about this). Although, of course, many mental activities can be pursued for their own sake in ways that have no religious bearing, if they are relevant to being mindful, to realization of One Mind, they are important. That the phenomenal is indeed an aspect of One Mind implies that they cannot be ignored or "transcended."

The third thing to notice is that doubt about method arises in the context where the potential practitioner already wants to practice. Given the connection of the doubt about method with the doubt about principle, both doubts can be said to arise at the point where the transition from "undetermined" to "determined" faith is in question. That is, the grasp and practice of One Mind through both its aspect is the key step in "determining" faith and moving on with confidence in One Mind, both as grasped intellectually and as the object and medium of committed practice. This refers back to the discussion where it is pointed out that intellectual and moral preparation for faith among the "undetermined" is qualitatively different from that of "determined." Without cognitive appreciation of that peculiar unity of One Mind and two aspects, without the sagacious appreciation of the cosmological and ontological dimensions of life and the ability to hold both in focus, those "undetermined" people have faith "blindly." The faith of the "determined" is no longer "blind."

Yet we must recur to the problem raised in Section II, concerning faith, backsliding, and will. Is it not still possible for the cognitive appreciation of the validity to be forgotten, suppressed, or perverted? Is it not still possible for the disciplines of practice to be abandoned, dissipated, or perverted becoming magic and siddhis? Of course it is.

III. Forsaking Wrong Attachments

The Treatise on Awakening Mahayana Faith, and Wonhyo in his commentary, raise the question of doubt in the context of treating the larger issue of why there is a religious problem. To repeat a line quoted above, "the reason why sentient beings fall into the sea of life and death for so long and do not hasten to the shore of Nirvana is only because of doubts and wrong attachments." In keeping with the *t'i-yung* construction exploited so consistently by Wonhyo, we may appreciate the entire question of doubt to be the *t'i* side of a unitary phenomenon for which wrong attachments are the *yung* side. That is, correcting doubts with the proper faith is the inward side of correcting wrong attachments with proper relations to the world. If we press this construction hard, it is possible to say that one and the same "activity of the spiritual life" can be viewed either as correct cognitive grasp of basic reality and disciplined practice in this grasping or as realistic affective orientation to the world (no wrong attachments).

This interpretive move has two consequences. One is that the intellectual-faith side cannot be viewed as merely intellectual or cognitive, because that would be to take it in abstraction from the process which is also a matter of action guided by attachment or nonattachment. This is one way by which the mentalistic metaphors are stretched beyond their ordinary compass.

The other consequence is that the affective dimension of attachment and nonattachment cannot be viewed plainly as matters of desire or will. Rather, reflecting the mentalistic imagery, affectional disposition is expressive (*yung*) of the cognitive center. As it is stated in *The Treatise on Awakening Mahayana Faith*:

> All evil attachments originate from biased views; if a man is free from bias, he will be free from evil attachments. There are two kinds of biased view: one is the biased view held by those who are not free from the belief in atman; the other is the biased view held by those who believe that the components of the world are real.[29]

This is not the place to undertake a full-scale study of Wonhyo's "forsaking attachments." *The Treatise*, however, is not a fertile ground for such a study, particularly one undertaken with the interests developed here. That section of *The Treatise*'s third chapter called "The Correction of Evil Attachments" is a brief, disappointing discussion of the wrong attachments that result from incorrect opinions. Its emphasis is solely on the way affectional attachments are a function of cognitional errors; it does nothing to correct the intellectuality of the faith side of spiritual life with a deeper notion of affection. If one wants to see mentalistic faith set in balance with will and desire, one will not find it here. As far as the *t'i-yung* interpretation suggested above is true, the emphasis is all *t'i* and virtually no *yung*.

This chapter begins by observing that Buddhism is not just metaphysics but a tao of faith. What this might mean in Mahayana has now been explored in some detail, at least in connection with one text. We have discussed faith (*hsin-hsin*) as preparation of the "undetermined" for the (*fa-hsin*) faith of the "determined" who have realized One Mind. It was suggested that, contrary to *The Treatise*, "determined" faith is not immune to backsliding. Although one may not "slide back" to a cognitive experience innocent of the cognitive realization of One Mind, one may forget, distort, or pervert the realization. The noncognitive aspects of spiritual life might fail to be brought in line with cognitive progress. It is now possible to say that one may still have or acquire many wrong attachments even though one *knew* they were misplaced *if* one thought by means of the theory of One Mind-two aspects.

Faith has also been discussed as a matter of belief that triumphed over doubt, and doubt has been analyzed as doubting that the "principle" of faith is one and that there is a definite method with which to begin practice. This discussion has shown not only the importance of correct understanding of principle – One Mind with two aspects – but also the way by which cognitive faith is but the inner reality of a life whose outside expression is first practice and then, on a larger scale, affectional activity without wrong attachments. It should be stressed here that both cognitive activity and life without wrong attachments can be nondualistic. That is, thinking with a good hypothesis is not thinking *about* the hypothesis as an object but thoughtfully taking in the world *through* the hypothesis, a form of simple thinking. Thus, also, affectional orientation toward the world need not make a thing the object of desire, defining the desirer; but the orientation may, if not "wrongly attached," be an appropriate response to the worth of the thing. *The Treatise* is indeed a subtle, profound road into the Buddhist experience of nondual reality.

If one looks to see the Western experience of real life expressed and confirmed here, that person will be disappointed. Through many modes of expression, the West has experienced the religious problem not only as ignorance – the Mahayana analysis of ignorance and enlightenment is only more thorough and subtle than the West's, not contradictory – but also as perversity of will and corruption of desire. Given the quasi-independence of the faculties involved in psychic integrity – will – from those in knowledge and in desire, even cognitive faith has been appreciated in the West as prey to will's pride. If these extracognitive dimensions of experience have their warrant for being taken seriously in spiritual concerns, then *The Treatise*, and perhaps the tradition it forms, is unbalanced and biased. Are the Western and Buddhist tao's simply alien? Are they naturally irrelevant?

The *need* for those dimensions stressed in the West is apparent in *The Treatise*. The discussion of forsaking wrong attachments in that text is insufficient to bear the weight of paralleling doubt with wrong attachments as implied in the *t'i-yung* construction. Compared with the balanced analysis of phenomena in contrast with suchness, subtlety and detail is simply lacking for the problem of nonattaching. Furthermore, as is suggested above, wrong attachments both consist in and derive from considerably more than bad hypotheses or biased views. It may well be argued that wrong attachments involve both positive desires for unworthy objects – the faculties involved in desire not being identical with those of cognition – and a perverse will that seeks to obtain psychic integrity by making unreal connections (attachments). The most unreal connection is pride of place that misconstrues one's rather humble participation in process as the establishment of an ego.

There is a small irony in that our investigation of faith in Mahayana has led the discussion again and again to problems or practice. Perhaps there is some redundancy in the phrase "tao of faith and practice." The irony is compounded in the next chapter, which investigates practice as it bears on the study of religion, finding itself driven to develop a theory of cognitive experience in religion.

Chapter Eleven
The Daimon and the Tao of Practice

OW CAN SCHOLARS in the field of religious studies understand religions which claim that special spiritual practice is necessary in order to grasp their profound truths? Obviously, by practicing. That is the answer of the monastic and confessional traditions of both East and West. Although most contemporary scholars would find it boring to study a religion seriously without first trying it out, there are two reasons why this kind of scholarship-plus-practice is inadequate for giving weight to scholarly understanding. First, most religions are too distant in culture or time for a scholar to practice them exactly as the people who formulated them did. Second, should a scholar, by great luck or effort, transcend that distance, this would in turn create such a distance from modern scholarly methodology that the authority of objectivity would be cast into doubt. Is this an insurmountable paradox of understanding?

This chapter explores the crucial encounter of daimon and tao, in four steps. The first is to formulate the problem in a specific way, using the Mahayana Buddhist doctrine of two levels of truth. The second analyzes that doctrine as a philosophical strategy. The third analyzes how spiritual practice bears on the content of philosophical concepts. And the fourth returns to the role of practice in scholarship.

I. Two Levels of Truth

The doctrine of two levels of truth is a common theme in most forms of Mahayana. Different schools used it for different purposes; accordingly, it came to mean different things. Vaguely and in general, the higher truth (*paramārthasatya*) concerns the claim that things are empty; that is the absolute, or irrelative, truth. The lower truth (*samvrtisatya*) is the truth of the turning changing world of samsara; as *laukikasatya*, it is the truth of ordinary people. The main point made by the doctrine is that both higher and lower truths are true. One version of this is that One Mind has two aspects, higher and lower, as we see in Chapter 10. The doctrine has often been used as a dialectical tool to refute two forms of heresy. One form says that emptiness is the only truth, and against this the truth of ordinary people's changing world is asserted. The other form says that the reality of *dharmas* is the only truth, and against this the higher truth of absolute emptiness is asserted.

This dialectic of two levels of truth has achieved extraordinary subtlety. Consider Fa-tsang's use of it in a quotation from the fourth chapter of *Hundred Gates to the Seat of Ideas of the Flowery Splendour Scripture*:

> Matter has no substance; this is Emptiness. If emptiness is spoken of apart from matter, it would mean that there is no false matter in the realm of worldly truth, and that because of false matter there is the True Emptiness in the realm of absolute truth. If matter is spoken of apart from Emptiness, it would mean that there is no True Emptiness in the realm of absolute truth, and that because of True Emptiness there is false matter in the realm of worldly truth. Now, it is only necessary to understand that True Emptiness means that matter is false and has no substance. Emptiness is not so called because there is no matter.[1]

Defending the reality of consciousness-only, Hsuan-tsang appeals to the two levels of truth doctrine:

> *Objection*: Is the nature of consciousness-only not also empty?
> *Answer*: No. . . . We say dharmas are empty because the [so-called] real dharmas erroneously conceived on the basis of transformations of consciousness are contrary to reason. We do not say dharmas are empty because there is no nature of consciousness-only realized by correct and indescribable wisdom. If there were no such consciousness, there would be no worldly (relative) truth, and if there were no worldly truth, there would be no absolute truth, for the Two Levels of Truth are established on the basis of each other. To reject the Two Levels of Truth is to have evil ideas of Emptiness, a disease the Buddhas consider to be incurable.[2]

Earlier, Seng-chao applied the dialectic of the two levels of truth to the distinction between existence and nonexistence that so occupied the Three Treatise School:

> The *Fang-kuang ching* says, "According to the absolute truth, no affair is accomplished and no thing is attained, but according to the worldly (relative) truth, affairs are accomplished and things are attained." Now, ac-

complishment is a false name [indicating the relative aspect of] accomplishment, and non-accomplishment is the real name [indicating the absolute aspect of] accomplishment. Since it is the true name, although it is true, accomplishment does not exist. And since it is a false name, although it is false, accomplishment is not nonexistent. Therefore what is said to be true (absolute) is not necessarily existent, and what is said to be false (relative) is not necessarily nonexistent. The two terms are not the same but the principles are not different. Therefore the scripture says, "Are absolute truth and worldly truth different? The answer is, No." This scripture directly elucidates the absolute truth to make clear that [things] are not existent, and elucidates worldly truth to make clear that [things] are not nonexistent. Does it mean to say that because there are the two levels of absolute and worldly truth, there are two different kinds of things?[3]

These intellectual and dialectical employments of the doctrine of the two levels of truth are cited here to indicate the diversity of its uses. Three more citations indicate a special line of argument I will develop for the problem of scholarship. The first is from the great dialectician of the Three Treatise School, Chi-tsang:

When it is said that dharmas possess being, it is ordinary people who say so. This is worldly truth, the truth of ordinary people. Saints and sages, however, truly know that dharmas are empty in nature. This is absolute truth, the truth of sages. This principle [of worldly versus absolute truth is taught] in order to enable people to advance from the worldly to the absolute, and to renounce [the truth] of ordinary people and to accept that of the sages. This is the reason for clarifying the first level of twofold truth.[4]

Chi-tsang went on to say that since the distinction between being and nonbeing is a duality, the whole of it belongs to worldly truth on another level of understanding, while absolute truth is nonduality as such. But even beyond that, said Chi-tsang, the distinction between duality and nonduality is mere worldly truth, and the absolute truth is to avoid both one-sided duality and "central" nonduality.

Setting aside the content of Chi-tsang's discussion – the existence-duality problem – the operative force of his argument is to move people from the worldly to the absolute level at each of three levels. Ordinary understanding is misunderstanding. This point differs from the emphasis in the schools cited above, which defends the integrity of both levels of truth. In some way, even Chi-tsang must say that the two levels are a duality that must be transcended, with the result that it is a mistake to think one can move from worldly truth to absolute truth.

Moreover, most Buddhist tradition strenuously objects to saying worldly truth must be abandoned. Yet the distinction between ordinary people and sages rests precisely on which world of truth they occupy, and Chi-tsang urged advancing from one to the other. Does this mean scholars should become sages?

The second citation is from the great Indian master represented by Chi-tsang in China. Nagarjuna wrote:

> The teaching by the Buddhas of the *dharma* has recourse to two truths: the world-ensconsed truth and the truth which is the higher sense. Those who do not know the distribution of the two kinds of truth do not know the profound "point" in the teaching of the Buddha. The highest sense [of the truth] is not taught apart from practical behavior, and without having understood the highest sense one cannot understand *nirvāna*.[5]

The overall motive behind Nagarjuna's point is to criticize attachments either to the world-ensconsed truth alone or to the truth that is the higher sense. In keeping with his fourfold mode of argumentation, he would also say that one cannot affirm both truths; nor can one not affirm both truths. One should abandon all attachments that might lie behind affirming or denying anything positive or negative about the truths, and Chi-tsang's dialectic of abandoning attachments to every level of interpretation of the two levels of truth is very much in the spirit of Nagarjuna's thought.

Nevertheless Nagarjuna did say, according to my preferred translation (see Note 5 for this chapter), that the higher truth is taught in connection with practice or, rather, that the higher truth cannot be taught without practice. Those who do not know the higher truth, and the distribution of the two kinds of truth, all of which cannot be known without practice, cannot understand Nirvana. Since Nirvana and related basic doctrines are among the most important things scholars would like to understand about Buddhism, it would seem that the scholars must practice to understand. Again, let the qualifications be borne in mind: one should not become attached to higher truth or believe it supplants lower truth; and there may be a sense for Nagarjuna in which enlightenment is altogether different from grasping truths. Nevertheless, to become sagacious about Nirvana, one must at least grasp higher truth, which ordinary people do not do. Perhaps one does this, among other ways, by practice.

The writers cited so far employ the doctrine of two levels of truth in highly intellectual, dialectical ways even when, as in the case of Nagarjuna, the intent is to clear away intellect for the concrete results of practice. It might be assumed from this that the doctrine is wedded, positively or negatively, to truth in a narrow cognitive sense and thus is not well related to practice as Nagarjuna wanted. Consider this final citation from *The Awakening of Mahayana Faith*, clearly a devotional tract expressing the concepts and symbols of a practicing community. The text speaks of the Buddha-Tathagatas who belong to the realm of

> the absolute truth, which transcends the world where the relative truth operates. They are free from any conventional activities. And yet, because of the fact that sentient beings receive benefit through seeing or hearing about them, their influences [i.e., Suchness] can be spoken of [in relative terms].[6]

People would like to attain the state of the Buddha-Tathagatas, and the text explains the influence or grace coming from those beings in the absolute truth. The Buddha influence is the correlate of the personal practices of concentration and discrimination advocated in the text, and mentioned in Chapter 10 above. This influence takes different forms, depending on the state of those being influenced. The text continues:

> The influences [of Suchness] are of two kinds. The first is that which is conceived by the mind of ordinary men and the followers of Hinayana [i.e., the influence of Suchness as reflected] in the "object-discriminating consciousness." This is called [the influence of Suchness in the form of] the "Transformation-body" (Nirmanakaya). Because they do not know that it is projected by the "evolving mind," they regard it as coming from without; they assume that it has a corporeal limitation because their understanding is limited.
>
> The second is that which is conceived by the mind of the Bodhisattvas, from the first stage of aspiration to the highest stage, [i.e., the influence of Suchness as reflected] in the mentality which regards external objects as unreal. This is called [the influence of Suchness in the form of] the "Bliss-body" (Sambhogakaya). . . . These excellent qualities were perfected by the pure permeation acquired by the practice of *pāramitās* and the suprarational permeation [of Suchness]. Since the influence is endowed with infinite attributes of bliss, it is spoken of as the "Bliss-body."[7]

The Awakening of Mahayana Faith goes on to scale ordinary people and Bodhisattvas at various stages of attainment and, in later sections, to discuss various forms of practice appropriate for people at various stages. However much it qualifies the point by means of the higher truth that Nirvana and samsara are the same, this text distinguishes ordinary people from those spiritually advanced by their position on the scale from "the world where relative truth operates" to the "realm of absolute truth" which transcends that relative world. Whereas both truths are true in their proper contexts, only the more spiritually advanced can see both contexts in their "distribution," as Nagarjuna put it. To get from the ordinary position where only relative truths hold (and then misleadingly) to the higher position where both truths hold (under proper distribution), one must engage in the proper practice.

The community from which arose *The Awakening of Mahayana Faith* had its own particular interpretations of the two truths and its own special rubric of practices. Generalizing slightly from this, we can state the problem for the scholar: To understand the heart of the Buddhist vision (e.g., the best influences of the "Buddha-Tathagatas"), it seems necessary to live out the life of a Bodhisattva. Much of this problem can be generalized for the study of any sophisticated religion. To understand participation in Christ, for instance, one must attain to his mind. Only those who are accomplished in a specific degree at a specific practice can understand the entire truth taught or revealed by the religion.

This is an unfortunate situation for scholars who want to understand religions such as Mahayana Buddhism, yet who cannot claim the requisite enlightenment through practice. There are, in fact, two difficulties. First is that any claim a scholar makes as to what *higher truth* means is subject to being disputed, not on the basis of evidence but solely because what it claims differs from what is claimed by someone who possesses accomplishment in practice or who is said to possess such accomplishment. This usually turns scholarly discussion into a wrangle about authority. The second difficulty is that the scholar cannot engage in discussion as to whether what is claimed for the higher truth is indeed true, for the scholar's participation is blocked by the counterassertion that the truth of the claims for higher truth cannot be seen without the accomplishment in practice. Although these two difficulties are related, one about meaning and the other about truth or plausibility, the second is of greater interest here. Both the higher truth itself and the doctrine of the two levels of truth are often expressed as philosophical claims. As such, they have alternatives which the scholar needs to articulate and which thus put the original claims in need of critical evaluation. We may therefore examine the scholar's dilemma when the doctrine of the two levels of truth is approached as a problem in philosophy.

II. Two Truths as a Philosophic Claim

The two-truths doctrine takes up and relates an abstract perspective on both the visionaries of the higher truth and the captives of the lower truth. With little practical enlightenment about the higher truth, a scholar can still understand the difference in perspectives that can be made by devoted spiritual practices. The scholar can follow the detailed descriptions of what happens at various higher truths in terms of the transformations effected by practice and evaluate whether these meanings can be asserted truly on the basis of the evidence and the insight produced by the practice, albeit abstractly. If the philosophical perspective is self-conscious about its abstractness, the scholar need not experience the higher levels of practice or the higher truth itself to understand its meaning, evaluate the conditions under which it could prove itself true, and determine whether the conditions are fulfilled in the mass of spiritually accomplished practitioners to which tradition defers. Philosophers of science who are not themselves physicists do much the same thing to understand physics and evaluate the claims of physicists to higher truth.

Notice that the philosophical character of the distinction between the two truths is made possible by mediation of spiritual practices between lower and higher levels. If the two states were not related by a mediating structure, only the standpoint of the inclusive higher state could allow for distinction. This state of affairs obtains in the orthodox Calvinist claim that the damned and the elect are not structurally connected but are disjoined only by an apparently arbitrary divine will: the meaning of election is open only to the elect. But in Mahayana Buddhism (as in Arminian Calvinism), the lower truths of ordinary people and the higher truths of the practically enlightened are polar extremes on a continuum of analyzable experiences correlative with specificable practices. Understanding higher truth is a matter of degree; thus it is to be attained *abstractly* through analysis of the stages of practice. The poles of the two truths, in fact, need function only as ideal constructs. Most scholars of religion while not claiming great accomplishments in practice, have to some degree frequently engaged in practices personally or vicariously and have had their experience opened by the dialectic of ideas about a higher truth, its emptiness, lack of mediation, the vision of nonduality, and so forth. As teachers, scholars attempt to give their students at least a sense for higher truth. They probably find few if any students so blindly "ordinary" that talk about the nonrelative does not strike a responsive chord. Thus the place where the philosophical distinction between higher and lower truths is significant is somewhere in the middle of the life of spiritual practices. This was, in fact, the audience for which the Chinese sutras and commentaries were written – interested seekers after understanding not yet attained.

The question of evaluating claims made for higher truth, in contrast to that of understanding them, is greatly complicated by the abstractness of the philosophical distinction. Philosophy grasps a given meditational experience not in its concreteness but as a type. Philosophical claims about the conditions for experience and its effects are reinforced by knowledge deriving from other members of the type. Philosophy has access to a wide range of mutually checking data precisely by virtue of its abstraction. A philosopher's personal experience is at best a guiding sense of taste, not evidence that counts in its own right. The experience that counts is the funded experience of one or several religious traditions to which abstract categories give philosophers access.

Consider the higher truth discussed in Hua Yen Buddhism, that all things, including those past and future, interpenetrate and are coresident in one another. This seems patently false in ordinary experience for which the future is at least partially external to and dependent on crucial determination in the present. As Fa-tsang worried, the Bodhisattva's vows might not be serious enough if consummatory Buddhahood is already resident in the mere proclamation of the vow.[8] From an abstract philosophical standpoint, however, the Hua Yen claim for interpenetration can be seen, as Chapter 9 argues, as an attempt to articulate a sense of togetherness underlying and presupposed by relations involved in causation, spatial juxtaposition, and temporal distinctions. Recognition of interpenetration as ontological togetherness enables philosophers to connect it not only to subtle experiences of unity in Buddhism but to similar experiences in other traditions. Whether these experiences are similar cannot be ascertained simply from the fact that they are all instances of a sense of ontological togetherness. By means of determining how well say, the language of creation *ex nihilo* articulates the ontological togetherness experienced in the West, additional evaluative perspectives are gained on the claims for higher truth. True, no philosophical perspective can present its judgments as anything more than hypotheses based on the arguments presented.

To summarize this line of thought, philosophy can present interpretations of what the higher truths are supposed to mean and what warrants they have. If these interpretations are called mistaken, that amounts to making another claim, that they leave out some crucial experience or that they are incompatible with the best way to understand something else. Because the philosopher's claim is abstract and open to assessment, in principle, there should never be a time when an opponent rejects the philosopher's view on the grounds that the philosopher has not attained to higher truth through practice. Logically, rejection should take the form of showing specifically what the philosophical interpretation does not account for or what otherwise valuable accounts it ruins.

Let us return to the original question, Just what kind of understanding does philosophy give of higher truth? On the positive side it may be said to provide ever corrigible interpretations of the meaning of truth. Also, it provides access for those from other experiential traditions to engage in dialogue about whether formulations of the Mahayana higher truths articulate what they claim and are dialectically adequate relative to other formulations. Philosophy allows the assertion of higher truths to enter a community of theological dialogue transcending both the authority structures and the sociological structures of specific examples of Buddhist tradition.

On the negative side, by virtue of their abstractness, philosophical interpretations lead away from the concreteness and directness of experience as they are founded on spiritual practice. In practice, one does not possess one's experience as a type but as the experience itself. The experience of singular suchness in Mahayana – in contradistinction to experience of relation through marks, types and tokens – is the aim of practice. Since the religious aim is not to get the philosophical meaning of the experience but to attain singular experience itself, the philosophic approach to the two truths, by definition, is not an understanding of the religious aim. It is just the opposite: an understanding of something other than the religious point. Philosophic expressions of the two truths, even when given by such masters as Nagarjuna and Fa-tsang, are also contradictions of the experience to be attained in practice, which the assertions of the truths are supposed to express. Understanding the exact religious content of the higher truth cannot come from the philosophical treatment of the doctrine of two truths, whatever else may be understood that way.

III. Concepts in the Higher Truth

We are accustomed to think of concepts, particularly the refined concepts used to make assertions of the sort used in the higher truths, as defined by references and other concepts and as learned through a combination of explicit definition and acquired use within a language. All this may be true, but it obscures a deeper truth—namely, that *concepts are instruments for having an experience*. Plato pointed out that certain experiences are impossible without antecedently having the concepts to recognize their elements; but the converse point is also true: it is impossible truly to think concepts without having already the concrete elements for the concepts to organize into intentional experience. Practice is important because it supplies necessary ingredients for the concepts in the higher truths to organize. Without the necessary ingredients, one cannot truly think the concept as an experiential instrument; one thinks it only as a counter in a language game.

Let us say, by stipulative definition, that an experience is a complex feeling. The feeling may have one or several of a great many modes—for instance, of sensation, perception, willing, active doing, wondering, reflecting, inferring, or meditating. Whatever the mode, an experience at a given moment is a unified feeling. What is felt, though, is extremely diverse. Everything a person could possibly feel at the moment is either (1) integrated into the single feeling or (2) explicitly excluded by virtue of the form that integrates all the rest. As integrated, the components of a feeling fit together in their actual conjunction; this integration can be analyzed reductively to dyadic relations. Sometimes the components can be mediated by something beyond their togetherness in the given feeling, as when something has another meaning for something else. But that mediation requires a further feeling with another integration which itself can be analyzed into dyadic relations. As a vast complex of dyadic relations whereby components felt fit together, a feeling can be called a "contrast." The immediacy in a feeling contrast is the suchness or singularity that some religions, particularly Mahayana Buddhism, take as the mark of true reality. In ordinary experience we are not often aware of feelings themselves but rather of the directionalities and implications of feelings, their relativities.

Despite the notion that feelings are immediate contrasts, they have an organization whereby some components relate other components to still others. For instance, most feelings have the form of arranging focal elements against a background. The background may have many layers of depth, and it may include emotional and referential forms of keeping the elements of a distance from the focus, as well as the more obvious spatial and temporal forms. Each feeling has a "world" in the sense that it organizes all it can possibly include in a contrast that arranges *most* items so they support the focal importance of a *few* items. When we verbalize feelings we usually mention the focal items; but a little reflection indicates that the foci depend for their importance within the feeling on the array of other items not usually noticed. An experience is an experience of things in a world. Despite that a feeling component can mediate between various things, putting them in relations they would not have without it, it is directly and unmediately together with the things it mediates.

A concept is a rule for organizing other components of experience so they can be thought together. To think a concept in an experience is to use it as an organizing rule for some of the components felt in the experience. The feeling content of a concept consists in what it organizes; this is distinct from the implications that may be drawn from the concept in context by later thinking experiences. As a rule, a concept fits in a network of other concepts as the many rules of a game fit together. The network relations between concepts are what move us from one conceptual thought to the next; language reflects less the content organized by a concept than the network of relations between concepts. The network of relations forms the continuous fabric of experiences so that concepts become available at the right time to organize feelings. The flow of words in a speech prepares the listeners for the right next word, with the right concept, to organize the feeling the speaker intends at the right time.

The appropriateness of the concept according to the network of concepts is different from its organization of a complex content within an experience. Therefore, the ability of a person to speak well, using the concepts appropriately, is not necessarily a sign that the person has properly organized the direct feeling at hand. Components may be missing or distorted that are crucial elements of the concept within the feeling. In that case, the concept is thought within the experience, placed there because of its network conceptual connections with other experiences but functioning to organize only some of its proper contexts.

The content of a concept within a feeling consists of many things ordered according to the rule form of the concept. Of course, with general concepts such as "emptiness" or "absolute reality in contrast to phenomenal reality," most of the directly related components are other concepts – for instance, conditioned coorigination and arising and ceasing. These concepts, in turn, continue branching out into other concepts, on and on without specifiable limit. But the concepts are not limited to other concepts; they include particular experiences in which the concepts were thought, with all the emotional, kinaesthetic, and environmental orientations of the other experiencs. Further, there are all sorts of feeling components lacking the rule-form universality of concepts which, themselves, are organizational components of concepts. The concept of "scarlet," for example, needs to organize some visual sights of scarlet things; otherwise, it can be used only by way of its network connections, as it is by the blind man who says scarlet is like the sound of a trumpet. More to the point about higher truths, there are components that come from meditative experiences of focusing on feelings as such without their relativities, from Abhidharma training in isolating experiential components, from experiences focusing on the lack of importance of differences between things. To think "emptiness" is to think within it much else that it organizes.

Concepts are among the most important experiential forms by virtue of which our experience has value. By organizing its components, a concept allows the experience to feel all those components together. Without the concept, perhaps some of them would have to be eliminated. Specifically, each concept organizes its components in its own way; some concepts are better than others because they allow for enjoyment of more better components or the same components organized so as to better enhance each other. The value in an experience, in its immediate intensity, is the sum of its components as organized in a complex contrast. Concepts are necessary organizing forms for the cultural elements of experience, as well as for experiential components present by means other than brute force – for example, through memory or distant anticipation.

Because it is possible to focus on a concept in experience due to its network implications with other concepts, but without providing all the necessary component elements, we must distinguish genuine conceptual feeling from conceptual sentiment. Because of their intricate branchings of components within components, concepts make clearer a feeling by providing access from one component to another. The focal concepts of an experience allow a host of components to be appreciated in one complex feeling. This supposes, however, that the components are available to be experiences by means of the concept, and that may not always be so.

Consider an experience of love between a husband and wife, a sexual moment but also one filled with emotional ties of love, the sense of their struggle together to raise a family. Let us suppose that early in childhood the husband had a traumatic experience in which his mother washed out his mouth with soap for telling a lie. Ever since, he has associated women touching his mouth not with oral pleasure but with pain, punishment, and guilt. Part of making love to his wife involves kissing her, which he does, feeling the sensations but not the deep satisfactions of sensual oral fulfillment. He kisses because he knows he should; it is part of the "concept" of loving his wife. But because it does not make the sensual pleasures of kissing present, he does not feel the content of the kiss. Rather, he kisses out of "sentiment," thinking he ought to feel something which he doesn't. Though genuine in perhaps all other dimensions of love, the kissing part of the husband's love is mere conceptual sentiment; though maybe not as important, the merely sentimental element prevents the husband from loving with full value, with clarity and access to all the dimensions of love, until he provides himself with the experience of genuine oral satisfaction that can be integrated in his lovemaking. Although our concepts are put in place by the network connections we develop in learning to speak, they receive their deep contents only through much more profound education.

The rationale for spiritual practice in aspiring to higher truths should now be apparent. Whereas philosophical dialectic can present these concepts according to their network of connections, and whereas they can show how to relate them to possible experience, without various practices certain crucial components of those concepts are missing and the concepts are only sentiments, not true feelings. The unpracticed person can know higher truths in a sentimental way, and may even have the fawning devotion to them connoted by the word "sentimental" that comes from feeling a lack of real content; but spiritual practice is necessary for achievement of the content, step by step, branch for branch, that makes those truths genuine truths. The negative side of spiritual discipline is involved in getting rid of blocks to true feeling, such as the husband's association of kissing with pain, punishment, and guilt. The positive side is the actual attainment of new experiences which can provide the content necessary for a conceptual feeling to be genuine. An important way to characterize a well-practiced, enlightened person is to say that that person feels all the world without the impediment of sentiment. The feeling is clear and unblocked throughout, with each component giving access to the others. This is one meaning of "samadhi," feeling together. Whereas not many scholars perhaps are enrolled in the pursuit of spiritual practice, most are midway through an education that increasingly opens sentiment up to genuine feeling; therefore, they can appreciate how the practical pursuits of a spiritual path might directly lead to the genuine feeling of things through the concept of higher truth.

IV. Scholarship in Practice

If we had been looking for a way to ease the burden of unenlightened scholars attempting to understand religion, we have not found it in this role for practice. Consider the following. The practices of Mahayana Buddhism, say, as embodied in the *Treatise on Awakening Mahayana Faith*, are very particular. They include prescriptions from texts known to that community and not those from later or distant texts. They include personal examples of saints directly known to the community and of which we have only fanciful records. The conceptual background for the practice of that community was the Yogacara and Tathagatagarbha traditions as they locally fed in, not the conceptual traditions forgotten by them or reduced to formulas, nor the subsequent commentaries on *The Treatise on Awakening Mahayana Faith* that interpreted it according to later concepts. *The Awakening Mahayana Faith* community had a particular cultural body nourished by traditions that were never exactly the same again. Its cultural body was particular, given profound spiritual content by the community's spiritual disciplines, also never duplicated precisely. Although the higher truth concepts of One Mind-two aspects are dialectically available for consideration by other cultural bodies, including our own, in their original religious concreteness they are available only with the cultural body of their original community.

Later communities might put the text to even better use than did the original community. They might develop even richer spiritual disciplines with an even greater appeal. But understanding each religion means entering into its own body, because what there is to understand comes from the flesh of its own experiential practice and cultural matter. The extent to which we can enter the body of that religion limits the extent to which we understand its higher truths, in the sense that they depend on practice.

One might be tempted to conclude at this point that one must be an accomplished, practicing sixth-century Buddhist to understand the higher truths of sixth-century Buddhism. But something is wrong with this conclusion. What is wrong is not the necessity of becoming embodied in Buddhist flesh (that is right!) but the inference that *understanding* sixth-century Buddhism is compatible with sixth-century Buddhist flesh. Understanding Buddhist culture as a religion is part of *our* twentieth-century, modern, scholarly flesh, not of ancient Buddhist culture. It is *our* culture that moves from sentiment to true feeling *by scholarly engagement with other cultures*. This is not to suggest that the authors of

The Treatise did not understand what they were saying or doing; but they did not understand it as a religious culture in the way we would like to. Their understanding as such is intended to provide the content for their higher truths. Our understanding attempts to objectify this process as something which religion is.

The thesis suggested by the discussion of basic concepts is that each culture is a kind of body embodying basic concepts, in the sense of providing the content for the concepts to be experienced, and the content of the content, and so on.[10] Each cultural body is particular. It has a structure organized by the basic concepts and draws its specifics from the physical and historical conditions of its time. The metaphor of *body* perhaps is misleading, though it calls attention to the role of concepts embodied in culture. What misleads is the suggestion that a culture's concepts are coherent. In fact, most cultures have clusters of coherent concepts but only adventitious conjunction and overlap, or even irrelevence, between the clusters. There is a looseness about cultures that is hidden by the organic connotations of body. It is also misleading to think of cultures as static. Most cultures are constantly changing the components of their fabric, sometimes even the great organizing concepts.

To counter the rigid unity connoted by *body* perhaps we should say that cultures are perspectives on things, with each culture differing from others, not necessarily in the components but in the way the components are organized; the organization of the components comes in the basic concepts. Cultures differ from one another by differences in perspectives. They change by changing perspective. Individuals within cultures presuppose the cultural concepts to some degree, but it is only the rare individual who achieves much consciousness about them. Those who do are then able to inhabit their culture with ease and clarity. They not only embody it; their own experience epitomizes it, as is the case with great writers and artists and heroes. To understand cultures is to understand them relativistically, to enter into each as much as possible and take up its perspective, putting on the experiential content as a body embodying the culture's concepts.

Now, our own culture is just as much a particular body – a definite, historically conditioned perspective – as any other. It arises out of the Enlightenment and the Industrial Revolution. It confronts past and present cultures; it has certain hermeneutical tools of engagement while lacking others it surely would be good to have. One thing seems clear, however: we cannot understand religions other than those undergirding the community of Western scholarship *as they understood themselves*; for we relativize all cultures including our own, even in their religious components. It is not possible for us to avoid this scholarly relativizing without abandoning the perception of history that is such an important defining element of our own cultural body. To do so, we would have to lie about our own historical conditioning.

By and large, premodern and non-Western cultures are not historically relativistic. The historical books of the Bible and the Chinese chroniclers gave their cultures a sense of history; but it was all history as if within the standpoint of their own cultures, assuming their own culture's historical body, unaware that cultural distance marks fundamental difference in cultural meaning. Mahayana Buddhism, especially in its tantric lines, has emphasized the diversity of worlds, each ruled by its own set of basic concepts, or Tathagata, and reached by an imaginative hermeneutic leap. But the Buddha worlds are reached by imagination or magic, not by encountering data, interpreting texts, or reconstructing through archaeological digs. The worlds of Buddha are not alien historical realities with empirical integrity to be respected.

Few if any cultures besides our own contain the fundamental religious concept of deep piety in the face of actual historical difference; but that piety is the religious center of our own relativism. It is a mistake to distinguish our culture's struggles for profound religion from its struggles with scholarship. As a mode of piety before other cultures, understanding is one of our greatest achievements.

Is it possible, then, for scholars to address the theological question of truth? The notion of truth has undergone a vast change as Western culture emerged from its premodern forms and become modern. Whereas the premoderns understood truths to be either absolute and irrelative to cultural or historical differences, or somehow illusions, the moderns have slowly come to view truth as context-dependent; or, to use the earlier language, truths are always assertions that are meaningful and true *within a perspective.*

In principle, the answer to the question of understanding the higher truths of Buddhism might be this: Through our own practice and imaginative projections we can, in part, enter into the perspectives of the cultures guided by those truths, giving significant content to their concepts. Aided by the distance of our abstract philosophical understanding of the concepts, we can articulate and move through diverse perspectives. But, practically speaking, there is always a limit to our entrance into a culture that itself is innocent of objectifying relativism. We cannot go to that home again while retaining our integrity as contemporary scholars. This limitation should not suggest that our own piety, which includes understanding the alien character of Mahayana Buddhism, is not worth its own effort. We must view the labor of modern scholarly understanding as part of our own culture's religious practice. Genuine perspectival understanding of an alien culture such as classical Chinese Buddhism is as much a higher truth at the end of *our* practice, abstractly available to all but filled with content only for the practiced, as the higher truth of the absolute and phenomenal realms filled the accomplishment of practice in the original community of *The Awakening of Mahayana Faith*.

Doubtless, all will have perceived the irony in stating this essentially secular view of objective religious scholarship in the homiletical form of the remarks above. The conclusion of the argument is that the secular scholar's approach to understanding even the most esoteric alien doctrine is itself a form of piety defining in part a religious mode of life. Consider what led us to this conclusion. The preceding section argues that the having of concepts is twofold. First is a grasp of the meaning of the concept through the network of other concepts in which it is enmeshed. Second is the enjoyment of the content of the various feelings which that concept's rational structure integrates into a single complex feeling. This, in itself, explains the ironic situation in which some people exhibit virtuosity in the dialectic of meanings with no serious content, while others can have depth of content yet are ignorant of the implications of what they say and believe. These are two levels of truth, to extend the metaphor; a good scholar will not affirm one without the other except through the impiety of poor scholarship.

As Section II indicates, however, possessing concepts is significant because the concepts are correlated according to a scale of practice and enlightenment, the "distribution of the two senses of truth," as Nargarjuna said. This, in turn, is ironic, because the statement that philosophy can know *un*experienced extremes by means of a *conception* of the practice connecting them makes sense only to people who are partially engaged in the practice and who therefore are not mere conceptual adjudicators.

What is *not* intended as irony is the claim that the discussions employing the doctrine of the two levels of truth are aimed at those midway between contentment with the ordinary truth and full appreciation of higher truth. The conclusion to be drawn here is that what scholars of religion can understand is only what can be registered from their historical perspective, given their modes of involvement in the subject. What is important in scholarly understanding, however, is not any kind of reiteration of the original texts; for, if we do not understand it in its original statement, we fool ourselves by believing that enlightenment comes from repetition of a statement in a new language. What is important is achievement of a new locus of religious significance, our own scholarly interpretation, new creations of the holy out of practices, scholarly piety toward the old.

Postscript

IKE THE SNAKE of Abraxas, our argument has curled around and swallowed its tail. Chapter 1 states that, in the study of religion, theology derives no authority from the tao itself that can stand over against the critical questions of the daimon. Chapter 11 ends by defining the contemporary daimon's passion for objectivity in religion, particularly alien religions, as a special and unique piety. The intervening chapters introduce speculative tools for establishing a perspective on religions. Some chapters argue down from the speculative theory of divine creation to possible instantiations in Christianity, Buddhism, taoism, Confucianism, and, to a lesser extent, Hinduism. Other chapters argue up from the dialectic within the religions and their philosophical contexts to the conception of creation. All of the arguments were fragments of cases, partial, at best exemplary, and always subject to counterarguments to the effect that other considerations are more important. I do not doubt that any of the arguments presented in this book can be refuted or shown to be not as important as I think. On the other hand, there is much to be learned about religion by thinking of it from the perspective of these arguments. In particular, the usefulness and legitimacy of philosophical theology, in its place, has been demonstrated.

I. The Daimon in the Tao

As with all circular routes, concluding the argument of this book leads to the next step, once one has realized that we have returned to a new version of the starting point. The next step is to ask how we can determine whether seriousness about "understanding the alien" is true piety for our contemporary tao, of faith and practice. Our argument has moved from opposition of tao and daimon to an inclusion of the daimon within a strange kind of tao. That is, the development and perfection of the

235

daimon of critical investigation of religion incorporates itself as part of a new piety, a new tao. The question is, How do we understand this new piety, this part of a tao to which scholarly piety is relevant?

The question in this case of true piety and alienation is raised from the side of the tao rather than from that of the daimon, as in the previous circle. Is this contemporary tao, which includes scholarly piety about the alien, a true tao? Is it authentic? Do faith and practice in that path lead us to the presence of divinity, to enlightenment, or to whatever it is that tao discovers as the religious object?

It is too soon, and we are too close, to make the kind of historical, aesthetic, cultural judgment we make in identifying "great religions of the world." Since this is our own tao, however, for better or worse, and since the critical daimon is within it, we can press the question in a certain way.

Let me begin with a necessary condition argument. The condition for having a true tao in the contemporary postmodern world is that it include the free and unconditioned play of the critical daimon. This claim rests on a conception of the locus of religion's power within thinking culture and life.

Thought has at least four dimensions, each with its own forms, norms, and functions and which are discussed in the chapters above. The most obvious dimension (sometimes the only obvious one) is thinking as interpretation or assertion. Its form is intentional or judgmental, supposing a relevant distinction between what is asserted and that to which the assertion refers. Its norm is to be true in assertion. Its function has to do with the social, political, and personal functions of discourse. Closely related to the dimension of assertion is that of envisagement. Its function is to grasp the diverse elements of its subject in such a way that thought has access from one element to another. Its form is theoretical, that is, abstractions that create routes of access. Its norm is unity of the sort associated with theory. Theories need not be true to be theoretical, as the valuable plurality of metaphysical systems attests; an *asserted* theory should, however, be true. Not all assertions need have theoretical sophistication, as perceptual judgments sometimes indicate; but since theoretical forms are nearly always used in assertion, incoherence is likely to impede truth.

The third dimension of thinking – in fact, the foundation on which the others rest – is imagination. I use the word *imagination* here roughly as Kant did – to mean the basic activities of synthesis by which various causal impingements of the environment are transformed into the stuff of experience. The goal of imagination is engagement. Images, the basic forms of imagination, are the terms in which experience is taken up; they constitute the basic orders of the world. In fact, they constitute the world in a crucial sense. Experience orders what otherwise would be merely mechanical pushes into a world with spatial and temporal dimensions, values and interests, vectors of forces and possibilities with various degrees of attractiveness. The function of imagination is to supply this order so that the other dimensions of thinking have structure and horizons in which to exist. This is not to say that the world is a solipsistic, subjective construct or that there is no external world; rather, it is to say that the way human beings experience external elements is to "worldize" them. Any consideration of the truth of a particular assertion about what is real is based on, and therefore relative to, its own imagery, its own fundamental imaginative structure. Of course, one can identify an imaginative structure itself, articulate it in an appropriate series of assertions, and inquire whether it is true or authentic. If it is found wanting, and if it is part of the imaginative base of the culture doing the criticizing, then we have a situation of a culture attacking its own foundations, a situation with which we are familiar. If, in the process of critical thinking, we should arrive at an assertion of what would constitute a better imaginative structure, the assertion alone does not accomplish the restructuring of our imagination. Having an imaginative structure must come before assertion; the cultivation of imagination lies more in the province of religion and art than in that of interpretive inquiry. Insofar as our imaginative structures are reasonably coherent, the articulated statement of them is something like a theory, an envisionment. But a theory is even more abstract and formal than are most ordinary assertions about imaginative structures; so they cannot be identified with the structures themselves. The special advantage of a theoretical statement of imaginative structures is that it can be subjected to evaluation when critical inquiry treats it as a complex assertion. Though conditioned by each other, interpretation, theory, and imagination cannot be reduced to each other or replace each other functionally in experience.

The fourth dimension of experience generally can be called the "pursuit of responsibility." It consists in judging and guiding the activities of thinking so as to aim at the relevant goals in appropriate ways. Thus it criticizes the relationships between other dimensions of thinking, making sure that mere imaginative structures are not taken for assertions, that mere assertions, true or not, are not taken for comprehensive visions, or mere visions for truth or imaginative content. Specifically, the pursuit of responsibility organizes all dimensions of thinking to perform their roles vis-à-vis each other. In itself, it asks whether the structure of imagination, the content of one's assertions and the formal structure of envisionment, are important, the best possible: not just engaging, true and unitarily perspicuous, but *important*. This dimension's goal is the *good* relative to the situation; its form is dialectic, its function to achieve what Plato called justice among the diverse parts of thinking.

How does a tao of faith and practice relate to these dimensions of thinking? If the critical daimon is to be contained and fulfilled within a contemporary tao, how is that manifested in the four dimensions of thinking?

II. Four Loci of the Tao

Religion as a cultural phenomenon is most prominent in imagination. Although there is nearly always assertive content, religion is imaginatively structured by ritual behavior, repetitive telling and hearing of mythic statements or religious cosmologies and specific practices of prayer, meditation, fasting, ascetic discipline, and religiously motivated good works. In something like the sense explained by Peter L. Berger, these practices create the world.[1] They give structure to those syntheses by which we take the "external" to be a world. They name certain things as important and make legitimate the suppression of others, and they do so by forming capacities for valuing and disvaluing. These practices connect certain things and disconnect others. They contribute to the way imagination distinguishes focal elements from background elements.

To be sure, many things beside religion contribute to the formation of imagination. Most sociologists, anthropologists, and phenomenologists of religion suggest that religion particularly affects a world image at its boundaries. Death, suffering, birth, change of life in the sense of coming of age or abandoning competence, marriage, and so on have emotional power that threatens the ordinariness of imaginative structures; the world image of a culture or a tao has religious elements at these boundary junctures. Religious practices are also involved in imaging fundamental social conditions. For instance, where subsistence is the overriding problem, myth, ritual, and spiritual disciplines relate to fertility or hunting. They relate to social order, hierarchy, and kingship in such societies as the ancient cities of Mesopotamia, the Indus valley, and central China where irrigation agriculture was capable of producing some security of subsistence. When societies seem to work well economically and politically, but people feel dislocated, alienated, and filled with the dread of a meaningless existence, religious practices focus on personal salvation, fulfillment, and perfection. Because societies have evolved cumulatively through something like this set of problems (though far more complex), the resulting religious practices form imagination with each successive layer of culture sedimented down. In Christianity, for instance, Jesus, who called individuals to follow him for salvation, is proclaimed king and lord in religious practices that include reenacting his execution, symbolically eating his flesh, and finding new life in his rebirth.

Insofar as religious cultures differ, they do so most significantly in their structures of imagination. Concrete taking up of the world is at the opposite end of the spectrum of abstraction from the speculative theories in which religious cultures might agree. Differences among imaginative structures are impossible to arbitrate except as translated into assertions. For instance, it has often been observed that the cultures of Western religions have a linear sense of time in which people live definitely and finitely and just once. Eastern religious cultures have a more cyclical, or eternal, time sense in which each person's lifetime is experienced as connected with earlier and later lifetimes, so that no one lifetime has the ultimacy it does in the West. This is not just (or even) a difference in theories of time. It is not only a difference in time senses presupposed in making assertions. It is a difference in worlds. Assuming that the distinction is roughly correct, people in Eastern religious cultures experience themselves fundamentally differently from the way people in the West do. They have different worlds, where that means they take up items as experienced with different temporal orders. At this imaginative level it makes no sense to say that one side or the other is right or wrong; temporality simply is one way for Eastern cultures, another for the West. Since communications media and vigorous economic activity influence the imaginative structure of time, and since these are becoming common to both East and West, perhaps a common time sense will develop. If it does, one or both cultures will have to change how it experiences being in the world. Congruence or overlap of some parts of different world images might encourage greater congruence; on the other hand, so far as we understand these things, radical differences in other elements might lead the apparently congruent to diverge.

If we are to occupy an authentic, contemporary tao of faith and practice, it must have a set of religious practices—a cult—that reaches to the boundaries of the imagination and addresses the most critical problems of our lives. Without a cult, a tao of faith and practice can only be a quasi-intellectual affair. However much we might think about religious matters, our contemporary imaginative structure will be formed by other than religious elements and by leftover religious practices of which we are unaware. Therefore, a contemporary tao must include a cult which is in some kind of continuity with the great historic cults whose presence at our boundaries is formed by the same history that formed our present boundary situation. There are many such cults, East and West, and they are irreducibly different at crucial points.

No religion has static religious practices over a long time. Even if the words or the ritual remain the same, the historical context introduces novelties. The eucharist about which Paul wrote to Corinthians involves little or no significance for the ecclesial authority and office of the celebrant, an element that became central to the eucharist within a few hundred years. Further, traditions borrow elements of cult back and forth, as the history of religious symbolism attests. Every tradition is syncretistic in some way and to some degree. In our own time, techniques of prayer and mediation are passed back and forth between East and West in experiments that sometimes lead to enrichment of the cultivated imagination.

Nevertheless, I see no possibility at the present time for an authentic tao of practice to be constituted by any elements of cult soon to be common to the world's great religious cultures. Each element of cult requires for authenticity too much of the rest of the cult from which it rose historically. By themselves, the common elements are superficial in the sense that they do not reach boundary points or fundamental problems. They need the enrichment of the rest of their cultic heritage. Therefore, an authentic contemporary tao of faith and practice needs to be a Buddhist tao, a Christian tao, a Jewish tao, a Vendantic tao, a Neo-Confucian, or a taoist tao even if all of them involve sitting in zazen. It cannot be enough merely to take a little of each (and of several other candidates) in a syncretistic life-style if, when one's best friend dies, one's imagination is thrown back on fragmented second-hand childhood imagery. On the other hand, it is virtually impossible to devote oneself wholly to several cults, not only because of limitations of time and energy but because of the requirement of living in several concrete cultic worlds. If one does not experience them as different worlds, either one has not reached the depths of the cults, or they are not truly different in forming imagination and any cult alone would be sufficient.

To make matters more confusing, today it is inadequate, I believe, to devote oneself wholly to one historic cult in isolation from others. The reason is that precisely the situation for which each great religious tradition is to provide imagination structure is the historical situation that brought the cultures together. Either each religious cult perceives itself together with the others or it has not caught up to the problem of imagination in the situation. In between isolated cults irrelevant to the situation and superficial cults that fail to address the religiously important elements of imagination, lies a large field of possibilities.

Here, then, is the argument for a cult of "respect for the alien." If one's authentic tao must come from a great tradition and aim at a situation common to all, then the cultic piety of respecting others as different is essential. The cultic means – the practices themselves that form imagination around the other *as other* – are simply the various relevant disciplines of study. The resulting understanding of other religions as other is valuable, not just for its prudential use but because it empowers one to comport oneself imaginatively in one's own tradition toward the other while allowing the other to remain *other*. Understanding itself moves out from the dimension of assertion to that of imagination. With the possible unhappy exception of symbiotic Judaism and Christianity, no religions have acknowledged understanding of the alien to be a kind of piety; nor have they made it part of their cult. Thus my suggestion requires modification of any tradition which one might call one's own. Further, the distinction between one's own tradition and an alien one is complicated by recognition of the other as in the process of change, not as a static entity. Study of other traditions, especially from a historical perspective, even with these ambiguities and those noted in Chapter 1, must be part of an authentic contemporary tao. Otherwise, the tao fails its responsibilities to imagination.

With respect to the interpretive dimension of thinking, most major historic religions, under prodding by the daimon, have at least initiated the critical formulation of the suppositions and expressions of their cultic practices. The radical character of internalizing the daimon to the process of religious self-understanding is most problematic for religious authority. It appears – thus far, at least – that personal autonomy is at the heart of the daimon's prodding. One is responsible for oneself and cannot cast that responsibility on another. Most great religious traditions on this agree. But in practice, most have also advocated the cultic importance of the master and disciple relationship. This relationship takes numerous forms, but all involve a way of transferring "authorship" of significant spiritual works to master from disciple. In a basic sense, a contemporary tao of faith and practice embracing the daimon cannot allow abrogation of personal responsibility in the master-disciple relationship.

In what sense, in what bad sense, is a master an authority? As long as the master teaches cultic practices that have no serious interpretive or assertoric content, there is no problem of authority. In this sense, the master is merely a teacher able to convey a cultic skill or power. Insofar as there is a serious interpretive content to the relationship, though, the disciple may be asked (or forced) to accept the assertions on the authority of the master. That would be irresponsible except in ways in which the daimon would approve of respecting the greater experience of others. Any serious tao of faith and practice is a long, complex path to follow; it is almost inconceivable that separation of cognitive from noncognitive content could be sustained. What a contemporary seeker could not do while retaining the authenticity of the tao is to turn the direction of the path over to a guru. That would inevitably require turning over critical responsibility as well. To put the problem another way, the acceptable model of the guru is not the fulfilled devotee who has come to the end of the path but the professor who teaches the means to know other cultures (and other things) while also teaching the critical tools to relativize and judge the teaching. The reason the "enlightened master" cannot be a guru in the traditional sense is that ascertainment of what enlightenment consists in is a matter of critical judgment and responsibility for making that judgement cannot be left to the disciple. The content of what constitutes the tao is a matter of interpretation.

Sweeping generalizations such as those in the preceding paragraph need to be recognized for what they are. No one can prescribe for another individual the next step in spiritual life. People's needs are diverse. There is a time for engagement and a time for solitude, a time for critical judgment and a time for casting the burden of direction on others. There may be times for ascetic mortification and times for inducing visions with drugs; but, on the whole, a contemporary tao that internalizes the daimon must find models of learning and guidance that do not deny the autonomy required by critical judgment. If a crucial part of contemporary cult is learning about alien paths, then at least one of the crucial models of learning and guidance is that of the daimonic teacher.

The interpretive dimension of thinking includes not only verbal assertions but assertions that shade into action. Religion is involved in moral action in at least as complicated a set of ways as is suggested in Chapter 2. The point I want to make here is that religious judgment is involved in behavior toward other religious traditions. Not only does one think about the aliens, one acts in various ways toward and with them. To gain a critical purchase on what is involved in such moral interaction, it is necessary to get a higher view – that is, a vision. One needs a theory in order to gain access to the values of another tradition in an interchange with one's own. The more diverse the traditions, the broader the theory. The situation of morality leads from interpretation alone to unified envisagement.

The major thesis of this book is that an abstract systematic conception of creation offers the formal means for providing access from one tradition to another. If the arguments given have some merit, then philosophical theology is a discipline for moving from the theoretical perspective of creation to each of the major tao's of faith and practice. Philosophical theology can motivate the other disciplined methods for studying religion to the cultic activity of understanding the alien, enabling each to be specified by the metaphysical perspective. Is philosophical activity itself a cultic activity? It often has been in the past where it performed an apologetic role. According to the requirements for respecting the critical daimon, philosophical theology can never undertake an apologetic task for a particular tao. The closest it can come is to be self-conscious about its own contribution to a contemporary tao of which the daimon is a part.

Religion bears on thinking's dimension of responsibility in ways that can only be suggested here. They have to do with the responsibility of people for finding or forming a tao that does indeed engage people with the world. That is, people have a religious responsibility to develop imaginative structures that organize the content of our experience into a world, particularly at its boundaries and its problematic points. Since the content of experience is always changing, often in important ways, there is a continuing responsibility for world construction in imagination. As a cultivator of imagination, this responsibility in religion is subtly connected with responsibilties in philosophy and art.[2]

This section is motivated to explore how the four dimensions of thinking informed by the daimon pose requirements for a contemporary tao of faith and practice. Because religion moves principally in the dimension of imagination, discussion there is lengthiest; even there, it is still only a sketch. With respect to imagination, a contemporary tao must engage all those things that must be imaged in the contemporary world, both in its historical roots (which are diverse and require diverse contemporary taos) and in its novelties, particularly the novelty of intercultural challenge. Regarding interpretation, a contemporary tao must respect the integrity of critical judgment and be wary of forms of authority that would undermine that judgment. With respect to the scale of envisionment needed for a perspective on the encounter of world religions, a contemporary tao requires something like the dialectical method of moving from common abstractions to diverse specifications, a method found in the concept of philosophical theology I have advocated. With respect to responsibility itself, a contemporary tao must express the more basic religious responsibility to face divine things, the boundaries and fundamental problems.

III. Silence and the Sufficient Conditions

Section II discusses certain conditions necessary for an authentic contemporary tao which internalizes the daimon. Even if the necessary conditions are met, they are not sufficient. For sufficiency, a tao must be born of the commanding presence of the divine. As the phenomenologists of religion have said, a tao is formed in response to the awesomeness, terror, and uncannyness of the *mysterium tremendum*. A tao itself contains and presents the divine while at the same time somehow taking a distancing attitude toward itself and construing itself as merely a means, a path, to the divine. It may be misleading to speak of the "divine," which perhaps is too Western a word. What I mean by it, however, is that which brings one into proper contact with boundaries and problematic points. One can think of birth and death, of the encounter of diverse cultures, without believing anything ultimate is to be found there. But if we are faced with them suddenly as ultimate, *that* is the presence of the divine. Even the pursuit of personal happiness or salvation can be conceived nonultimately, as it is, in fact, by most materialistic people. But a sudden sense of ultimacy about one's happiness and worth, a sense that drove the Buddha to seek enlightenment, is what I mean by *divinity*; for, as several earlier chapters argue, the presence of the creator is in the ontological fact of existence. Boundary situations and the rest can shock us into recognizing that ontological facticity. A well-practiced tao is supposed to lead people to a continual awareness of the ontological aspect of everything whether it is at a boundary or not. To put the point the opposite way, the ontological character of the boundary situation can be perceived in everything from the Exodus to the Zen master's dung stick.

The question of sufficient conditions for a contemporary tao waits on the presence of this divinity. A *theory* of the ontological aspect of things is not the spiritual *presence* of things as ontological, even if the theory is believed. Is the divine present today so as to evoke a tao? The answer to this question must be ambiguous. Clearly for some people, the presence of the divine is as palpable as ever St. Francis or Hui Neng thought.

Sometimes this still shines in the imagery provided by one or another historical tao of faith and practice. Sometimes it is an imagery stretched out from science or the contemporary arts. Even among the most God-filled people today, however, at least in my experience and reading, there is a terrific tension between attaining the historical depth of a tao's cult while at the same time extending the cult to meet the requirements of imagination in contemporary experience. Most people are godless and taoless, or they play at religion cheaply. For them, God is silent, or lying, or dead. Usually, those filled with the Holy Spirit or conscious of the Buddha Mind are so only privately, not in ways that quicken our diverse cultures.

My postscript ends with this tentative empirical observation. Let me point out, however, that there are two clear alternatives to this way of leaving things.

Robert Scharlemann has written what must be the most persuasive argument since Josiah Royce for the presence of God in the possibility of reflecting on God. His recent *The Being of God: Theology and the Experience of Truth* claims that truth, as a relation between an asserted meaning and the reality to which it refers, can be experienced.[3] That is, truth becomes an object for a higher level kind of judgment which Scharlemann calls "reflection." To think about the fact of truth, however, is a higher-level judgment that he calls "reflexivity," a level at which the relation between meaning and reality is itself the object. God as the ground of meaning and reality, which are identical in being different and different though identical, is present and experienced as such in reflexivity. Only Anselm's fool would not understand what is experienced in reflexivity. Scharlemann is thus in a position to claim that the sufficient condition for a contemporary tao is, in fact, here, that the religious intellectual task is one merely of clearing away foolishness. His argument is much subtler than I have indicated, but he shares Tillich's confidence that ultimacy is present even if its material content is misconstrued.

For myself, I doubt that everyone has an ultimate concern. I also suspect that Scharlemann has placed religion's work too much in the interpretive dimension and too little in the imaginative. Only the interpretive dimension allows for an important distinction between the meaning of assertions and the reality they refer to. Yet religion's cults have mostly to do with cultivating imagination, imagination for which the question of truth or falsity is irrelevant or is added from the outside. "Successful" religion is not true but wholly engaged. From an empirical standpoint, Scharlemann's approach seems to take the mythic, ritual, and spiritual practices of the great traditions of faith and practice as almost adventitious. Yet they are the heart out of which even the intellectual elements of religious thinking arise. It is hard, as well, to see how to get from the God in reflexivity to the separate worlds of the great tao's of history.

The second alternative to my ambiguous ending is put forward in Thomas J. J. Altizer's *Total Presence*.[4] After years of recording and analyzing the absence, silence or death of God, Altizer has taken the extraordinary dialectical turn of finding the total presence of divinity in the final emptying of the private self.[5] Altizer has argued from the beginning that the life and death of God and of persons consists in a dialectical series of negations of self, other, and the presence of each to both. To sketch briefly the end of his story, the modern Western notion (or image) of the profoundly deep, private soul arose in counterposition to the notion of God as profoundly deep self. As Western mankind's "self" became increasingly private, isolated from others and according to Nietzsche, Freud, et al. even from its own consciousness, so God became Wholly Other and then vanished. Then, in our own century the fragmentation and privacy of the self turned back through art to make that privacy public. Joyce, Kafka, and others negated the privacy of the self by creating a literature about that isolation. Jazz music makes the private blues so public that the idiosyncracies of each person's privacy drop away and we are totally present in and to the world. That being true ontologically, God returns not as the Other Self but as Total Presence. My account butchers Altizer's nuanced historical dialectic, but his point is clear: The course of modern culture has come to the point where the very alienation from divinity about which seekers for a tao might worry has produced the presence of divinity itself. Whereas Scharlemann's dialectic is a logical one, showing that one cannot help but suppose the experience of God, Altizer's is empirical, arguing that what we have now, or are beginning to find, is God.

Again, I have my doubts. First of all, a dialectic of historical movements is intrinsically implausible to me. It requires a totalization of situations that seems false to the fragmentation, lack of coordination, and incommensurability for which there is so much evidence. Hardly any generalizations hold tightly enough of historical situations to sustain a dialectical argument of this sort. Since the engine of historical dialectic is totalizing negation of a totalized situation, fragmentation, lack of coordination, and incommensurability seem fatal to a dialectic of history. Second, if God is totally present, or total presence, why are so few aware of it? If God is totally present, then being asleep or fooled cannot be an excuse, for the spiritual blindness and foolishness must also be permeated by divinity. Speaking personally, I find the total presence of the divine in the same places Altizer does. Where Scharlemann's brilliance lies in logical dialectic, Altizer's lies in cultural discernment, if my own cultural tastes are the benchmark of brilliance. But then, why doesn't nearly everyone else agree? I have to conclude that, if Altizer and I are right in seeing God where he says, that is because of some limited and parochial, if unnamed, tao that we share. Thus I remain with my ambiguous empirical conclusion.

For all that, the present situation in the study of religion is an exciting chapter in the story of the daimon and the tao. The great taos of faith and practice are being transformed through understanding in various analytical ways. Furthermore, representatives of each are beginning to understand each other. The capacity for understanding others as alien, yet as subjects themselves, is one of the most valuable achievements of Western culture. That achievement itself may be, as has been argued, a critical element of an authentic contemporary tao. The achievement has been made possible, at least in part, by philosophical theology of the sort described and illustrated in this book. If I may conclude on a personal note, this is an extraordinary time for philosophical theology, a time when that calling elicits unbounded excitement and energy.

Notes

Introduction

1. Socrates' statement about his daimon, his divine protector, who prompted him to stop and reconsider whenever his thinking was awry, is recounted in Plato's *Apology*, at page 40, in the classic editions.

2. Perhaps the most consistently daimonic thinker today in the field of philosophy of culture is David Hall. See his *The Uncertain Phoenix* (New York: Fordham Univ. Press, 1982); and *Eros and Irony* (Albany: State Univ. of New York Press, 1982). In non-Western intellectual traditions the closest approximation to daimonic thinking derives from taoism. See, for instance, Kuang-ming Wu's *Chuang-tzu: World Philosopher at Play* (Chico, Cal.: Scholar's Press, 1982). Requiring a Confucian firmament to criticize, taoism never internalized the need for justifying positive assertions while at the same time putting them in a relative context.

3. For an account of theology as thoroughly daimonic yet orthodox, or at least in the service of truth for Western religion, see David Tracy's *Blessed Rage for Order* (New York: Seabury, 1975). Van Harvey's *The Historian and the Believer* (New York: Macmillan, 1966) scrutinizes the problem that historical (daimonic) reason poses for a version of a contemporary tao of faith and practice.

4. This complex logical point (concerning vagueness) is discussed throughout this book, particularly in chapters 1 and 3. See also my discussion in *Reconstruction of Thinking* (Albany: State Univ. of New York Press, 1981), chap. 2.

5. Neville, *God the Creator* (Chicago: Univ. of Chicago Press, 1968). The theory of divine creation is related to a dialectic of spiritual development in *Soldier, Sage, Saint* (New York: Fordham Univ. Press, 1978); and is developed as a foil to process theology in *Creativity and God* (New York: Seabury, 1980).

6. Gilkey, *Maker of Heaven and Earth: A Study of the Christian Doctrine of Creation* (Garden City, N.Y.: Doubleday, 1959; Anchor ed., 1965). For Gilkey's treatment of the general problem taken up in this book, see his *Naming the Whirlwind: The Renewal of God-Language* (Indianapolis: Bobbs-Merrill, 1969).

7. Gilkey treats the connection between Christianity and Buddhism in philosophical theology in his *Message and Existence* (New York: Seabury, 1979), in the context of stating the content of Christian faith.

8. On the point of the "silence of divinity," see Thomas J. J. Altizer's *The Self-Embodiment of God* (New York: Harper, 1977). On the point of divine presence in private individuality and public life, see Altizer's *Total Presence* (New York: Seabury, 1980).

Chapter One

1. The uniqueness of theology as being Christian is, of course, oversimplified here. There are not only several significant parallels–compare Samkara's *Commentary on the Brahma Sutras* with the medieval Christian commentaries on the *Sentences of Peter Lombard*–but also significant crossovers. For instance, the first modern work of critical biblical scholarship, the method that has had a determining influence on Christian theology in the last 200 years, was by Baruch Spinoza, a Jew. True, Spinoza was not at the center of the rabbinic tradition, but he fits into the great heritage of independent Jewish thinkers, from Philo to Buber and Fromm with whom Maimonides, the paradigmatic Jewish "theologian" had many affinities. In our own time, Rabbi Eugene Borowitz, professor at Hebrew Union College in New York, explicitly undertakes theology as a sort of intellectual work involving "a mediation between Jewish tradition and some external way of thinking. In the past this sort of activity has flourished when Jews found themselves in a hybrid cultural situation, e.g., Alexandria or Moslem culture." "Liberal Jewish Theology in a Time of Uncertainty, a Holistic Approach," *OCAR Yearbook*, 1977, p. 1. The "external way of thinking" Borowitz employs is the form of systematic theology in something like the Christian sense, applied to the "givens" of Jewish tradition. Where theology means something more precise than reflection in and about religions, as it is characterized in the Introduction of the present book, it makes essential reference to historical styles and norms of reflection.

2. An eloquent expression of the priority in religious studies of the scholarly encounter with religions alien to one's own tradition is Jacob Neusner's "Stranger at Home: The Task of Religious Studies" (published by the Department of Religious Studies, Arizona State Univ., Tempe, Arizona, 1979).

3. This position clearly is close to Tillich's famous description of theology in his *Systematic Theology* (Chicago: Univ. of Chicago Press, 1951), vol. I, Intro. pp. 3–68. But whereas Tillich was comfortable with the phrase "theological circle," I hope for only a "theological mosaic" and whereas he called *correlation* in theology a "method," though denying it an a priori status, I think *method* is too strong, as the next paragraph urges. Finally, Tillich is more sanguine than I about sustaining a clear difference between a contemporary "situation" and religious "answers."

4. The general point about argument as "making a case" was developed by Stephen Toulmin in his *The Uses of Argument* (New York: Cambridge Univ. Press, 1958) and was applied to theology by Van A. Harvey, *The Historian and the Believer* (New York: Macmillan, 1966).

5. The best discussion of Peirce's theory of community and inquiry with a sensitivity to religious and theological issues is John E. Smith's *Purpose and Thought* (New Haven: Yale Univ. Press, 1978); see also *Perspectives on Peirce*, ed. Richard J. Bernstein (New Haven: Yale Univ. Press, 1965). Smith's early "Religion and Theology," in Peirce, *Studies in the Philosophy of Charles Sanders Peirce*, ed. Philip P. Wiener and Frederic H. Young (Cambridge: Harvard Univ. Press, 1952), pp. 251–67, is also important.

6. See Hall's *Eros and Irony* (Albany: State Univ. of New York Press, 1982), chap. 3, "The Myth of Consensus."

Chapter Three

1. See Charles Sanders Peirce, "A Neglected Argument for the Reality of God." in *Collected Papers of Charles Sanders Peirce*, ed. Charles Hartshorne and Paul Weiss (Cambridge, Mass.: Harvard Univ. Press, 1935), vol. VI, pp. 311–26, 332–39.

2. A historical study of the concept of the holy spirit is not the topic of this chapter. The chapter arises out of the context of the discussion of the American Theological Society at its 1978 meeting in which the following historical papers were discussed in manuscript: "The Spirit in Primitive Montanism" by Walter J. Burghardt (S.J.); "The Holy Spirit in 16th Century Anabaptism" by Gabriel Fackre; "Who or What Is the Holy Spirit?: The New Testament" by Paul Meyer; "The Holy Spirit and the Church Fathers: A Sketch" by Richard Norris; "The Joachite Doctrine of the Spirit and the Expectation of the Third Age" by Rosemary Ruether; and "A Note on Ruah Ha-Kodesh in Rabbinic Thought" by Lou H. Silverman. For published, general accounts of the Holy Spirit in trinitarian thinking, see C. C. Richardson, *The Doctrine of the Trinity* (Nashville: Abingdon, 1958).

3. The great book of process cosmology is Alfred North Whitehead's *Process and Reality* (New York: Macmillan, 1927), which has been developed systematically for theological use by John B. Cobb, Jr. in *A Christian Natural Theology* (Philadelphia: Westminster Press, 1965). My own development of a cosmology is to be found in *The Cosmology of Freedom* (New Haven: Yale Univ. Press, 1974).

4. See my *Creativity and God: A Challenge to Process Theology* (New York: Seabury, 1980).

5. Within the technical details of process cosmology, elimination of the process God requires developing alternate categories for solving the problems Whitehead solved by suggesting that God supplies the lure which provides an original subjective unity to any occasion. To defend a creationist theory of God, as I do, requires showing how divine creation enters the creative process, a topic discussed in Chapter 3 and in chapters 8 and 9.

6. For a thorough discussion of this point, see the treatment of causation in Harold F. Moore, Robert Neville, and William Sullivan "The Contours of Responsibility: A New Model," in *Man and World*, 5/4 (November 1972), 392–421.

7. In this connection see John E. Smith's essay, "Is Existence a Valid Philosophical Concept?", in his *Reason and God* (New Haven: Yale Univ. Press, 1961).

8. The distinction between the ontological dimension of things and the relative cosmological dimension is suggested by Josiah Royce in his discussion of the *what* and the *that* in *The World and the Individual* (New York: Dover, 1959), First Series, Chap. 2.

9. The ontological concept of mutual relevance, important in this and the next section, is explored thematically in my *God the Creator* (Chicago: Univ. of Chicago Press, 1968), exp. chapters 2, 3, and 9.

10. See Chapter 6.

11. For an explanation of harmony as value, see my *Cosmology of Freedom*, chap. 3, and *Reconstruction of Thinking* (Albany: State Univ. of New York Press,

1981), chaps. 3–8; the latter also explores the following points concerning engagement, interpretation, envisagement, and responsibility.

12. For a precise analysis of integrity in this sense, see *God the Creator*, chap. 4, and chap. 6 of the present book.

13. For an elaborate analysis of the theory of indeterminacy and freedom, see *Cosmology of Freedom*, chaps. 5, 6.

14. What is proposed here as a supposition is the conclusion of a long argument in *God the Creator* which need not be rehearsed. In the explication of the logic of the supposition, the discussion below summarizes more detailed treatment in *God the Creator*, particularly in chaps. 1–4.

15. Chapter 4 relates this trinitarian conception to categories of orthodox Christian theology.

16. Hegel properly recognized the implication of the world in God's own determinate character but perhaps failed to appreciate the difference between the ontological creation of determinate things and causal relations among them.

17. Not appreciating this distinction, Whitehead was led to treat God as a being within the cosmos. His principles for understanding the cosmos itself are merely empirical generalizations that do not account self-referentially for themselves. See *Creativity and God*, chap. 3.

18. For a logical analysis of the concept of essential and conditional features, see *God the Creator*, chap. 2 and App.

19. For a defense of this view, see chap. 4.

20. See *Reconstructions of Thinking*, chaps. 1, 2.

21. Peirce's most succinct discussion of this concept is in "A Neglected Argument for the Reality of God," in *Collected Papers*.

22. The general point here, as well as the electron example, are derived from Hilary Putnam, *Meaning and the Moral Sciences* (London: Routledge and Kegan Paul, 1978), lectures I, II.

23. Two points must be made here about the existential quality of human life relative to the problematic status of belief within a community of inquirers. First, as John E. Smith points out in his *Experience and God* (New York: Oxford Univ. Press, 1968), positive answers to basic religious questions are framed in the "anthropological dimension." The particular history and context of oneself and one's group provides the terms in which the divine may be encountered. We should expect, therefore, that a divine person would follow the prophetic and kingly models in first-century Palestine and not the medicant model of India. Further, the precise sense in which one might relate to Jesus or to rabbinical authority depends, say, on the details of one's personal history. One's particular experience is therefore expected to be idiosyncratic and is publicly accessible and understandable as such, insofar as that history is understandable. Hermeneutic discovery of some alien tradition is not so much more difficult than hermeneutic recovery of the tradition of one's cultural ancestors, as current public canons of historical scholarship illustrate. The other side of Smith's position is that the idiosyncracies of positive religious encounters are public and communicable precisely because there is a universal religious dimension to experience. Not universal religious experience (religious experiences are always particular) but a religious dimension is universal to all cultural experiences. Smith defines this as a quest for the ground and goal of human experience. (The questions asked in the first paragraph of Section I, articulations of the "problem of God," are ways of parsing this.) The

universal dimension provides a common reference point for inquiry by those whose positive experiences differ.

Second, any given inquirer's religious life is positive and definite, whereas the available positions in the ongoing religious inquiry are tentative and hypothetical, at best, plausible. Put another way, the religious life demands commitments now, not promissory notes. Despite the fact that some people historically have been definite in their beliefs, in the course of theological reflection the intellectual significance of beliefs has come to be seen as that of merely provisional hypotheses in an ongoing inquiry. This suggests that the existential dimension of belief is not identical with the intellectual dimension. Two suggestions seem plausible immediately. First, a good portion of religious beliefs serves to orient one to the symbols and imagery with which religious practice forms the imagination. In religious practice, liturgies, rituals, scriptural recitations, and prayers serve to form the imagination in ways that govern how the world is engaged. Imaginative engagement comes before critical interpretation and, strictly speaking, makes no claim for truth. Whereas ascertainment of the truth status of religous belief may well be tentative, the existential employment of the beliefs in forming imagination can be definite. Second, another part of religious belief serves to orient commitments of action and life-style. In extreme times, religious belief directs the faithfulness that invests martyrdom. In this respect, however, tentativeness of religious belief is no different from tentativeness of belief in another sphere. Many spheres – for instance, politics – involve life-and-death decisions. Requirements for wholehearted actions based on a partial understanding is a natural ambiguity of life. It should be noted that referring beliefs to the contexts of imagination and action does not solve all the problems of existential life with tentative theology. To a Jew in Buchenwald, the question how God could allow the Holocaust to happen must have been a "living, forced, momentous option" for self-understanding, yet it was not clear how to answer it. And the brute, fact is, it still is not clear.

Chapter Four

1. This chapter systematically expands the concept of creation used illustratively in chapters 1–3, paying more attention to the roots of the concept in the Christian tao.

2. Even Schleiermacher, concerned as he was to preserve the dogmatic truths in the doctrine of the Trinity, expressed his frustration at making internal sense of the doctrine. "The ecclesiastical doctrine of the Trinity demands that we think of each of the three Persons as equal to the Divine Essence, and *vice versa*, and each of the three Persons as equal to the others. Yet we cannot do either the one or the other, but can only represent the Persons in a gradation, and thus either represent the unity of the Essence as less real than the three Persons, or *vice versa*." *The Christian Faith*, tr. Mackintosh and Stewart (tr. of 2d ed.; Edinburgh: T. & T. Clark, 1928, prop. 171, p. 742.

3. See John E. Smith's excellent analysis of the ramifications of this point in his *Reason and God*) (New Haven: Yale Univ. Press, 1961), chap. 7, esp. pp. 153–56.

4. As John H. Leith argues: "Heresy is so important a factor in the origin of

creeds that it tempts the commentator to exaggerate its role. As was said long ago, creeds are signposts to heresies." *Creeds of the Churches*, ed. J. H. Leith (Garden City, N.Y.: Doubleday Anchor, 1963), p. 9. Leith's introductory essay, "The Creeds and Their Role in the Church," is very instructive.

5. See Schleiermacher, *Christian Faith*. If the doctrine were not speculatively inept, as he thought it, it is unlikely that he would have distinguished it so sharply from experience. He would have been more sympathetic to Calvin's treatment (*Institutes of the Christian Religion* 1, 13, 3–5), which holds speculation to interpretation of scriptural experience.

6. *God the Creator* (Chicago: University of Chicago Press, 1968), chap. 4.

7. Ibid., pp. 74–88.

8. Ibid., pp. 44–50 and App.

9. The theory of norms is discussed at length in my *Reconstruction of Thinking* (Albany: State Univ. of New York Press, 1981), especially chaps. 3, 4, 6, 7.

10. Thomas J. J. Altizer's *The Self-Embodiment of God* (New York: Seabury Press, 1977) is the most original twentiety-century trinitarian claim that God becomes God by speaking or acting. My position is in basic agreement with Altizer's. Whereas Altizer distinguishes the three features temporally, however, I take them to be features of the act itself: God is Spirit.

11. Cf., namely, Justin's *First Apology* 8 and Irenaeus' *Against Heresies* 1, 10, 1; also Eph 1–3. J. N. D. Kelly states: "at this period the title 'almightly' connoted God's all-pervading control and sovereignty over reality, just as 'Father' referred primarily to His role as creator and author of all things." *Early Christian Doctrines*, 2d ed. (New York, 1960); p.83.

12. That is, the Apologists. See Kelly, pp. 100–104.

13. Kelly, pp. 83–87.

14. See Aloys Grillmeier (S.J.), *Christ in Christian Tradition* (New York: Sheed and Ward, 1965), pp. 27–35.

15. See Prov. 8:30–31; even Sir. 24:8–29, which declares that wisdom is to dwell with Jacob and Israel, and likens wisdom to a vine with abundant fruit (John 15:1–11), does not go so far as to assert an incarnation of wisdom. Wisdom, it says, is the law of Moses (24:23). Interestingly, for Ben Sira (24:21), those who eat wisdom hunger for more and those who drink it thirst for more, whereas for John's Gospel, those eating and drinking of Christ shall neither hunger nor thirst (6:35) – an unexpected pragmatic benefit of incarnate spiritual sustenance.

16. The theme of the lordship of Jesus means not only that Jesus rules the world but also that the world is a glorifying expression of God because it is ruled by Jesus Christ. This lies behind Jesus's remark (to the Father): "All mine are thine, and thine are mine, and I am glorified in them" (John 17:10 RSV); the work Jesus has accomplished (John 17:4), with the further work of the Spirit (John 16:14–15), makes those whom the Father has given Him (John 17:9) the proper possessions of the Father ("all mine are thine"). Cf. Paul's doctrine in Colossians. Speaking of Jesus, he says: "For in Him all the fulness of God was pleased to dwell, and through Him to reconcile to himself all things" (1:19–20 RSV). Again: "For in Him the whole fulness of deity dwells bodily, and you have come to fulness of life in Him, who is the head of all rule and authority" (2:9–10, RSV).

17. Hence the supreme importance of the early credal statements in Matt. 16:16; Acts 17:3; and John 11:27. Cf. also, Luke 2:11; Acts 2:36, 9:22; and John 20:31).

18. The incarnation of the World first came to clear expression in John's gospel, generally recognized as a late New Testament writing.

19. See Rabbi Richard L. Rubenstein's essay "Thomas Altizer's Apocalypse," in *America and the Future of Theology*, ed. William A. Beardslee (Philadelphia: Westminster, 1967), pp. 32–40. The central Jewish objection to Christianity now derives from the history of Christian-Jewish relations.

20. For the technical use of the term *normative*, see my "Intuition," in *International Philosophical Quarterly* 7 (1967) 556–90, esp. pp. 581–89.

21. Gen. 1:2–3. This passage can mean that the Spirit of God moving over the face of the waters was the condition for His Word ("Let there be. . . ") being spoken. This gives a functional interpretation to the concept of *Word*. The writer of the passage was not a logos Christologist.

22. This claim has a cosmological generality not directly expressed in Christian scripture. But see Rom. 14:17: "For the kingdom of God does not mean food and drink but righteousness and peace and joy in the Holy Spirit" (RSV). See also the numerous passages where the Spirit is the power by which God does something, e.g., Matt. 1:18; Acts 20:28; Rom. 5:5, 15:13–16.

23. In this and the following discussions of Christological and trinitarian controversies, historical problems are subordinated to dialectical ones. The following books give adequate historical accounts of the positions discussed: J. N. D. Kelly, *Early Christian Doctrines*; C. C. Richardson, *The Doctrine of the Trinity* (Nashville: Abingdon, 1958), a careful criticism of the doctrine; Claude Welch, *In This Name: The Doctrine of the Trinity in Contemporary Theology* (New York, 1952).

24. Cf. Kelly, *Early Christian Doctrines*, pp. 139–40.

25. Ibid., pp. 140–42. See Ignatius' argument (*Epistle to the Trallians* 10–11): "But there are men who do not believe in God, that is, they have no faith. If, as they declare, His suffering was only an illusion (it is they themselves who are mere illusion), why then am I a prisoner, and why do I pray to fight with the beasts? I would then be dying in vain . . . . For it is through the cross that Christ in His passion calls all of you to be His members. Hence the head cannot be born without limbs, for God promises us unions, that is, Himself." *The Fathers of the Primitive Church*, ed. and tr. Herbert A. Musurillo (S.J.) (New York: Mentor-Omega, 1966), p. 75.

26. Cf. Kelly, *Early Christian Doctrines*. See esp. the references to Paul of Samosata in Grillmeier, *Christ*.

27. Historically, Patripassianism was the result of monarchianism – for instance, in Noetus of Smyrna and Praxeas (see Kelly, *Early Christian Doctrines*, p. 120); Grillmeier, *Christ*, p. 144; Tertullian, *Against Praxeas*, ed. and tr. Ernest Evans (London, 1949). Consequently, the mediating function of the Spirit that I attributed to the position is a historical distortion, as is the distinction implied between the Father and the nondivine elements in the Son. What is of interest here is the structure of the problem.

28. Welch, *In This Name*, App. A. pp. 293f. For a discussion of the general issues, see Kelly, *Early Christian Doctrines*, chap. 10.

29. Kelly, *Early Christian Doctrines*, pp. 107–15; Welch, *In This Name*.

30. The battle cry of Arians, *ēn pote hote ouk ēn*.

31. Without some form of order, Sabellianism, in one guise or another, is the result.

32. For example, Arius' argument on its dialectical side was that the Father alone is unoriginate or self-existent and that everything else is dependent, including Christ. The opposing argument was that the Father is both unoriginated (*agenētos*) and unbegotten (*agennētos*), that the world is originated or created, and that Christ is merely begotten, not originated. The opposing argument, however, depends on making out the created-begotten distinction we are dealing with. See Kelly, *Early Christian Doctrines*, pp. 227–31.

33. Thus, Arius, in denying that to beget (*gennān*) differs from to create (*poiein*), said the Son is created *ex nihilo*.

34. *Metaphysics* 1074b27.

35. See *God the Creator*.

36. It is interesting that this is exactly how Athanasius saw the issue. As Kelly says (*Early Christian Doctrines*, p. 243), "In Athanasius's approach philosophical and cosmological considerations played a very minor part, and his guiding thought was the conviction of redemption." The metathesis of Chapter 4 of the present work is that only highly abstract philosophical theology such as is implied in the theory of creation can preserve the concrete history and experience of religion. The fallacy of misplaced concreteness is always committed where concrete problems are treated as abstract, and vice versa. Chapter 11 enlarges on this point.

37. See *God the Creator*, pp. 220–35.

38. Cf. the quotation from Ignatius in note 25. If bodily men are united to God, it must be through a bodily Christ.

Chapter Five

1. For a detailed analysis of one part of this shift in interest, see Peter C. Hodgson's *Formation of Historical Theology: A Study of Ferdinand Christian Baur* (New York: Harper & Row, 1966).

2. See, for instance, James's *Varieties of Religious Experience* (New York: Mentor, 1958), p. 395; *A Pluralistic Universe* (New York: Longmans, Green, 1909), pp. 311ff.; *Pragmatism* (New York: Meridian, 1955), "Pragmatism and Religion," esp. p. 192; and *The Will to Believe and Other Essays* (New York: Dover, 1956), "Reflex Action and Theism," exp. ff. 134–36.

3. For instance, *Process and Reality* (New York: Macmillan, 1929), ff. 519–33; and *Religion in the Making* (New York: Macmillan, 1926).

4. See, for example, *The Divine Relativity* (New Haven: Yale Univ. Press, 1948); and *The Logic of Perfection* (LaSalle, Ill.: Open Court, 1962).

5. See *Modes of Being* (Carbondale: Southern Illinois Univ. Press, 1958), intro., chaps. 4, 12; also *The God We Seek* (Carbondale: Southern Illinois Univ. Press, 1964).

6. *A Christian Natural Theology* (Philadelphia: Westminster, 1965).

7. See *Christ without Myth* (New York: Harper & Row, 1961), chap. 4; and *The Reality of God* (New York: Harper & Row, 1966).

8. See Paul Tillich, *The New Being* (New York: Scribner's 1955), "The Paradox of Prayer," pp. 135–38.

9. For an alternate account of freedom in Christianity, as interpreted by

philosophical theology, see Carl G. Vaught's *The Quest for Wholeness* (Albany: State Univ. of New York Press, 1982).

10. The problems are answered, after a fashion, in my *Cosmology of Freedom*, chaps. 4–7.

11. See the splendid elaboration of this orthodox point in Julian N. Hartt's *Christian Critique of American Culture* (New York: Harper and Row, 1967), Part II.

Chapter Six

1. This is a theme of John E. Smith's fine book *Experience and God* (New York: Oxford Univ. Press, 1968). See also his essay "The Experiential Foundations of Religion," *Reason and God* (New Haven: Yale Univ. Press, 1961), pp. 173–83.

2. See, for example, *The Book of Mencius*, 2A:6, 3A:5. There are many editions and translations of this book; one of the best is *A Source Book in Chinese Philosophy*, ed. Wing-tsit Chan (Princeton: Princeton Univ. Press, 1963).

3. I defend this in *Reconstruction of Thinking* (Albany: State Univ. of New York Press, 1981), esp. chap. 2.

4. Hans Jonas has a fine treatment of many complexities in the history of the doctrine of creation *ex nihilo* in his "Jewish and Christian Elements in the Western Philosophical Tradition," in *Creation: The Impact of an Idea*, ed. Daniel O'Connor and Francis Oakley (New York: Scribner's, 1969), pp. 241–58. It is interesting that, in discussing the Scotistic idea of creation (of which my hypothesis is a version), Professor Jonas argues that the doctrine that the divine intelligibles are products of the divine will leads to the relativizing of values to human will when faith in the divine will fades. Another way of looking at the contingency of intelligibles, and of all values is to say that they are known only empirically, not a priori. To conclude, as so many do, that divine voluntarism entails conventionalism is to assume that experience cannot be a source of important knowledge.

5. 1. Non-being then existed not nor being:
    There was no air, nor sky that is beyond it.
    What was concealed? Wherein? In whose protection?
    And was there deep unfathomable water?

6. Who knows for certain? Who shall here declare it?
    Whence was it born, and whence came this creation?
    The gods were born after this world's creation:
    Then who can know from whence it has arisen?

7. None knoweth whence creation has arisen;
    And whether he has or has not produced it:
    He who surveys it in the highest heaven.
    He only knows, or haply he may not.

Hymn x. 129, *A Source Book in Indian Philosophy*, ed. Sarvepalli Radhakrishnan and Charles A. Moore (Princeton: Princeton, Univ. Pres, 1957).

6. See, for instance, the *Brhadāranyaka Upanisad*, II, iii; or III, viii.

7. This whole world the illusion-maker (*māyin*) projects out of this.
    And in it by illusion (*māya*) the other is confined.

Now, one should know the Nature (*Prakriti*) is illusion (*māyā*).
And that the Mighty Lord (*mahesvara*) is the illusion-maker (*māyin*).
Svetāsvatara Upanisad IV, i, 9–10. Radhakrishnan and Moore, *Source Book*.

8. See the *Mādhyamika-sāstra* by Nagarjuna, esp. chap. 1, in *The Concept of Buddhist Nirvana*, ed. Th. Stcherbatsky (London: Mouton, 1965). Chap. 8 of the present book expands on this point.

9. Ibid., chap. 25. See also, Seng-chao's treatises, "The Immutability of Things" and "The Emptiness of the Unreal," in Chan, *Source Book*.

10. Compare Fa-tsang's "Treatise on the Golden Lion" in Chan, *Source Book*, for instance, with the Western doctrine that determination is by negation of the otherwise unlimited pure act. See chap. 7 of the present book for a more careful discussion.

11. See Nicolas Berdyaev's discussion of Jacob Böhme's contribution to the notion of freedom and creation in *The Beginning and the End*, trans. R. M. French (New York: Harper Torchbook, 1957), pp. 104–17.

12. *Vedātra Sūtra* I, i, 2, in Radhakrishnan and Moore, *Source Book*.

13. Samkara's commentary on *Vedānta Sūtra* I, i, 2, also in Radhakrishnan and Moore.

14. Nagarjuna, in Stcherbatsky, Seng-chao, in Chan, *Source Book*.

15. A strictly logical exposition of the speculative hypothesis would be to say in the first proposition that determinate things are created and in the second that the creator is indeterminate and divine. Because of the lay of the evidence, however, I have chosen a different division. The religious evidence for creation of the world makes reference to a creator; thus the creator must be included in a discussion of creation *ex nihilo*. The *character* of the creator, however, may be left vague until it is considered in a separate proposition.

16. David Burrell, for instance, argues for this approach in his "Religious Life and Understanding," *Review of Metaphysics*, 32 (1969), pp. 690–95. The assumption that a self-defeating or contradictory statement is a "nonstatement" in his. Other philosophers might want to reserve *nonstatement* for referring to statements so ill formed as to be unintelligible. A contradiction, after all, must be a fairly clear assertion if it can be recognized as contradictory.

17. The Tao (Way) that can be told of is not the eternal Tao;
The name that can be named is not the eternal name.
The Nameless is the origin of Heaven and Earth;
The Named is the mother of all things.
Therefore let there always be non-being so we may see their subtlety,
And let there always be being so we may see their outcome.
The two are the same,
But after they are produced, they have different names.
Chan, *Source Book*, p. 139.

18. Tibetan Buddhism is perhaps the most picturesque form of Mahayana in terms of mythical beings and places. See the *Tibetan Book of the Dead*, ed. W. Y. Evans-Wentz (London: Oxford Univ. Press, 1927). The editor's introduction contains a splendid explanation of the three "bodies," or *kayas*, pp. 10–18.

19. See, for example, the glorification of Krisna in the *Bhagavad-gītā*.

20. These rough characterizations of Buddhist notions such as absoluteness, emptiness, and suchness are inherently unsatisfactory. Buddhism, as diverse as Christianity, is grasped on so many levels that what is assertion for some people

is merely symbolic "expedient means" for others. The level of understanding selected here is where obvious comparisons of East and West present themselves. Chapter 9 and the Postscript deal with paradoxes of interpreation in detail.

21. See William H. McNeill, *The Rise of the West* (Chicago: Univ. of Chicago Press, 1963), pp. 157–66. See also Sabatino Moscati's *Ancient Semitic Civilizations* (New York: Capricorn, 1960).

22. This point is perhaps overstated by Oscar Cullman in *Christ and Time,* trans. Floyd V. Filson, rev. ed. (Philadelphia: Westminster, 1964), where he treats the Hellenic sense of time as cyclical. A superbly nuanced general study of Eastern people's sense of the disposition of the world is Hajime Nakamura, *Ways of Thinking of Eastern Peoples,* ed. Philip P. Wiener (Honolulu: East-West Center Press, 1964). If the comparison is not too simplistic, the Eastern time sense is symbolized by the overturning wheel of the mandala, the Western by the beams of the cross, representing life as an intersection of eternal action and linear history.

23. In this view of metaphysical hypotheses, I follow that of Charles S. Peirce expressed in "A Neglected Argument for the Reality of God," Peirce, *Collected Papers,* 6.452–93.

24. Tillich, *Christianity* (New York: Columbia Univ. Press, 1963).

Chapter Seven

1. See the *Tao Te Ching,* any ed., chap. 1.

2. See the beginning of Chou's explanation of the *Diagram of the Great Ultimate,* for instance in Wing-tsit Chan's *Source Book in Chinese Philosophy* (Princeton, N.J.: Princeton Univ. Press, 1963), p. 463.

3. See Francis H. Cook's *Hua-yen Buddhism: The Jewel Net of Indra* (University Park, Pa.: Pennsylvania State Univ. Press, 1977), chap. 7; Garma C. C. Chang's *The Buddhist Teaching of Totality: The Philosophy of Hwa Yen Buddhism* (University Park, Pa.: Pennsylvania State Univ. Press, 1971), part 2, sec. 1; and Frederick J. Streng's *Emptiness: A Study in Religious Meaning* (Nashville: Abingdon Press, 1967), inc. his translation of Nagarjuna's *Mūlamadhyamikakārikās.*

4. See N. J. Girardot, "The Problem of Creation Mythology in the Study of Chinese Religion," *History of Religions,* 15/4 (May 1976), pp. 289–318.

5. See Chen's "Nothingness and the Mother Principle in Early Chinese Taoism," *International Philosophical Quarterly,* 9 (1969), pp. 391–405; "The Origin and Development of Being (Yu) from Non-Being (Wu) in the *Tao Te Ching,*" *International Philosophical Quarterly* 13/3 (September 1973), pp. 402–17; and "Tao as the Great Mother and the Influence of Motherly Love in the Shaping of Chinese Philosophy," *History of Religions* 14/1 (August 1974), pp. 51–63.

6. One of the strongest passages for an interpretation based on transcending temporality is the *Tao Te Ching,* chap. 40: "All things in the world come from being. And being comes from non-being." Translated by Chan in the *Source Book.*

7. See Hsu's article, "Two Kinds of Changes in Lao Tzu's Thought," *Journal of Chinese Philosophy,* 4 (December 1977), pp. 329–55. This thesis is reflected in

his "Laotzu's Conception of Evil," *Philosophy East/West* 26/3 (July 1976), pp. 301–16; and less in his "Laotzu's Conception of Ultimate Reality: A Comparative Study," *International Philosophical Quarterly*, 16 (June 1976), pp. 197–218.

8. See Chang Chung-yuan's brilliant attempt to correlate taoism and Whitehead's process philosophy, in *Creativity and Taoism: A Study of Chinese Philosophy, Art, and Poetry* (New York: Harper, 1970; orig. ed., Julian Press, 1963), esp. chap. 1.

9. See the eighty-first chapter of the *Tao Te Ching*.

10. *Hsun Tsu: Basic Writings*, trans. by Burton Watson (New York: Columbia Univ. Press, 1963), p. 46.

11. Ibid., p. 44.

12. Fingarette, *Confucius: The Secular as Sacred* (New York: Harper, 1972), p. 43.

13. Ibid., chap. 3.

Chapter Eight

1. Whitehead himself, as well as Charles Hartshorne, John B. Cobb, Jr., and many others, have discussed connections between process philosophy and Buddhism. See, for instance, Whitehead's *Religion in the Making* (New York: Macmillan, 1926); Hartshorne's *Creative Synthesis and Philosophic Method* (La Salle, Ill.: Open Court, 1970); and Cobb's *The Structure of Christian Existence* (Philadelphia: Westminster, 1967) and *Christ in a Pluralistic Age* (Philadelphia: Westminster, 1975). For several critical dialogues on this issue, see *John Cobb's Theology in Process*, ed. David Ray Griffin and Thomas J. J. Altizer (Philadelphia: Westminster, 1977). A thorough critical analyses of process philosophy and Buddhism is that by Altizer, discussed at length in chap. 9 of the present book. The most original and thorough full-scale study of process philosophy and Buddhism, especially of Hwa Yen Buddhism, is Steve Odin's *Process Metaphysics and Hwa-Yen Buddhism: A Critical Study of Cumulative Penetration Versus Interpenetration* (Albany: State Univ. of New York Press, 1982).

2. Chang Chung-yuan and David Hall have explored this point, emphasizing the prominence naturalistic cosmology gives to the aesthetic dimension of human experience. See Chang's *Creativity and Taoism: A Study of Chinese Philosophy, Art, and Poetry* (New York: Harper, 1970); and Hall's *The Uncertain Phoenix* (New York: Fordham Univ. Press, 1982) and *Eros and Irony* (Albany: State Univ. of New York Press, 1982).

3. Two excellent studies of Wang have been published recently: Julia Ching, *To Acquire Wisdom: The Way of Wang Yang-ming* (New Yrk: Columbia Univ. Press, 1976); and Tu Wei-ming, *Neo-Confucian Thought in Action: Wang Yang-ming's Youth (1472–1509)* (Berkeley: Univ. of California Press, 1976).

4. A fine example of such spadework is *Self and Society in Ming thought*, ed. William Theodore de Bary and the Conference on Ming Thought (New York: Columbia Univ. Press, 1970). A much more innovative attempt to understand Confucianism as a profound and viable philosophy in contemporary terms is Tu Wei-ming, *Humanity and Self-Cultivation: Essays in Confucian Thought* (Berkeley: Asian Humanities Press, 1979), esp. chaps. on Wang Yang-ming.

5. In Wang Yang-ming, *Instructions for Practical Living and Other Neo-Confucian Writings*, trans. with notes by Wing-tsit Chan (New York: Columbia

Univ. Press, 1963). I give the page references to Wang's "Inquiry" in this book because of references to other writings here. Professor Chan's translation is reprinted in his *Source Book in Chinese Philosophy* (Princeton: Princeton Univ. Press, 1963), to which I refer for writings of other philosophers. The "Inquiry" is short enough that a reader with only the *Source Book* can quickly locate the passages cited.

6. Chu Hsi was the great systematic synthesizer of Sung Neo-Confucianism. Just as Thomas Aquinas provided the great synthesis of medieval Christian responses to Aristotelian and Arabic thought, so Chu brought together the Confucian incorporation of Taoism and Buddhism. His editions and interpretations of the Chinese classics were the basis of the civil service examinations in China from 1313 to 1905! Selections of Chu's writings are found in Chan's *Source Book*; Chu's *Philosophy of Human Nature* is translated with notes by J. Percy Bruce (London: Probsthain & Co., 1922). For background see Dr. Bruce's *Chu Hsi and His Masters: An Introduction to Chu Hsi and the Sung School of Chinese Philosophy* (London: Probsthain & Co., 1923); also Professor Carsun Chang's *The Development of Neo-Confucian Thought*, vol. 1 (New York: Bookman Associates, 1957).

7. Wang, *ibid.*, p. 272. The Chinese phrase ta jen means "great person," with no gender suggested; Wang meant to say that both women and men could become great. Also, the standard translation *great man* reflects not only English-speaking chauvinism but subsequent Chinese chauvinism. My text uses the gender-absent form.

8. Ibid.

9. *Book of Mencius*, 2A:6. In Chan, *Source Book*, p. 65.

10. For a brief biography and exposition, see Bruce's *Chu Hsi and his Masters*, chaps. 2, 6.

11. Chan, *Source Book*, p. 463.

12. See Whitehead's *Science and the Modern World* (New York: Macmillan, 1927). For a complete if popular development of themes of "vibration" in Eastern thought and modern physics, see Fritjof Capra's *The Tao of Physics* (Berkeley: Shambala, 1975).

13. See Antonio T. de Nicholas, *Four Dimensional Man* (Stony Brook, N.Y.: Nicolas Hays, 1976); and Ernest G. McClain, *The Myth of Invariance* (Stony Brook, N.Y.: Nicolas Hays, 1976).

14. See Sophia Delza, *Tai Chi Ch'uan: Body and Mind in Harmony* (New York: David McKay, 1961), App.

15. See Chan, *Source Book*, pp. 95–114.

16. *Ibid.*, p. 466. The internal quotation is from *Analects* 12:1, in Chan, p. 38.

17. Whitehead, *Process and Reality* (New York: Macmillan, 1929), part I, chap. 2, sec. 3.

18. Whitehead, *Adventures of Ideas* (Cambridge, Eng.: Cambridge Univ. Press, 1933), chap. 16.

19. Chan, *Source Book*, p. 463.

20. Ibid., p. 465.

21. See Chu Hsi's *Philosophy of Human Nature*, bk. 2. For an assessment of Chu's place in the Confucian tradition, see Tu Wei-ming's *Humanity and Self-Cultivation*, Ch. 9, which advances the revolutionary view that Chu was aberrent from the Confucian-Mencian tradition and that Wang Yang-ming represented the more faithful lineage.

22. Wang, p. 272.

23. Ibid., p. 273.
24. Ibid. Wang's general line of argument concerning the origin of evil was originally developed by Chang Tsai (1020-1077); see, for instance, Chang's *Correcting Youthful Ignorance*. See also, chap. 6 in Chan, *Source Book*, pp. 507-15.
25. Although this particular interpretation is original with Wang, Ch'eng Hao wrote: "The man of *jen* forms one body with all things without any differentiation. Righteousness, propriety, wisdom, and faithfulness are all (expressions of) *Jen*," in his essay "On Understanding the Nature of Jen (Humanity)," in Chan, *Source Book*, p. 523.
26. The "item" in the *Great Learning*, "loving the people," can also be translated "renovating the people," which was Chu Hsi's preferred rendering. Wang argued that it means *both* loving in the sense that a parent loves a child and renovating in the sense of arousing "the people to become new," a phrase from a later portion of the *Great Learning*. See Wang, pp. 5-6.
27. Ch'eng Hao, for instance, wrote: "Everyone's nature is obscured in some way and as a consequence he cannot follow the Way. In general the trouble lies in resorting to selfishness and the exercise of cunning. Being selfish, one cannot take purposive action to respond to things, and being cunning, one cannot be at home with enlightenment. For a mind that hates external things, to seek illumination in a mind where nothing exists is to look for a reflection on the back of a mirror." From "Reply to Mater Heng-chu's Letter" in Chan, *Source Book*, p. 526. Chi Hsi said: "Whatever remedy you find for the distraction and distress of the Mind you cannot regain its lordship. You must perceive and understand the principles of the universe without the slightest admixture of selfish motives, then you will succeed . . . . Otherwise, you will find that selfish desire becomes like a live dragon or tiger, impossible to master," in *Philosophy of Human Nature*, p. 247; see also pp. 264-66. Wang Yan-ming discussed desires throughout the *Instructions for Practical Living*; see, for instance, part II, sec. 161, pp. 140-41.
28. Wang, *Instructions*, p. 274. In his *Investigation of Things*, Wang wrote: "The highest good is the original substance of the mind. It is no other than manifesting one's clear character to the point of refinement and singleness of mind. And yet it is not separated from the events and things. When Chu Hsi said in his commentary that (manifesting the clear character is) 'the realization of the Principle of Nature to the fullest extent without an iota of selfish human desire,' he got the point." From Wang, *Instructions*, p. 7; the parenthetical clarifications are supplied by Chan, the translator.
29. Chu was not as "externalistic" as Wang sometimes made him out. Chu wrote: "The mind embraces all principles and all principles are complete in this single entity, the mind. If one is not able to preserve the mind, he will be unable to investigate principle to the utmost. If he is unable to investigate principle to the utmost, he will be unable to exert his mind to the utmost." Quoted in Chan, *Source Book*, p. 606.
On the other hand, as is discussed below, Chu Hsi believed that we must investigate external things if we are to understand principle thoroughly. "From the most essential and most fundamental about oneself to every single thing or affair in the world," he wrote, "even the meaning of one word or half a word, everything should be investigated to the utmost, and none of it is unworthy of attention. . . . There is no other way to investigate principle to the utmost than to pay attention to everything in our daily reading of books and handling of

affairs. . . . To investigate principle to the utmost means to seek to know the reason for which things and affairs are as they are and the reason according to which they should be; that is all. If we know why they are as they are, our will will not be perplexed, and if we know what they should be, our action will not be wrong. It does not mean to take the principle of something and put it in another." Chan, *Source Book*, pp. 610–11.

30. Whereas Chu distinguished the "reason for which things and affairs are as they are" from the "reason according to which they should be" (Note 29), Wang emphasized an identity of fact and value in things' reasons or principles. All Neo-Confucianism stressed the continuity of value with fact in experience.

31. See Whitehead, *Process and Reality*, part 2, chap. 3, sec. 1, pp. 126–30. Here, for instance, Whitehead says that the " 'order' in the actual world is differentiated from mere 'givenness' by introduction of adaption for the attainment of an end." See also my *Reconstruction of Thinking* (Albany: State Univ. of New York Press, 1981), chaps. 2, 4, 7 for a defense of the view that all thinking and experience entails valuation.

32. See, for instance, Chu Hsi's *Philosophy of Human Nature*, bk. 1. "The Nature and the Decree," passim. Wang treats the theme throughout his *Instructions for Practical Living*, for instance, in part 2, p. 96.

33. See Bruce's discussion of the Great Ultimate in his *Chu Hsi and His Masters*, chap. 6.

34. For a sustained criticism of process theology on this point, see my *Creativity and God* (New York: Seabury, 1980), chap. 4.

35. Wang, pp. 274–75.

36. Ibid.

37. Ibid.

38. Ibid.

39. That Whitehead's basic categories are empirical generalizations without demonstrated normativeness is argued in connection with the category of the ultimate, in *Creativity and God*, chap. 3.

40. Cited in Wang, p. 276.

41. This is not to suggest that the Neo-Confucianists believed that a sage could control completely through efficient causes. Still, they believed that control was not limited by the responses of others if one's own character is perfected to manifest principle clearly.

42. Wang, p. 277.

43. Ibid.

44. Ibid.

45. See *Cosmology of Freedom*, chaps. 9, 11.

46. Fingarette, *Confucius: The Secular as Sacred* (New York: Harper Torchbook, 1972).

Chapter Nine

1. Kenneth K. S. Ch'en recounts the historical encounter of Buddhism and taoism in his *Buddhism in China* (Princeton: Princeton Univ. Press, 1964), esp. pp. 48–67. An interesting discussion can be found in Joseph Needham, *Science and Civilization China*, vol. 2 (Cambridge, Eng.: Cambridge Univ. Press, 1956),

pp. 408–19, where it is argued that Buddhism was responsive to the naturalism of taoism but that Buddhist insistence that impermanence means illusion was rejected by the taoists and later by the Neo-Confucianists. Needham believes that the Buddhists' rejection of the world helped inhibit the development of science in China. As I argue, however, it is not necessary for Buddhism to claim that the world is illusory or that it should be fled, even if influential Chinese Buddhist thought and practice claim just that.

2. See Dilworth and Silverman, "A Cross-Cultural Approach to the De-Ontological Self-Paradigm," *Monist*, 61 (1978), 82–95.

3. Process philosophy offers few resources for embodying Buddhism as a transcendental turn. Some reasons for this are explored in the present book. Steve Odin's *Process Metaphysica and Hwa-Yen Buddhism: A Critical Study of Cumulative Penetration and Interpenetration* (Albany: State Univ. of New York Press, 1982) uses a naturalized theory of imagination to transform transcendental phenomenology into a naturalistic tool for interpreting Buddhist experience.

4. As a general historical comment, I might note that Buddhism before its encounter with the West had a certain ranking or set of rankings of what is important in the Buddhist heritage. Responding to Western thought, different things might emerge as important, and what was previously thought to be important may sink and become trivial. This is one way in which a tradition changes through encounter. My point in the text is that, whereas the epistemological elements are important in responding to the transcendental tradition in the West, conceptions of nature and reality are important in the selective encounter with process philosophy.

5. A straightforward, clear analysis of ancient agreements and disagreements can be found in Edward Conze's *Buddhist Thought in India* (Ann Arbor: Univ. of Michigan Press, 1967), pp. 134–58.

6. I will try to make the presentation of process philosophy general enough to apply to all or most of those who have been decisively influenced by Whitehead's theory of causation by prehension. Whitehead's central text is *Process and Reality* (New York: Macmillan, 1929). The classic analysis of it is William Christian's *An Interpretation of Whitehead's Metaphysics* (New Haven: Yale Univ. Press, 1959). A fascinating new commentary is Elizabeth M. Kraus, *The Metaphysics of Experience: A Companion to Whitehead's Process and Reality* (New York: Fordham Univ. Press, 1979).

There is significant disagreement among process philosophers as to whether the loss of subjective immediacy with the attainment of "satisfaction" is significant. Although I claim it is, and reflect this in my exposition, Hartshorne and his followers claim it is not. See Hartshorne's discussion in *Creative Synthesis and Philosophic Method* (LaSalle, I.: Open Court, 1970), p. 118 *passim*. My particular development of the process philosophy of nature can be found in *The Cosmology of Freedom* (New Haven: Yale Univ. Press, 1974), parts 1 and 2. The problem of subjective perishing is central to the argument of Charles Hartshorne, John B. Cobb, Jr., and Lewis S. Ford, "Three Responses to Neville's *Creativity and God*," in *Process Studies*, 10/1 (Spring 1981).

7. For an analysis of Whitehead's relation to the Western tradition, see Charles Hartshorne and William L. Reese's *Philosophers Speak of God* (Chicago: Univ. of Chicago Press, 1953).

8. David Dilworth calls Whitehead's metaphysics "probably the most sustained philosophical articulation of the conception of reality as process in either Eastern

or Western traditions." "Whitehead's Process Realism, the Abhidharma Dharma Theory, and the Mahayana Critique," *International Philosophical Quarterly*, 18/2 (June 1978), p. 152.

9. Altizer, "The Buddhist Ground of the Whiteheadian God," *Process Studies* 5/4 (Winter 1975), p. 230; Dilworth, "Process Realism."

10. Whitehead, *Process and Reality*, p. 30.

11. Dilworth, "Process Realism", 155; Whitehead, *Process and Reality*, p. 28.

12. Dilworth's analysis depends in part on a paper by Justus Buchler, "On a Strain of Arbitrariness in Whitehead's System," *The Journal of Philosophy*, 66 (1969), pp. 589–600. Buchler maintains a doctrine of "ontological parity," to the effect that anything that is real is just as real as anything else. The "arbitrary strain" he criticizes in Whitehead is that, for the latter, some things are more important or interesting than others; but Buchler does not distinguish between degrees of reality and those of value. Nor does Buchler deal comprehensively with Whitehead's distinction between coordinate analysis, for which all things are in ontological parity, and genetic analysis, for which each concrescence establishes ontological priorities.

13. Dilworth directs his argument against the alleged ultimacy of actual occasions. Perhaps Whitehead's eternal objects could be said to have "own being." Still, Whitehead said that, apart from God's primordial envisionment of them, eternal objects are completely indeterminate; so they cannot have "own being" in *that* sense. Perhaps, then, they have "own being" as graded possibilities in the divine vision. In that case, however, their determinate reality would depend on the divine envisioning decision, and "own being" would have to be derived from God's "own being." Whitehead is not consistent regarding his theory of God and the claim that God must exemplify the characteristics of actual occasions. If God does the latter, then God too is temporal and has no "own being." If God *does* have "own being" of primordial conceptuality, that is a mystery otherwise unrelated to Whitehead's account of process. For an attempt to reach a satisfactory doctrine for Whitehead, see Lewis S. Ford, "Whitehead's Categoreal Derivation of Divine Existence," *Monist* 54/3 (July 1970), pp. 374–400, and his "Neville on the One and the Many," *Southern Journal of Philosophy* 10/1 (Spring 1972), pp. 79–84.

14. Dilworth follows Conze, *Buddhism: Its Essence and Development* (New York: Harper, 1959), p. 130, in noting that the root meaning of *sunya*, "empty," is "swollen," from the root *svi*.

15. *Mūlamadhyamakakārikās*, XXIV, 8; trans. Frederick J. Streng in *Emptiness: A Study in Religious Meaning* (Nashville: Abingdon Press, 1967), p. 213.

16. A subtle discussion can be found in William Johnston's *The Still Point: Reflections on Zen and Christian Mysticism* (New York: Fordham Univ. Press, 1970).

17. Streng, *Emptiness*, pp. 139–46.

18. Dilworth, "Process Realism," pp. 162–63.

19. Ibid., 167–69.

20. Dilworth's approach reflects a Kantian and neo-Kantian interpretation of paradigms. Although I am enthusiastic about its comparativist possibilities, I have criticized the Kantian bent in "Specialties and Worlds," *Hastings Center Studies*, 2/1 (January 1974).

21. See the fine first chapter of Whitehead's *Process and Reality*.

22. Nagarjuna, I, 4.; the translation is in Streng, beginning at p. 183.

23. Ibid., I, 5–6.

24. Ibid., I, 7.
25. Ibid., I, 8.
26. Ibid., I, 9.
27. Ibid., I, 10.
28. Ibid., I, 11.
29. Ibid., I, 13.
30. Ibid., I, 14.
31. Streng, p. 167.
32. Altizer, "Buddhist Ground," pp. 235f.
33. Ibid., p. 230.
34. See *Process and Reality*, pp. 124, 374f., 443; on pp. 94f., Whitehead says: This doctrine of organism is the attempt to describe the world as a process of generation of individual actual entities, each with its own own absolute self-attainment. This concrete finality of the individual is nothing else than a decision referent beyond itself. The "perpetual perishing" of individual absoluteness is thus foredoomed. But the "perishing" of absoluteness is the attainment of "objective immortality.". . . Continuity concerns what is potential; whereas actuality is incurably atomic. . . . So far as physical relations are concerned, contemporary events happen in *causal* independence of each other. . . . The contemporary world is in fact divided and atomic, being a multiplicity of definite actual entities. These contemporary actual entities are divided from each other, and are not themselves divisible into other contemporary actual entities.
35. Chang, *The Buddhist Teaching of Totality: The Philosophy of Hwa Yen Buddhism* (University Park, Pa.: Pennsylvania State Univ. Press, 1971), pp. 122f.
36. Ibid., p. 156.
37. Francis H. Cook, *Hua-yen Buddhism: The Jewel Net of Indra* (University Park, Pa.: Pennyslvania State Univ. Press, 1977), p. 73.
38. Ibid., p. 112. The Fa-tsang text is his treatise, *Hya-yen i-ch'eng chiao i fen-ch'i*, trans. Cook from the *Taisho* ed., no. 1866 in vol. 45; this passage is at 489b.
39. Ibid., pp. 115f.
40. Hartshorne, p. 198.
41. I argue this thesis in *The Cosmology of Freedom*, chaps. 1–6.
42. Chang, p. 156.
43. The difficulty with Whitehead's philosophical theology is that he still proceeded to treat God only cosmologically, maintaining a distinction between creativity and God.

Chapter Ten

1. This title follows Professor Sung-bae Park's translation of the Chinese title, *Ta-ch'eng ch'i-hsin lun*. Except where explicitly noted, however, the discussion here follows the translation of the entire text by Yoshito S. Hakeda (New York: Columbia Univ. Press, 1967), who renders the title, *The Awakening of Faith in Mahayana*. The original is controversially attributed to Asvaghosha. I am no sinologist or scholar of Buddhist philology; thus my interpretations should be taken with a grain of salt. Yet when an early draft of this chapter was presented to a conference of real sinologists and philologists of Buddhist texts, my inter-

pretation was closer to each of the other scholars than any of them was to each other.

2. See Sung-bae Park's *Buddhist Faith and Sudden Enlightenment* (Albany: State Univ. of New York Press, 1983), chap. 5.

3. Hakeda trans., p. 81.

4. Park, *Buddhist Faith*, chap. 5.

5. Ibid.

6. The classic modern analysis of this point is Paul Tillich's *Systematic Theology*, vol. 2 (Chicago: Univ. of Chicago Press, 1957), esp. pp. 44–59. See also my *Soldier, Sage, Saint* (New York: Fordham University Press, 1978).

7. Park, *Buddhist Faith*, chap. 10.

8. Hakeda trans. p. 86.

9. Ibid., pp. 86–87.

10. Ibid., p. 39. Hakeda's brackets.

11. See Hakeda's commentary, on p. 89.

12. Park, *Buddhist Faith*, chaps. 5, 10.

13. Wonhyo, *"Treatise on Awakening Mahayana Faith,"* comb. ed. with the *Running Commentary* and the *Expository Notes*, as cited and trans. by Sung-bae Park in *Buddhist Faith*.

14. Trans. Park, ibid.

15. Ibid.

16. Ibid.

17. The first association of *t'i* with *yung* is usually said to be in Wang Pi's *Commentary on the Lao-tzu*, chap. 38. Wang Pi's point was that nonbeing gives rise to being or substance and that substance has nonbeing in the sense that the tao is its function.

18. In Wing-tsit Chan's translation,

> What Heaven (*t'ien*, nature) imparts to man is called human nature. To follow our nature is called the Way (Tao). Cultivating the Way is called education. . . . Before the feelings of pleasure, anger, sorrow, and joy are aroused it is called equilibrium (*chung*, centrality, mean). When these feelings are aroused and each and all attain due measure and degree, it is called harmony. Equilibrium is the great foundation of the world, and harmony its universal path.

From *A Source Book in Chinese Philosophy* (Princeton, N.J.: Princeton Univ. Press, 1963), p. 98.

19. The text says, "Each of these two aspects embraces all states of existence. Why? Because these two aspects are mutually inclusive." Hakeda trans., p. 31. Concerning knowledge of this distinction, see the discussion of "permeation" in chap. 3 of Hakeda's trans., pp. 54–64.

20. Plotinus, *The Enneads*, esp. the *Fifth Ennead*. For critical discussions, see Paul Weiss, *Modes of Being* (Carbondale, Ill.: Southern Illinois Univ. Press, 1958), chap. 10; and my *God the Creator* (Chicago: Univ. of Chicago Press, 1968), pp. 83–88.

21. For instance, in Hakeda's trans., "That which is called 'the essential nature of the Mind' is unborn and is imperishable," p. 32; "[the essence of Suchness] knows no increase in ordinary men, the Hinayanists, the Bodhisattvas, or the Buddhas. It was not brought into existence in the beginning nor will it cease to be at the end of time; it is eternal through and through"; pp. 64–65.

22. See Hakeda's trans., p. 34.

23. Ibid., pp. 38–42.
25. Ibid., pp. 56–68.
26. Ibid., pp. 38–39.
27. See *Reconstruction of Thinking* (Albany: State Univ. of New York Press, 1981), chaps. 1, 8; and *Soldier, Sage, Saint*, chap. 3.
28. In Park, *Buddhist Faith*, chap. 4.
29. Hakeda trans., p. 74.

Chapter Eleven

1. From chap. 4, sec. 2 of the *Hundred Gates*, trans. by Wing tsit Chan in his *Source Book in Chinese Philosophy* (Princeton: Princeton Univ. Press, 1963), p. 420. An equally dialectical use of the doctrine was made by the T'ien-t'ai writer Hui-ssu, responding to the criticism that the emphasis on harmony destroys the distinction between the two levels of truth:

> *Question*: If substance and function are not different, it can only be said that the Two Levels of Truth (worldly or relative truth and absolute truth) involve each other. How can worldly truth also involve worldly events?
>
> *Answer*: By saying substance and function are not different, one does not mean collecting the different functions of many particles of dust to form the one substance of the lump of clay. It merely means that within the level of worldly truth, every event or character is the total substance of absolute truth. Therefore we say that substance and function are not different. Because of this meaning, if absolute truth involves completely all events and characters within the level of worldly truth, at the same time every single event or character within the level of worldly truth also involves completely all events and characters within the level of worldly truth.

From *The Method of Concentration and Insight*, chap. 2, trans. by Chan, ibid., pp. 403f.

2. From Hsuan-tsang's *Treatise on the Establishment of the Doctrine of Consciousness-Only*, trans. Chan, ibid., p. 389.

3. From chap. 2 of *Seng-chao's Treatises*, trans. Chan, ibid., pp. 353f.

4. From his Treatise on the Two Levels of Truth, chap. 1, trans. Chan, ibid., p. 360.

5. *Mūlamadhyamakakārikās* 24:8–10; Streng trans. in *Emptiness: A Study in Religious Meaning* by Frederick J. Streng (Nashville: Abingdon, 1967), p. 213. The word in the last sentence, translated "practical behavior," is *vyavahāra-satya*, Hakeda translates it as "conventional truth" in his quotation of the sentence in *The Awakening of Faith* (New York: Columbia Univ. Press, 1967), p. 69. The rationale behind Hakeda's translation is that *vyavahāra* occurs frequently in compounds having to do with legal practice and regulated business affairs. It means ordered, regulated, or informed activity. The Buddhist commentarial tradition generally sides with Hakeda's interpretation and concludes that Nagarjuna's point was only to preserve convention. I think it is a mistake to emphasize the order without the activity and therefore translate the phrase as though it meant the truth that comes from the order in affairs. The emphasis should rather be on the activity as ordered by the truth. Here, *vyavahāra-satya* means spiritual practice ordered by true discipline, which is better conveyed in Streng's translation. Richard Gard, in private comments, has pointed out that *satya* means "be-

ing"; thus the interpretive dispute is between being a practicer and being a conventional person. Attaining higher truth is attaining enlightened being.

6. *Awakening of Faith*, Hakeda trans. p. 68.

7. Ibid., pp. 68f.

8. See the discussion of this topic in chap. 9.

9. Roughly speaking, this account follows Whitehead's in *Process and Reality* (New York: Macmillan, 1929); more precisely, it follows my *Reconstruction of Thinking* (Albany: State Univ. of New York Press, 1981).

10. The notion of a cultural "body" is derived from the language of Antonio de Nicolas in *Avatara* (New York: Nicolas Hays, 1976), esp. chap. 6.

Postscript

1. Berger, *The Sacred Canopy: Elements of a Sociological Theory of Religion* (Garden City, N.Y.: Doubleday Anchor, 1969). See also, Peter L. Berger and Thomas Luckmann, *The Social Construction of Reality* (Garden City, N.Y.: Doubleday Anchor, 1967).

2. For a thorough discussion of the imaginative parallels and continuities of responsibility in art and religion, see Thomas R. Martland, *Religion as Art: An Interpretation* (Albany, N.Y.: State Univ. of New York Press, 1981).

3. Scharlemann, *The Being of God: Theology and the Experience of Truth* (New York: Seabury, 1981).

4. Altizer, *Total Presence: The Language of Jesus and the Language of Today* (New York: Seabury, 1980).

5. Altizer's early, famous statement is *The Gospel of Christian Atheism* (Philadelphia: Westminster, 1966). The most scholarly presentation, focusing on Hegel and Blake, is *The New Apocalypse: The Radical Christian Vision of William Blake* (Michigan State Univ. Press, 1967). Altizer argues the case in the form of a systematic theology that opens into a theology of world religions (or, at least, Buddhism as well as Christianity), in *The Descent into Hell: A Study of the Radical Reversal of the Christian Consciousness* (New York: Seabury, 1979; orig. Lippincott, 1970). The most systematic philosophical statement is *The Self-Embodiment of God* (New York: Harper & Row, 1977).

Index